Finding Your Seat

Finding Your Seat

A Zen Handbook

Amala Wrightson

Kathryn Argetsinger

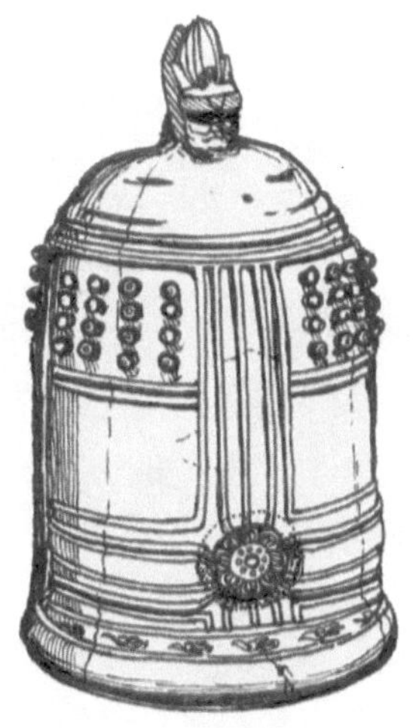

AUCKLAND

THE AUCKLAND ZEN CENTRE

2020

TO HEAR LIVE PODCASTS OF AMALA-SENSEI'S TEISHOS
AND TO LINK TO THE COMPLETE ARCHIVE OF HER TALKS, VISIT
aucklandzen.org.nz/Home/podcasts

CONTENTS

Contents

Dedicated with respect and gratitude to

ROSHI BODHIN KJOLHEDE

who for thirty-four years has selflessly, fearlessly
taught the truth of the Dharma for the
welfare of all beings

*   *

*

PREFACE

THERE is a lot of confusion about what Zen is. Go into any bookshop and look for the Zen books, and you may find them under 'Psychology', 'Philosophy', 'Eastern Religion' or even 'Self-Help'. The Internet abounds with Zen lists, such as '6 steps to a Zen attitude', '6 tools to enjoy your job like a Zen monk', or 'How to Zen your body'. One list includes:

> 5. Visualize a positive outcome.... Use a picture to visualize what you want. If you need a new or better car, take a picture of your ideal car at a dealership. Tape it to your fridge or bathroom mirror so you can see it everyday.

Needless to say, Zen has nothing to do with visualisation or acquiring a newer or better car. But then what is it? This has been a perennial question within Zen itself. Often the question is framed as 'What is the meaning of Bodhidharma's coming from the West?'[1] The responses have been many. The ancient Chinese master Joshu replied, 'The oak tree in the garden.' If he were here in Auckland Joshu might have said, 'The pōhutukawa at the water's edge.' Another master, Kyorin, replied to the same question, 'Sitting long and getting tired.'

That response neatly brings us to *Finding Your Seat*, which is a handbook for people interested in taking up authentic Zen practice (a large part of which involves sitting and getting tired), and finding out for themselves what Zen is. As with all handbooks, it will have succeeded when the reader has indeed found her seat and put the book down.

In *Finding Your Seat* we explore the way Zen is practiced in a particular community, the Auckland Zen Centre Sangha. It is just one style of practice among many, but we hope it gives a sense of context, of Zen as something we do, often with others, and in a particular place and time.

Often Zen and other Buddhist practices are understood as therapies, and this is not altogether unjustified. The Buddha is sometimes referred to as the Great Physician and his Four Noble Truths as diagnosis, prognosis, prescription and course of treatment for relieving the sufferings of the human condition. People often come to Zen hoping to find some relief

---

1. Bodhidharma (483–540), the founder of the Zen school. See further in the Glossary.

from their ills and many find it. But for those who seek it, there is more. Our practice can deepen from the therapeutic into the religious as we discover that it offers us not just relief but transformation of our whole being – a transformation that happens both gradually and at times with sudden insights. And, as we are able to put our faith in this process more and more wholeheartedly, the teachings, or Dharma, permeate our lives. We become Dharma vessels, not only benefiting from the teachings, but being of benefit as well.

If you have read certain Zen books you may think of Zen as highly iconoclastic and be surprised to learn that it involves chanting, bowing and other rituals. Two stories may serve to illuminate this. The first comes from Tibet:

> One day an old man was circumambulating Reting Monastery. Geshé Drom said to him: 'Sir, I am happy to see you circumambulating, but wouldn't you prefer to be practicing the Dharma?'
>
> Thinking this over, the old man felt he'd better cover himself by reading some Buddhist scriptures. While he was reading in the temple courtyard, Geshé Drom said: 'I am happy to see you reading the Dharma, but wouldn't you prefer to be practicing it?'
>
> At this, the old man thought that the best way to cover himself would be to meditate single-pointedly. He put aside his reading and sat on a cushion, his eyes half-closed. Drom said: 'Good to see you meditating, but wouldn't you rather be practicing the Dharma?'
>
> With nothing else left to do, the old man asked: 'Geshé-la, please, how should I practice the Dharma?'
>
> 'When you practice,' Drom replied, 'there is no distinction between the Dharma and your own mind.'[2]

Here is the second story, from twentieth-century America, told by Lawrence Shainberg in *Ambivalent Zen*. Shainberg is showing his elderly parents around the small zendo of his teacher Kyudo-roshi in Soho, New York City. He is 'translating' for his hard-of-hearing father who has trouble with Kyudo-roshi's eccentric English and for the Roshi who struggles to understand the father's southern accent. Just as they are leaving, his father, who is skeptical about all things religious, says:

2. From *Miscellaneous Advice of the Kadampa Masters*, quoted in Stephen Batchelor, *Buddhism Without Beliefs* (New York: Riverhead Books, 1997), p. 55.

'Ask him has he read Krishnamurti.'

'Yes, of course,' says Roshi when I've relayed the question. 'Very intelligent! Beautiful words!'

'Tell him Krishnamurti hates spiritual practice or any kind of formal meditation.'

Laughing, Roshi offers him a friendly pat on the shoulder. 'Yes, yes, very intelligent, I feel same!'

'Then what's all that about?' says dad, waving his hand in the direction of the zendo, 'the cushions! The altar! The Buddha and the flowers and the candle! How can he maintain the establishment if he doesn't believe in formal meditation?'

Once again Roshi doesn't wait for me to translate, 'Please you tell him — I have no idea.' [3]

He gives a similar response when asked why he prays every morning for the wellbeing of each member of the zendo and bows to the Buddha and to an image of his teacher Soen Nakagawa-roshi:

'I have no idea. When I pray I just pray.' [4]

As both stories suggest, Zen (or the Dharma) has nothing to do with mere ritual, but at the same time ritual done wholeheartedly has everything to do with Zen. Practice entails embodiment. Whether sitting in meditation, chanting sutras, bowing to Buddhas — or, indeed, whether chopping vegetables or digging the garden — activity undertaken with the full engagement of body and mind holds the key. It is our hope that the guidelines and teachings offered in *Finding Your Seat* will help you to find a path towards wholehearted engagement with the circumstances of your own life, and that the book will be of use both for those who seek a pathway out of personal suffering, and for those who discover the meaning and joy in quietly relieving suffering wherever they can.

AW

3. Lawrence Sheinberg, *Ambivalent Zen* (New York: Pantheon, 1995), p. 257.
4. *Ibid.*, p. 252.

Finding Your Seat

INTRODUCTION

✳ ✳ ✳

I take refuge in Buddha. I take refuge in Dharma. I take refuge in Sangha.

TO take refuge in Buddha, Dharma and Sangha has been, through the ages, the means of formally entering upon the path which the Buddha pointed out. Throughout the Buddhist world, these three are known as the Three Jewels, the Three Treasures, or the Triple-gem, and, in taking daily refuge in them, followers of the Buddha Way give voice to their faith and their aspiration to awaken. So too at the Auckland Zen Centre, two and a half millennia and 12,000 kilometres distant from the time and place in which the Buddha Shakyamuni first offered his teachings, the chanting service begins each day with this triple recitation.

Although Buddhist teachings are vast, and the meaning of the Triple-gem may be expounded on many different levels,[1] at the simplest, most literal level, *Buddha* refers to the historical teacher Shakyamuni ('the sage of the Shakya clan'), *Dharma* refers to his teachings, and *Sangha* to the community of his followers. The community that Shakyamuni gathered around himself was a group of celibate home-leavers, who, possessing nothing of their own beyond a robe and a begging bowl, were supported by the food offerings of lay followers. A long process of historical change underlies the transition from this organisational structure to the one we find 2500 years later in Auckland. In each country through which the Buddha's teachings have passed, Buddhist institutions have been shaped by the particular cultural orientations, needs and yearnings encountered there. In Buddhism, this is not seen as a problem, but rather as a reflection of the basic teaching of *anatta*: that things lack a fixed, permanent shape, and are instead the products of particular causes and conditions. It is not yet 100 years since Westerners began to take up Buddhist practice in their home countries in any numbers, and barely over a decade and a half since a Zen Centre was established in New Zealand. Thus the Auckland Zen Centre is both heir to an ancient and venerable teaching tradition while at the same time a very new institution, one that is only beginning to discover the forms and structures best suited to carrying on this work in New Zealand today.

1. See Chapter 5, pp. 101–104.

{ 3 }

In part, then, this book seeks to introduce the practice of Zen to a culture unfamiliar with its forms and functions, and to serve as a handbook for those setting out on the path of Zen, particularly at the Auckland Centre. At the same time, we hope that this book can offer a culturally appropriate, contemporary Zen approach to the timeless and profound teachings of the Buddha. Above all, we will be happy if any of what is written here may serve to encourage you in your own practice, in your own search, and your own discovery of your heart's inmost desire. With these ends in mind, it may be helpful to begin with the briefest possible sketch of how we got from there to here — from a group of wandering mendicants in ancient India to a community of householder practitioners coming together for daily meditation in the heart of the commercial-industrial Auckland suburb of Onehunga.

Though the Sangha that gathered around the Buddha was initially itinerant, as the years passed there was an increasing tendency, particularly during the annual rain retreats, for the monks or nuns to settle down in one location, often provided by a wealthy patron. This practice of settled or cenobitic living travelled with Buddhism to China. There, under the influence of teacher Baizhang Huaihai (720–814), monasteries of the Chan school (called the Zen school in Japanese)[2] became places where the monks or nuns engaged in farming, cooking and other types of work that made them at least partially self-supporting. Zen monasteries in Japan were initially based on the Chinese model, but during the Meiji period (mid-19th century) the social role of religious celibacy became a subject of political debate as the Japanese government sought to encourage modernisation and secularisation of the society as a whole. A law passed in 1872 allowed male monastics to marry, and this soon became the norm.[3] By the twentieth century, Japanese Zen novices would most typically spend about two to five years in a large training temple, living a traditional monastic life, but the majority would subsequently marry and settle down as the priest of a local temple, most often inheriting the position from their father.

2. The meaning of foreign language and technical terms (such as Chan, Dharma Heir, Roshi) may be checked in the Glossary found at the back of this book.

3. The story of this law and the social issues surrounding its passage is recounted in detail in *Neither Monk nor Layman: Clerical Marriage in Modern Japanese Buddhism* by Richard M. Jaffe (Princeton, N.J.: Princeton University Press, 2001).

This was the situation Philip Kapleau (1912–2004) encountered when he travelled from the United States to Japan in 1953 to study Zen. Of his two main teachers, Daiun Sogaku Harada and Hakuun Yasutani, the first was a celibate monk, while the second was a married man with five children who worked for many years as a primary-school teacher. These two teachers worked closely together (Yasutani was Harada's Dharma Heir), and their work was somewhat unusual, not only in their fusion of the two traditional Japanese Zen teaching lineages, Soto and Rinzai, into one unified way of practice (sometimes referred to as Integral Zen), but also in their interest in opening the practice of Zen meditation to lay people and to Westerners. Roshi Kapleau himself spent three years working with Harada-roshi and his monks in a strict training-monastery atmosphere, but completed his training with Yasutani-roshi while living with his wife and daughter in Kamakura.

After being invited to teach in Rochester, New York, Roshi Kapleau established the Rochester Zen Center in 1966. At least two other major Zen Centers were founded in the United States at close to the same time (San Francisco in 1962 and Los Angeles in 1967), and all three of these centres were institutionally quite distinct from anything that had preceded them in Japan. Offering meditation instruction and daily sitting opportunities for lay people, they also hosted residential training programs based on the monastic style of Asian training, but open to all who might wish to train for shorter or longer periods of time. As no similar training was available in New Zealand, Auckland-born Charlotte Wrightson, after meeting Roshi Kapleau and his eventual successor Roshi Bodhin Kjolhede in Europe in 1982, spent periods training at the Rochester Zen Center between 1986 and 2003, including full-time training from 1990 onwards. In 1999, she ordained as a Zen priest, taking the name Amala, and in 2004 returned to New Zealand to teach.

Since that time, the Auckland Zen Centre has offered workshops, practice opportunities, and intensive retreats for lay people, as well as a daily programme for those who are able to train full-time.[4] Roshi Kapleau's classic book, *The Three Pillars of Zen*, first published in 1966 and still in print, has always been available to those practicing at the Centre, and has stood in many ways as our inspiration and founding document. This book vividly describes the Zen training of its time and place, but there

4. See Chapter 7, p. 145.

has been a gradually increasing sense that this description, dating from more than fifty years ago, no longer entirely reflects our own style and approach. Though of course the underlying aspiration of Zen training remains always the same, the expression and methods of that training, like the institutions that embody it, must take the forms best suited to the needs, culture and orientation of the people doing the practice. It is in this spirit, then, that we offer this book, based around the teachings of Sensei Amala Wrightson, as an expression of the Zen being taught and practiced in Aotearoa today. These teachings have been compiled and the various chapter topics introduced by Kathryn Argetsinger, Amala-sensei's longtime student.[5]

In Auckland, our Centre takes its place alongside about fifty other Buddhist temples and centres, the majority of which have been established by immigrant groups from traditionally Buddhist countries. At these temples, services are generally conducted in the various Asian languages and the forms of practice hew closely to those of their particular homeland. Our own focus, on the other hand, has been on sharing the Dharma with those for whom it is culturally new — though this would certainly not describe all of our members. Nevertheless, as mostly newcomers to the Dharma, we feel privileged to be located in a city with such a diverse Buddhist community, and find that our own practice has been greatly enriched by our many contacts with this larger Sangha.

About Teisho and Koans

Each chapter of this book contains two parts. In the first part, you'll find some basic information about the topic of the chapter — information which we hope will be useful as you take up the practice of Zen or as you begin to find your way as part of a Zen Centre community. The second part of each chapter offers an edited transcription of a *teisho* given at our Centre and selected for its relevance to, or its ability to shed light on, some aspect of the chapter topic.

So what is a teisho? A teisho is a talk delivered by a Zen teacher, generally following a period of zazen (seated meditation). A teisho takes up a particular topic or text, chosen by the teacher in advance, but, although the teacher will normally do some research and note-taking in preparation for

---

5. For the forms 'Sensei Amala Wrightson' and 'Amala-sensei', see Glossary under Sensei.

the talk, a teisho is characterised by a greater degree of spontaneity than tends to be the case, for example, with a church sermon. In Zen parlance, a teisho is not simply a talk or a lecture, but is a 'presentation': the teacher aims through the teisho to give a verbal presentation or demonstration of the Dharma as it expresses itself in the particular moment and place of the teisho's delivery. The understanding is that the Dharma, the truth, is always *right here*, completely available to us, if we just turn towards it openly, and this the teacher endeavours to do. Traditionally a teacher delivers a teisho not facing the group, but rather facing the Buddha-figure on the altar. As Amala-sensei explains in one of her teishos:

> Normally if you're talking to people, you face them, and, if a lecture is being delivered, the understanding is that one person is speaking to a group of people. We could call this a conventional understanding; it takes place in the realm of convention. But a teisho aims to move us beyond that realm. It is not a talk given by a speaker to an audience. Rather, this talk takes place in the realm of oneness. We're all facing the altar together. We're all endeavouring to orient ourselves towards our True Nature, our Buddha Nature. We could say that we're all shoulder-to-shoulder at this workbench we call zazen, working together on the Great Matter. And it's for this reason that the teacher faces the altar. The teisho is an offering to the Buddha by the teacher of her understanding at that moment. And it is equally an offering to all the other Buddhas in the zendo – a Buddha speaking to Buddhas.

Teisho topics may be quite varied. Very often, though not always, the teacher will comment on a written text, and these may range from traditional Buddhist sacred books, through teachings of contemporary teachers, psychologists, historians, scientists or others, to news articles from the internet. In short, the texts taken up will be any that the teacher feels can help her to convey points of Buddhist teaching in the most direct and relevant way. Very typically a teisho will begin with some biographical or background information about the writer or protagonists of the chosen text. If the protagonists are ancient Chinese masters, the teacher often begins by relating some of the stories that have been handed down to us about them. Because of its in-the-moment nature, a teisho can often be quite conversational in tone. The teishos presented here are all edited, to one degree or another, for readability and organisation. To some extent, however, we have tried to preserve something of the conversational, spontaneous, and expressive tone that you would find in a live teisho.

In the teishos selected for this book, many of the core texts being commented upon are Zen koans. Though, at least in our tradition, relatively few of a teacher's teishos may take up a koan, students often find these koan teishos to be the most hard-hitting, suggestive, or profound, and so several of these talks are included here. It is important, then, to understand something of what a koan is and how koans are used in Zen training.

A koan is a Zen teaching story. Most of the koans that we work with in Zen have been handed down to us from the ancient Chinese masters, and the word 'koan' is the Japanese form of the Chinese word *gongan*, a term that comes from Chinese law, where it means 'public case' or precedent. Koans most often take the form of a pithy story recounting an incident or verbal exchange between a master and student, or between two masters. These stories are full of rich echoes as well as very specific teaching points, and they often contain a paradoxical element, something that does not make sense to our usual ways of thinking. The name 'public case' indicates that the story is public, not secret, and freely available to anyone who cares to investigate wholeheartedly. Each koan is a very particular window into the Dharma and has the potential to lead the meditator to a shift in consciousness.

> *This one instant, as it is, is the whole of eternity.*
> *The whole of eternity is this one instant.*
> *If you see into this fact,*
> *The one who is seeing has been seen into.*
>
> —Master Mumon, verse for *Mumonkan*, Case 47.

A monk asked Zen Master Yangshan Huiji, 'Can ultimate reality teach about itself?'

Yangshan said, 'There's nothing that I can tell you about this, but there is someone else who can.'

The monk said, 'Where is this one who can teach it?'

Yangshan pushed forward a cushion.

—Zen koan from the *Himitsu Shōbōgenzō*

CHAPTER I

Learning to Sit

THE CORE of Zen is a practice called zazen, literally 'sitting meditation'. In Japanese the word 'za' means a seat, while 'zen' is the Japanese pronunciation of the word that the Buddha himself used for 'concentration' or 'meditation', and which he taught as one of eight essential aspects of the path to liberation. Thus the Zen school of Buddhism is the one that puts a special emphasis on this aspect of the path.[1]

Since the time, over fifty years ago, that the first Western Zen centres were established, the practice of meditation has found increasing popularity and acceptance in countries where it would have been almost unheard of a century ago. Very often the practice of meditation is associated with stress reduction and better health. But it is important to understand that in Zen these things are viewed merely as possible side-effects of the practice. Rather, the more fundamental teaching is that zazen can open us to a direct, experiential understanding of our True Nature, uncovering more and more of our innate clarity, joy and loving-kindness.

Zazen is a way of working with both the body and the mind, and in Zen we view these two as intimately interconnected: what we do with

1. See further in Glossary under Chan and Eightfold Path.

our bodies affects our minds, and what we do with our minds affects our bodies. For this reason, instruction in zazen puts a strong emphasis on finding a relaxed but alert and stable meditation posture. Various traditional postures are taught that have been time-tested for supporting the qualities of body and mind that we seek in zazen. The text and images below (on pp. 19–24) provide a summary of these.

We can identify three main elements in any of the postures listed, and the first one is stability; we need to find a way to sit in which we can easily settle. A key to this is to have three points of contact with the mat or the floor. If we have less than three points of contact, we're wobbly. When sitting on a mat, the three points will be the seat and the two knees. In a chair, they are the seat and the two feet. But whether in a chair or on a cushion, establishing three solid points of contact is what allows us to let go and release into the posture. In reference to this Amala-sensei has said:

> If you think of a three-legged stool, you'll understand that if one of the legs is too short, the stool is going to be unstable, and that's how it is with our sitting posture as well. Ideally we are not 'holding it all together' when we sit; instead there's a sense of being held up by the floor or the earth, a sense of being grounded.[2]

After stability, the second element of zazen posture is uprightness. Just as a stable seat fosters a sense of groundedness and connection with the earth, so an upright spine expresses our human dignity and our aspiration to awaken. A properly aligned spine creates the poise that we need in order to be fully present and responsive. To find the correct alignment, we need to have our knees lower than our hips. In this way the pelvis can be placed at an angle that makes sitting up straight virtually effortless. To find this correct angle for the pelvis, make sure when you first sit down that you are sitting directly on your sitting bones and that your buttocks are thrust back ('your behind is behind'). To accomplish this, it can be helpful to lean forward as far as you can, place your hands under your buttocks and draw the flesh back. Then sit up slowly until your ears are aligned over your shoulders. Relax your shoulders. Check your head and neck also. Most Westerners tend to have the head too far forward to be properly aligned. Draw the back of the neck towards the back of your

---

2. Quotations in this chapter are from the October 2006 teisho 'Some Basic Points About Dharma Practice'.

collar as you move the head slightly upwards. This will make the chin angle down just a little bit. Sometimes it is helpful to imagine a string from the crown of your head pulling it upwards.

Two things come out of this uprightness. One is ease of sitting. When we're lined up correctly, we will not be creating unnecessary tensions in the body, and we will tend to experience fewer physical issues while sitting. The second is clarity of mind. Though it is certainly possible to meditate lying down – and while at certain times that may even be the best choice – in general, a lying-down posture will encourage sleepiness and a wandering mind. The same applies to other postures that are too relaxed, such as sitting in an easy chair. This is a main reason that sitting upright, usually without support for the back, has been the classic position for meditation down through the centuries.

At the same time, however, sitting up straight does not mean ramrod straight. The natural alignment of the spine is more like the stalk of a flower than like a stake; it needs to have some softness in it. This leads to the third and final point of posture, which is balance. Balance does involve the symmetry and physical alignment that we have already been discussing, but it also refers to a balance between tension and relaxation. Sitting in meditation involves an ongoing process of observing and adjusting the level of tension, or effort, of both body and mind. Our sitting needs to be taut without being tight. The Buddha used the image of a stringed instrument to make this point (see inset p. 14). If the strings of an instrument are too tight, you don't get a good sound and they may even break; but if the strings are too loose, you don't get any sound at all. Again, Amala-sensei says:

Remember that when we sit down to meditate, we are not trying to take a rest – on the contrary, we are trying to wake up! But at the same time, this waking up can only take place through a steady process of release: releasing the tensions, obstacles and delusions that bind us.

So, not too tight and not too loose.

The *mudra*, or hand position, taught in Zen is another way of working with the balance point between too tight and too loose. In this mudra, the hands are placed in the lap with the back of the left hand on top of the right palm, while the two thumbs touch each other so that an oval shape is formed. The thumbs should touch each other ever so lightly, as if a single

FINDING BALANCE

'Now what do you think, Sona. Before, when you were a house-dweller, were you skilled at playing the vina?'

'Yes, lord.'

'And what do you think: when the strings of your vina were too taut, was your vina in tune & playable?'

'No, lord.'

'And what do you think: when the strings of your vina were too loose, was your vina in tune & playable?'

'No, lord.'

'And what do you think: when the strings of your vina were neither too taut nor too loose, but tuned to be right on pitch, was your vina in tune & playable?'

'Yes, lord.'

'In the same way, Sona, over-aroused persistence leads to restlessness, overly slack persistence leads to laziness. Thus you should determine the right pitch for your persistence, attune the pitch of the [five] faculties [to that], and there pick up your theme.'

—*Anguttara Nikaya*, 6.55, translated by Thanissaro Bhikkhu

sheet of paper were held between them. Bringing the attention regularly to the mudra is a good way of checking on your mind state. You'll soon find that when you are feeling spacey, sleepy or unfocused (too loose), the thumbs will tend to either drift apart so that they are not touching at all, or else collapse into your palms so that the oval shape is lost. Conversely, if you're feeling stressed, agitated or bringing too much striving to your practice (too tight), your thumbs will tend to press into each other until their ends are pointing upwards instead of directly towards each other. Again, the oval shape is distorted.

The gaze, too, can help you to find and monitor a proper balance. In the Soto Zen tradition, we are taught to sit with our eyes open, but facing a blank wall, just as Bodhidharma, the fifth-century founder of the Zen school was said to do. Having the eyes open helps us to stay awake and alert (not too loose), while keeping the gaze down at approximately a 45-degree angle, keeping the eyes relaxed and the gaze soft, and facing a wall or a divider help us to avoid distraction or agitation (not too tight). Again, if you find yourself growing sleepy as you sit, it may help to open the eyes wider and raise the gaze; if you find yourself distracted or restless, it may help to lower the gaze and soften the eyes.

One of the reasons that finding a balanced and well-aligned posture is so important to the practice of Zen meditation in particular, is that, different to some other traditions, Zen puts a strong emphasis on 'no moving'. Because our aim is to settle the mind, we try to maintain a deep physical stillness while we sit. If something itches while we are sitting, we don't scratch; we just observe. If we experience some discomfort in a limb, or if our foot falls asleep, we don't change position, but simply stay as we are until the time that we have set for our round of sitting is up.

This can be a challenging practice, and it does come with some important caveats. Though some discomfort while sitting is to be expected when you are new to the practice, any sharp, shooting pain, especially while getting into a posture, is a signal that you need to change what you are doing at that moment. Likewise if any pain or numbness persists after a practice period ends, be sure to modify the way you are sitting. If your legs fall asleep in the course of a round, there is no cause for concern, but do not try to stand up until you have full feeling in them. Standing up quickly when the feet or legs are asleep can cause falls or injury.

Though it is important to be aware of these safety guidelines, it is also important to appreciate the power that resides in our willingness to remain still and to sit through whatever arises. Finding a posture that feels truly comfortable and natural takes time. None of us gets it all sorted out the first time we sit down, and, in fact, many of us continue to work on and refine our posture for as long as we practice. So our aim is always simply to find the best balance that we can for right now.

Once you have settled your body into your best possible posture for now, it is time to begin the process of settling the mind. In Zen the first practice assigned to newcomers is most often a breath practice. In this practice we bring our attention to the flow of the breath and keep it focused there moment by moment. This practice develops concentration while at the same time encouraging a natural settling and relaxation of the nervous system. Unlike some yogic practices, in Zen we do not try to control or manipulate the breath in any way. Though it can be helpful to begin the practice by taking a couple of slow, deep breaths, once you have done that, simply let the breath fall into its natural rhythm, whether long or short, shallow or deep. The Buddha himself is said to have taught breath practice with the following pithy instructions:

> Breathing in long, [the practitioner] understands: 'I breathe in long;' or breathing out long, he understands: 'I breathe out long.'
>
> Breathing in short, he understands: 'I breathe in short;' or breathing out short, he understands: 'I breathe out short.'

Keep the lips closed and breathe quietly through the nose. Pay attention to the physical sensations of the breath, not trying to visualise the breath or verbalise what is happening, but just experiencing the sensations of the breath flowing in and out. Remember, too, that your job is *simply* to experience the breath, not to control it or force it in any way. As long as you are bringing your full attention to the breath, or as much attention as you can, then you are doing the practice correctly.

When you first take up a breath practice, it can be helpful to count each of your inhalations and exhalations. Count up to 10, and then start again at 1 (inhalation = 1, exhalation = 2, inhalation = 3, and so on). This counting is taught as an aid to concentration and to help you check whether or not your mind has wandered from its task of following the breath. Remember, though, that the counting is not an end in itself; the main thing is your experience of and connection with the breath. Any time you lose the count, just start again at 1. Once you find that, during the course of an average practice period, you can keep the count without losing it for about 15 minutes, then you may want to try counting only at the start of each exhalation. As before, count each exhalation from 1 to 10 and then begin again at 1. This is a bit more challenging, as there is more space between each count during which the mind may wander. But at some point you will find that you can practice in this more spacious style, too, for about 15 minutes without losing the count; at that point, try dropping the counting altogether and just focus on the breath.

No matter which of these three styles you are working with, you will inevitably find your attention wandering away from the breath before long. When you notice that your attention has wandered, just gently bring it back. As Amala-sensei says:

In the end it really doesn't matter how many times you get pulled away from the practice. One hundred, two hundred, three hundred times in the space of a sitting – that's Okay. Every time we get pulled away is an opportunity to come back, an opportunity to cut those threads that bind us to our delusions. And it is the willingness to come back, over and over again, that is really the core of this practice. Thoughts will inevitably arise, and it would be wrong to say that we are trying to stop our thoughts when we practice – because, in fact, that's a futile exercise. The more we try and stop the thoughts, the more they will come, because by trying to stop them we are giving them attention. Rather, what we do is very akin to what people are doing in aikido and other martial arts. We use the energy of our unruly mind, and divert it, channel it, into the practice. We try to deflect our attention away from the thoughts and onto the breath. And when we notice that our mind is not on the breath, then we gently bring it back.

The word *gently* here is really key. Zen teacher John Tarrant once likened the way that we hold our practice to the way you have to hold a wet bar of soap. If you hold it too tightly it shoots out of your hand. Another analogy that Amala-sensei has used is to the way we hold a baby:

If you hold a baby too tightly you smother it. If you hold it too lightly you could drop it. And this analogy is particularly apt because it points to the nature of our relationship to the practice: to take care of it, to nurture it, to become intimate with it. That's how a mother will take care of a baby. She doesn't hold her baby out at arm's length and try to figure out what it needs. She holds it close, and as she holds it close, what's going on becomes apparent. So it's a matter of going lightly, but at the same time being fully attentive. Dharma teacher Pema Chodron describes the way that we concentrate on the breath as 'touching the breath'. We're not strangling the breath, we're not wrestling it to the floor, but touching it. Actually the breath is touching us, each time we inhale, and each time we exhale.

If you find your mind very busy, it helps to choose one point in the body where you can focus on the flow of the breath. In Japanese Zen, the point most often recommended for this purpose is the *hara*, that is, in the belly, about three finger-widths below the navel. Focusing on this area brings your centre of gravity into the abdomen and this can help you to get out of your head and your thoughts. With your mind centred deep in the abdomen and focused on the physical sensations of its gentle expansion and contraction, you will still hear sounds or see changes in the light, but these things will take place more and more at the periphery of your attention.

Gradually, as you continue to stay with the breath, you will find that you are becoming more aware of all the aspects and all the phases of the breath. What at first might have seemed somewhat boring or static actually becomes more and more interesting as you pay attention. You may notice an overall soothing and calming of the nervous system. And as the nervous system calms, the breath in turn becomes increasingly fine and subtle. This means that in order to continue following the breath, your attention, too, will need to become ever more finely tuned. This sets up a virtuous cycle: attention leads to greater calm and greater calm to closer attention.[3] However the quality of the attention remains key. Tensing up to grab hold of the increasingly subtle breath will break the cycle, as will letting yourself grow so calm that you become drowsy and begin to drift into dreams. As before, just the right degree of gentle focus will draw you deeper and deeper into oneness with your breath. Over time you will come to recognise the mental and physiological signs of this union.

The practice of following the breath is generally the first practice that is taught to those who take up zazen. And yet it would be a mistake to think of it simply as a beginner's practice. In fact, this is the practice that the Buddha is said to have been doing at the time that he realised full enlightenment. The potential of this practice is unlimited. So take your time with it, and give each breath your full care and devotion. You may feel that your mind is always scattered, jumping here and there. But just noticing that is the most important first step in practice. Your mind may be scattered, but it is your own scattered mind that has generated the aspiration to sit, and to explore.

In fact, we only have one mind. Just as we tend to divide up the world around us into self and other, me and them, so we do the same thing inside. We divide our mind into concentrated mind and distracted mind, divide ourselves into good Zen student and hopeless Zen student. But in fact there is only one mind. And our job in zazen is to keep shifting back, to keep reaffirming that basic nature of the mind, which is one. We do this through giving ourselves to the practice.

3. This process is discussed in detail by Vajrayana teacher B. Alan Wallace; see for example in *The Attention Revolution* (Boston: Wisdom, 2006), p. 48.

SEIZA

Kneeling posture. The cushion may either be placed flat or vertically (as pictured) in order to gain more height.

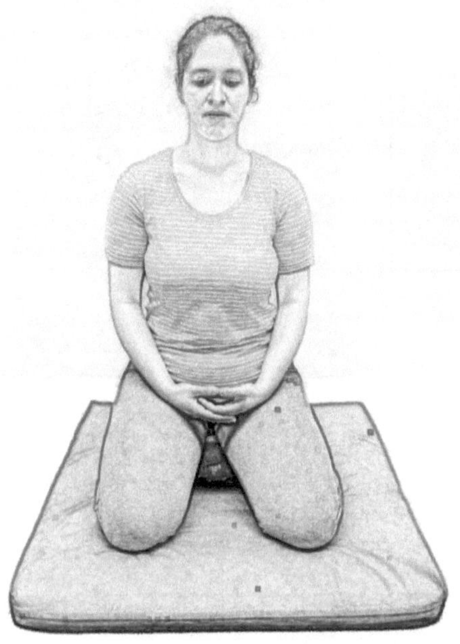

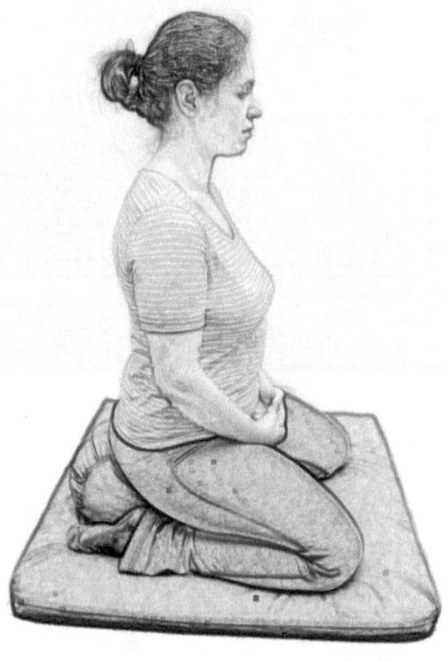

SEIZA WITH A BENCH

Kneeling with a bench. Feet may be placed inside or outside the legs of the bench.

BURMESE

One foot drawn in close to the centre of the body; the other foot placed directly in front of it on the floor.

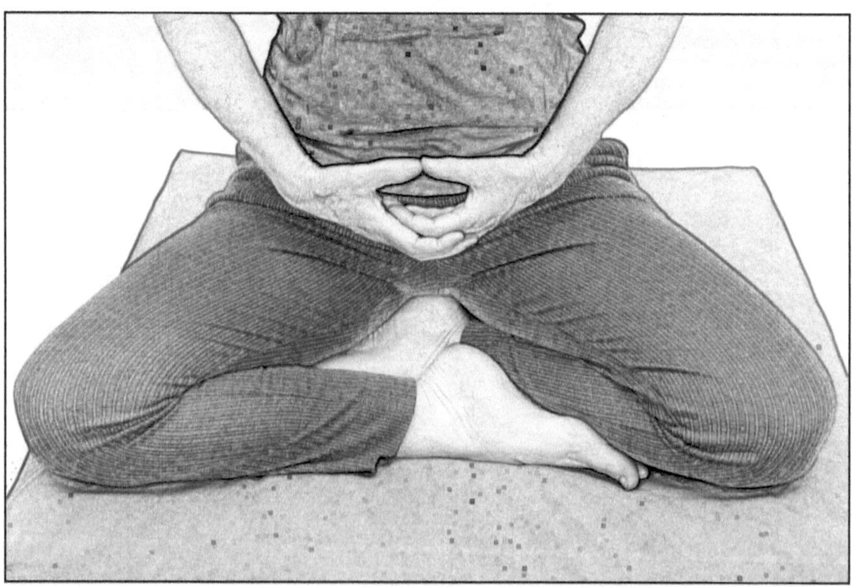

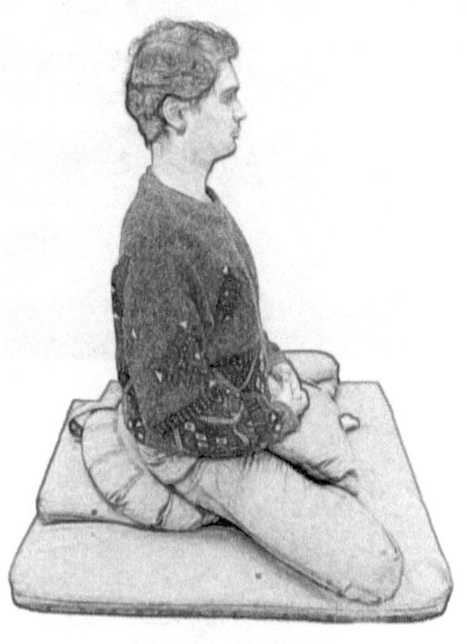

Notice the use of a small cushion for the hands whenever the lap is too far away to support the mudra comfortably. This prevents shoulder strain.

Note the straight neck and ears perfectly aligned over the shoulders.

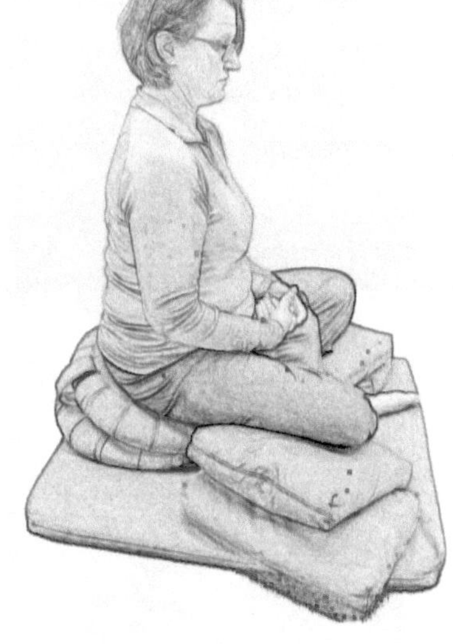

If the knees cannot comfortably reach the mat, they are supported by cushions. But note that they remain at least slightly lower than the hips.

QUARTER-LOTUS

One foot drawn in close to body; second foot placed on calf of first leg.

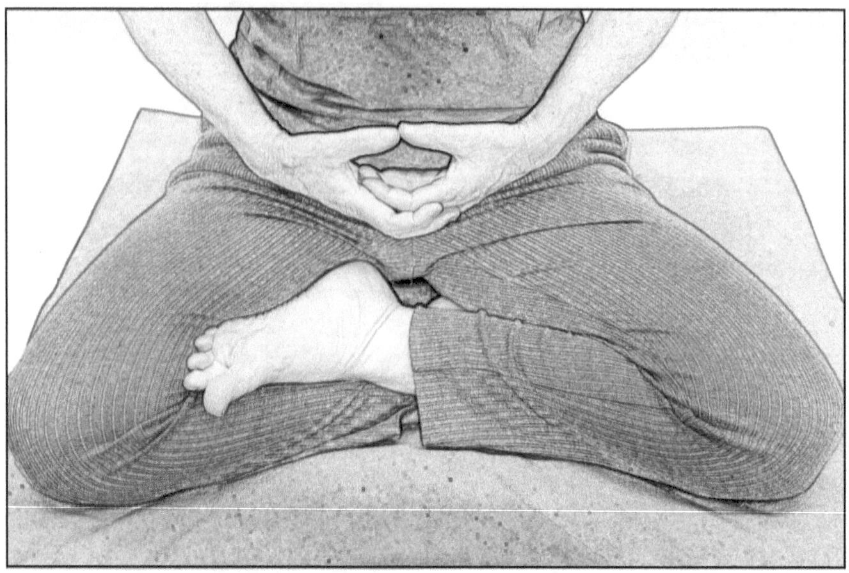

HALF-LOTUS

One foot drawn in close to body; second foot placed on upper thigh of first leg.
Make sure you can see the whole sole of the upper foot and wiggle the toes easily.
Don't twist your knee to achieve this; the key is in having open hips, for which some
hip-opening exercises may be necessary.

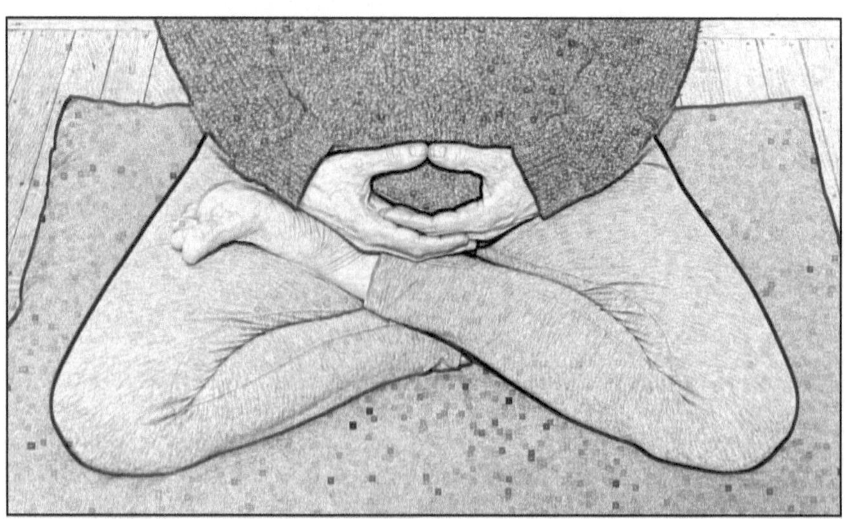

One foot placed on upper thigh of opposite leg; second foot placed on upper thigh of first leg. Caveats as for half-lotus.

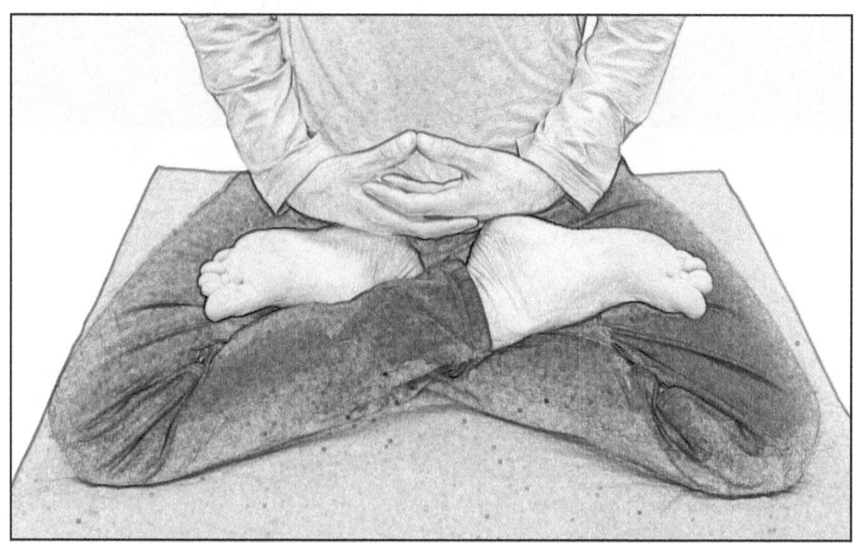

Sitting in quarter-lotus.

Sitting in full-lotus. This is a very stable posture that may not require much additional support.

CHAIR

Make sure that your weight is centred on your sitting bones, with the back upright and the upper body open and relaxed. Both feet should be flat on the floor and the knees slightly lower than the hips.

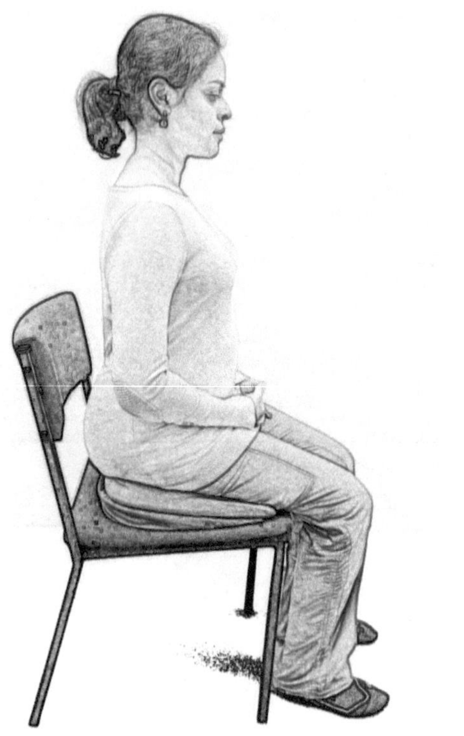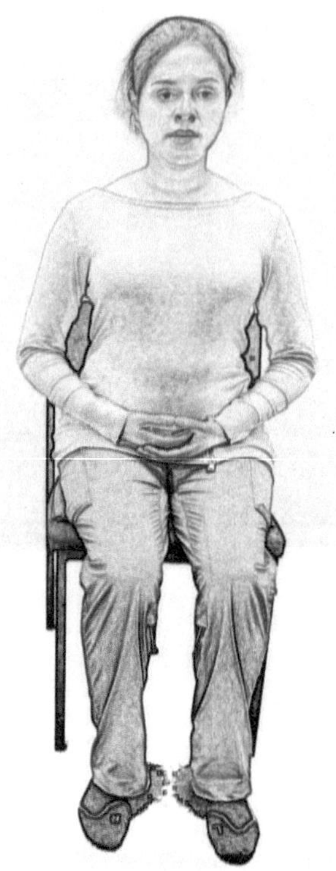

- If sitting on a cushion, both knees are firmly on the mat, and if sitting in a chair, both feet are firmly on the floor. These three points of contact (seat plus knees or feet) give the posture the necessary stability. If the knees or feet do not reach the floor they are supported by cushions.

- The hips are higher than the knees, so that a natural inwards curve can be maintained in the lower back. To find this curve it is often helpful to lean forward after sitting down and use the hands to stretch the flesh of the buttocks back, then sit up straight again.

- The hands are placed in the lap, left hand on top of right hand, with the thumbs lightly touching. It is often helpful to place a cushion or towel under the hands so that they may rest in position without pulling the shoulders forward.

- The shoulders are aligned over the hips, and the ears over the shoulders; the chest is open and the spine long. Imagine a string attached to the crown of your head gently pulling you upwards.

- The eyes are at least slightly open, lowered at about a 45-degree angle, the gaze soft and resting without strain.

- The belly is rounded with the breath flowing easily and naturally.

- Finally, take care when you sit to pay attention to your body's signals. Some discomfort while sitting is to be expected when you are new to the practice or when you are sitting for long periods, but if pain or numbness persists after the practice period ends, you should modify the way you are sitting. Sharp shooting pain while getting into a posture is a signal that you need to change what you are doing at that moment. If your legs fall asleep in the course of a round, there is no cause for concern, but do not try to stand up until you have full feeling in them. Standing up quickly when the feet or legs are asleep can cause falls or injury.

NOTE: Most bed and sofa pillows are too soft to support a stable sitting posture. If you don't own a zafu (Zen sitting cushion) or a bench, then a rolled-up blanket is usually the best choice.

TEISHO

* * *

Yangshan's Cushion
(2004–04–25)

In today's koan Master Yangshan encourages his student to put down his philosophical questions and attend to what is right in front of him. What might be revealed through the simple practice of sitting on a cushion?

The Dharma talk today will be on a koan called The Cushion. This is a koan presented by the thirteenth-century Japanese Zen master Keizan Jokin, and the case is as follows:

> A monk asked Zen Master Yangshan Huiji, 'Can Ultimate Reality teach about itself?'
> Yangshan said, 'There's nothing that I can tell you about this, but there is someone else who can.'
> The monk said, 'Where is this one who can teach it?'
> Yangshan pushed forward a cushion.
> When Guishan heard about it he said, 'Huiji brings out the activity of a sword.'[4]

We'll start by taking a look at the protagonists in this story. Besides the monk who asks the question and who is not named, we just have Master Yangshan, and then Master Guishan who adds his comment at the end. Guishan Lingyou was the teacher of Yangshan Huiji, and together these two were joint founders of the Guiyang school of Chan[5] in Tang Dynasty China. The Guiyang school was named for these masters, Gui-shan and Yang-shan; the 'shan' part of their names means 'mountain,' as each had taken his name from the mountain where he taught. Masters often did this, and this association of the teacher with the place is an interesting phenomenon, as the teacher takes on the name of something bigger than her- or himself, becoming identified with the local maunga, as Māori do.

4. From *The Transmission of Reality: The Himitsu Shōbōgenzō Koan Collection* by Keizan Jōkin-zenji and Mushin Daie-zenji. Translated by Yasuda Joshu Dainen-roshi and Anzan Hoshin-roshi. *Zanmai*, no. 12, p. 19 (1993). White Wind Zen Community www.wwzc.org. The Chinese names have been changed to Pinyin spellings.

5. For the words 'Zen' and 'Chan' see under Chan in the Glossary.

The Guiyang school founded by these two masters was known for its mellowness. Many of us, when we first learn about Zen, hear stories of the Rinzai masters who are famous for their shouts and blows, but the Guiyang school was very different. It was a subtle kind of teaching, and we'll see this in some of the exchanges that we're going to look at today. Another characteristic of this school was the use of circles. There are a number of koans involving the Guiyang masters where people employ the gesture of a circle, and there was apparently a manuscript containing a whole collection of circular symbols used to express the teaching. As we'll see, Yangshan himself became involved with that manuscript in quite a dramatic fashion.

Yangshan's Japanized name is Kyozan Ejaku[6] and his dates are 807–883.[7] He came from ancient Shaozhou which is in Guangdong province. This is the area we call Canton, in Southern China, where many of the earliest Chinese immigrants to New Zealand came from. His parents forbade him to become a monk, so Yangshan cut off two of his fingers, vowing that he would repay his filial obligations by seeking the Dharma. You can imagine the effect that such a drastic act would have on the parents. It would certainly get their attention! There are many stories about the fierce aspiration of men and women throughout the history of Chan and Zen.

Here is a story that takes place when Yangshan was with his first teacher Danyuan, before he went to work with Master Guishan, and since the story has some bearing on today's koan, I want to take a look at it:

6. Most Zen koans or teaching stories come to us from ancient China, and their protagonists are most often Chinese monks and masters. When the Japanese re-told these stories, they assigned the protagonists 'Japanised' names, as the Chinese names are difficult to pronounce (or to represent with the Japanese syllabary). For us as English speakers, the Japanese forms of the name are often more familiar and easier to remember. In the lineage of the Auckland Zen Centre, koans from the collections known as the *Mumonkan* (*The Gateless Barrier*) and the *Hekiganroku* (*Blue Cliff Record*) are studied using the Japanese names, while those from the *Shoyoroku* (*The Book of Equanimity*) are studied using the Chinese names. Thus, depending on the particular koan, the teishos in this book may refer to the protagonists either in Japanese or in Chinese. For the alternate name, please refer to the 'Names' Appendix in the back of the book.

7. Biographical information and anecdotes about this master, as well as about many of the other masters referenced in subsequent koans, comes from Andy Ferguson's important reference work, *Zen's Chinese Heritage: The Masters and Their Teachings* (Boston, Mass.: Wisdom, 2000).

Danyuan greatly esteemed Yangshan and said to him, 'Previously the national teacher Huizhong received the transmission of a total of ninety-seven symbolic circles from the Sixth Ancestor. He in turn passed these to me, saying, "Thirty years after I've died, a novice monk will come from the South who will greatly revive this teaching. When that time comes, pass the teaching on to him and don't let it end." Today I transmit them to you. You must uphold and preserve them.'

When he had finished speaking he passed the secret text to Yangshan. After receiving and examining the text, Yangshan burned it.

One day, Danyuan said to Yangshan, 'The symbols that I gave you are extremely rare, esoteric, and precious.'

Yangshan said, 'After I examined them, I burned them.'

Danyuan said, 'This Dharma gate of ours can't be understood by most people. Only the Buddha, the ancestors, and all the holy ones can fully understand it. How could you burn it?'

Yangshan said, 'After examining it, I fully comprehended its meaning. Then there was no use keeping the text.'

Danyuan said, 'Even so, when transmitting this to disciples, people of future times won't believe it.'

Yangshan said, 'If you'd like another copy that won't be a problem. I'll make another copy and give it to you. Then it won't be lost.'

Danyuan said, 'Please do.'[8]

Can you imagine the reaction of this elderly teacher who had been told by his teacher that a disciple would come who would preserve the secret teaching, and to whom he was to pass on this precious ancient text, and who then discovers that the student has burnt it? You have to put this in the context also of Chinese culture where there was enormous veneration paid to writing. But to Yangshan it seemed to be no big deal. He says, Okay, I'll write it out again and I'll give it to you.

Danyuan is obviously relieved. But what is this story pointing to? To understand this, we have to ask whether there is anything inherently valuable in these marks on a page that were given to Yangshan. What if he hadn't understood them? Would they have been transmitted if he'd just received the document? The fact that he fully comprehended these symbols meant that he could reproduce them, completely (though we have no way of checking!). So what was it that was transmitted? What was it that he understood?

8. Andy Ferguson, *Zen's Chinese Heritage* (Boston: Wisdom, 2000), p. 167.

Carl Jung emphasized over and over again that symbols are the best possible formulations we can make of something that is essentially beyond formulation, something that can't be fully tied down or completely expressed. So are the symbols important or not? Danyuan is concerned that without an actual text, people in the future won't give credence to the teachings they point to, but without their being comprehended they would be useless.

Now here's the story of when Yangshan met his primary teacher Guishan:

> Guishan asked Yangshan, 'As a novice monk, do you have a host or not?'
> Yanghan said, 'I have one.'
> Guishan said, 'Who is it?'
> Yangshan walked from west to east and then stood there erect.
> Guishan realised that Yangshan was extraordinary.[9]

Maybe we need to explain a little about this question that the teacher asks, 'Do you have a host or not?' On the surface of it, it might be that the teacher is asking the student, Do you have a teacher? Are you bound to any particular temple? But there's another layer to this. In Zen, guest and host are used as metaphors for our mind. The host is the one who doesn't go anywhere, who's always there; this is our essential nature. The guest is the stuff that comes and goes. So this is also a testing question. Guishan's trying to see what Yangshan's understanding is of his essential nature. And in the story, clearly Yangshan understands the underlying meaning of the question and he gives a beautiful demonstration that presents both guest and host together. He walks in the straight line from west to east and then stands tall.

Now this is a story about Yangshan after he had become a teacher:

> Zen master Yangshan entered the hall and addressed the monks saying, 'Each and every one of you, turn the light inward! Don't try to remember what I'm saying! For a beginningless eon, you have faced away from the light and been shrouded in darkness. The roots of delusion are deep. They're difficult to cut off and uproot. So [the Buddha] established expedient means to grab your attention. These are like showing yellow leaves to a crying child, who imagines they're gold and thus stops crying. You act as

9. *Ibid.*, p. 168.

though you're in a shop where someone sells a hundred goods made from gold and jade, but you're trying to weigh each item. So you say that Shitou had a real gold shop? Well in my shop there's a wide range of goods! If someone comes looking for mouse turds then I give him some. If someone comes looking for real gold then I give it to him.'[10]

What's he talking about here? Let's break it down a bit. First he says, 'The Buddha established expedient means to grab your attention.' Expedient means are all the teachings, all the different forms of teaching. They're not the direct experience of the truth, but they're ways of grabbing our attention, of getting us started on the path. The secret text of ninety-seven symbolic circles that Yangshan memorised was an expedient means.

And here he says, 'These are like yellow leaves given to a crying child who imagines they're gold and stops crying.' This is a beautiful image of expedient means. They're not the whole truth. But they're enough to stop the crying. Enough to grab our attention for long enough that we can step outside of our obsessions with our own problems for just a moment and turn towards something bigger.

And then, addressing himself to the monks Yangshan says, 'You think you're in a shop with all these different things you can choose from and you're weighing them up, picking this and picking that.' So what's wrong with this approach, this weighing up, this picking and choosing? The problem is that we've got to get past our discriminating mind. And the danger is that we latch onto this or that teaching and use our intellect to try and understand it. That's okay, but we've got to then go beyond the words to the thing itself. You can see this theme threaded through Yangshan's teaching. We have to go beyond the symbols, get to the real source of them. Where do they come from? What do they come out of?

Yangshan continues: 'Well, my shop's a general store. I've got all sorts of things in here. And I'll give you whatever you come looking for. If you want mouse turds, that's what you'll get; if you want real gold, that's what you'll get.' It's all to do with what we want. What do we really want?

But then, as the story goes on, a student stands up and says:

'I don't want mouse turds. May I have the Master's real gold?'

10. Ferguson, *Zen's Chinese Heritage*, p. 168.

Yangshan said, 'If you try to bite down on the head of a flying arrow, you can try until the year of the ass but you won't succeed.'

The year of the ass doesn't exist; if you take a look at the twelve Chinese signs of the zodiac, you'll see there's no ass in there. So he's saying, You can try for the rest of your life, but if you're trying to bite on something that you can't grasp, like an arrow in mid-flight, you're not going to succeed. We're told that at this the monk had no response. And Yangshan said:

'If you want to exchange something, we can make a deal. If you don't want to exchange anything then we can't.'

Another translation of this is, 'Business depends on demand.' He's bringing us back to this question of what we want. What are we looking for? Are we willing to exchange our cherished notions and attachments for awakening? Unless we're willing to give up our delusions, we can't awaken. We have to let them go, but we resist. There's a price to pay for freedom. But often we refuse to accept that everything changes and has no enduring substance; we rely on conditioned (and therefore impermanent and unreliable) things for our happiness; we act as if we were separate from the world around us.

Then Yangshan continues:

'If I truly speak of Zen, then there won't be a single companion at your side. How can this be if there's five or seven hundred in the assembly? If I talk about this and that and you strain your neck trying to pick something up, then it would be like fooling a little child with an empty hand. There's nothing authentic about it. Today I'm clarifying what is holy, which is not a matter of collecting and calming the mind. Instead you must practice to realize the true sea of self-nature.' [11]

This first statement can be taken in two different ways. He says, 'If I truly speak of Zen, then there won't be a single companion at your side.' Perhaps he's saying that there are very few who really want to hear the truth. Most people are going to be much more comfortable with easy explanations. So if I speak of the highest truth, not so many people will be listening, because it's going to push them back on themselves. Or another way to understand this is that he's saying, 'If you really hear what I'm saying, there won't be anybody else in the room. There won't be

11. *Ibid.*, p. 169.

any other. There'll just be you.' Or as the Baby Buddha said, 'Above the heavens, below the heavens, I am the only one.' Then Yangshan says, if I talk about this and that and you strain your neck trying to pick something up, then that's not what this is all about. This is not a matter of grasping something. 'Instead,' he says, 'you must practice to realise the true sea of self-nature.' More than just becoming calm and concentrated, we must *realise* the bottomless, immeasurably vast ocean of Buddha Nature.

Now let's go back to today's case. As we said, this koan is found in a collection compiled by Keizan Jokin, and Keizan also offers a commentary which we'll have a look at. Keizan was three generations after Master Dogen;[12] his dates are 1268–1325 and he's considered the second most important Japanese Soto Zen master after Dogen. So, the case again:

> A monk asked Zen Master Yangshan Huiji, 'Can Ultimate Reality teach about itself?'
> Yangshan said, 'There's nothing that I can tell you about this, but there is someone else who can.'
> The monk said, 'Where is this one who can teach it?'
> Yangshan pushed forward a cushion.
> When Guishan heard about it he said, 'Huiji brings out the activity of a sword.'

And here is what Keizan says in his commentary:

> This monk wasn't afraid to lose his life to that sword and so he spoke up. Yangshan didn't miss with the sword. He cut off the man's head before he knew he was cut.
>
> In just that moment when he pushes the cushion forward there is such subtlety. Can that cushion really be the one with the answer? Or is it really a cushion? And what about pushing it forward? Is that the one?
>
> Right here, how do you understand it? Look, I'm pushing a cushion forward now but do you really see it? (Whistles.) Like this! Look into it.[13]

---

12. Information about Master Dogen and other well-known masters may be found in the Glossary.

13. From *The Transmission of Reality: The Himitsu Shōbōgenzō Koan Collection* by Keizan Jōkin-zenji and Mushin Daie-zenji. Translated by Yasuda Joshu Dainen-roshi and Anzan Hoshin-roshi. *Zanmai*, no. 12, p. 19 (1993). White Wind Zen Community www.wwzc.org. The Chinese names have been changed to Pinyin spellings.

'This monk wasn't afraid to lose his life to Yangshan's sword, and so he spoke up.' This is the first point. Keizan is reminding us of the importance of asking, to be brave enough to ask your question. Maybe it's a silly question. It doesn't matter. Asking it, you'll find out. You'll get a response of some kind. So being ready and willing to stick your neck out and ask your question is very important.

Keizan then says, 'Yangshan didn't miss with the sword.' Guishan says so in his comment on the story too. But what is Yangshan cutting off here? We could say that he's cutting off all the avenues that the monk might pursue that are outside of him. The monk wants instruction from Yangshan about Ultimate Reality, but Yangshan doesn't oblige – how could he?

And, Keizan says, 'In just that moment when he pushes the cushion forward, there is such subtlety.' There is such subtlety all around us but we miss it.

Right here. [Pushing cushion forward.]

Can that cushion really be the one with the answer?

It's just a cushion, isn't it?

Is it really a cushion that he's pushing forward?

What's he saying?

Clearly, he's inviting the monk to be the one, to be the 'someone else' he mentions, the one who looks into Ultimate Reality. But also the whole truth is already right there in that pushing forward the cushion. It's all right there. Can you see it?

'What about pushing it forward? Is that the one?' asks Keizan. And as he pushes the cushion forward, he whistles. [Whistles.] And then his last words are, 'Look into it.'

That's our job; that's our job as Zen practitioners. To look into it. To look into ourselves. To sit. To stay with whatever is, even when we are not sitting. That's our job. This is one of the reasons why we put a lot of emphasis in Zen on no moving, because in not moving we get this opportunity to stay, to stay with whatever's going on, to sit with it, to see it. To stay with our vulnerability. To be with our pain. To experience our fear, and look at that. Because that's what *is* at this moment. That's Ultimate Reality teaching about itself.

Master Yangshan silently pushes forward a cushion. Blaise Pascal said, 'All of humanity's problems arise from man's inability to sit quietly in a room alone.' The cushion is a gift, a presentation of ultimate truth, and also a challenge. Can we stop all our manoeuvring, all our grasping at things, and look directly, nakedly? The healing happens right here, where we are now, and includes everyone. All we have to do is stop and look.

We'll stop here and recite the four vows.

*   *

*

Every day Zuigan used to call to himself, 'O Master!' and would answer himself, 'Yes?'

'Be awake! Be awake!' he would exclaim, and then answer, 'Yes, yes!'

'Do not be deceived by others, any day, any time.'

'No, I will not.'

—*Mumonkan*, CASE 12

CHAPTER 2

Establishing a Daily Practice

ONCE you have learned how to do zazen, the next step is learning to do it every day. The practice of zazen is simple — so simple that anyone can do it; and yet it is not easy — it is so difficult, in fact, that probably most people who have learned *how* to do it, *don't* do it. Zazen is not a quick fix for our problems. Though its potential is unlimited, it does require great patience, great persistence and a great determination to sit through whatever arises: pain, boredom, restlessness, fear — physical and emotional challenges of all kinds. Still, there is a direct relationship between the amount of sincere effort we put into our practice and the amount of transformation we'll experience in our lives. Daily practice is the key to seeing results from our meditation; zazen must become a part of one's life, almost as indispensable as drinking water.

At the Rochester Zen Center, week-long sesshin (intensive retreats) are offered quite frequently, generally six times a year. If someone were to come to all of those sesshins, they would be doing a lot of serious sitting.

And yet Roshi Bodhin Kjolhede, Abbot of the Center, has frequently said that if he had to choose between someone coming regularly to sesshin but never establishing a daily practice or someone with a daily practice who rarely came to sesshin, he would choose the latter every time.

For the beginner, there can be many obstacles to establishing this daily consistency in practice. The first apparent obstacle is often simply a lack of time. Our lives are already so busy and pressurised — in fact, this may be the very thing that made us seek out instruction in meditation in the first place. How can trying to insert one more activity, one more requirement, into our already over-scheduled lives possibly help?

In fact, it may not be so much a question of adding more in but at looking what we may be able to subtract, how we can simplify. We may have to honestly look at our own attitudes, coloured as they are bound to be by the attitudes of the society we live in. How can we justify taking time each day to sit and do nothing? Isn't it more important to be contributing, to be helping, to be doing something? Our social world is strongly oriented towards 'doing', but meditation is not about 'doing' but rather about 'being'. How can taking some time to simply 'be' each day help us with all that we want to 'do'? Most of us probably have a sense that increased calm, centredness, and focus will allow us to set clear priorities and goals and will be helpful to those around us as well as to ourselves as we move through our day. But in committing to a daily meditation practice, we really have to bring these beliefs to the forefront of our consciousness and actively place our trust in them. Even more importantly, learning to just sit for its own sake will be what truly sustains us in the long run.

In the meantime, there are many practical steps we can take that will help us to integrate a regular practice into our lives more smoothly. The first is finding a time to meditate that works with our daily timetable. It is important for most people to sit at the same time each day, as this allows the practice to become established as a habitual routine. If we decide instead that we will fit meditation in each day whenever we have the chance, it is very likely that the chance will never present itself.[1]

The classic time to sit is first thing in the morning. It is easy to make meditation a part of your morning routine simply by getting up a bit earlier

---

1. At least that is the case for most people. One exception can be parents with young children, when it often is a question of snatching a few minutes when the children are napping and not waiting for perfect conditions to arise.

(or by spending a bit less time reading the news or whatever else you might do in the morning that is not essential), and this way meditation practice will not be forgotten or skipped in the busyness of the day. Besides this practical advantage, the world tends to be especially quiet, calm and open in the early morning, which allows our minds also to manifest more of these qualities. We have just woken, so we are likely to have energy and alertness to offer to the practice, and, after a good rest, the mind tends to be relatively empty of the obsessive thoughts that will inevitably be triggered by the events of the day.

Just before bed is another good time to sit, and may be better for people who are simply not 'morning people'. Sitting at the end of the day can be a really good way to wind down – physiologically much more restful than watching a screen – and many people report that they sleep better after doing zazen in the evening.

Other times that work for some people are as part of a lunch hour (just before lunch) or immediately after coming home from work – again, a more helpful way to wind down than drinking a beer, for example. Find what works in your own life and then make a commitment to it. Remember that in finding what works, you do need to take into consideration those around you, and especially those you live with. For example, if your pattern is to spend some time catching up with your spouse as soon as you get home from work, then this is probably not the best time for your daily zazen. Your spouse is unlikely to be happy about being told that from now on instead of sharing some time together you will be going into another room and closing the door. Making sure that your practice harmonises with what is needed at home can be an important factor in helping establish a practice that will be sustainable over the long haul.

Besides finding a specific time, it can also be helpful to sit in a specific place. Choose a quiet place where you can close the door and not be interrupted. Ambient noise, such as traffic sounds or the refrigerator, are fine, but it is best if you can be out of earshot of conversations, music, or television. Sit facing the wall or a plain surface. If you have enough space to leave your cushions in place between sessions of zazen, that can be very helpful as you won't have to do a lot of set-up each time you want to sit. Many people also find it helpful to set up a small altar, or light incense or a candle; but this will depend on your circumstances and how much room you have available, and is certainly not a necessity.

It is important to begin your practice modestly. It is much better to start by sitting for 10 minutes at the same time and in the same place every day, as this will form the beginnings of a solid habit, rather than committing to an hour and not being able to complete the commitment. Often the hardest part is just getting to the mat. If you can get there with a 10-minute sit in mind, you may find that after 10 minutes you have no desire to get up. But whatever amount of time you commit to, do try to complete the whole of it. It is best to set an alarm, place it out of sight, and then just forget about time and focus on your practice. If you keep checking the time, not only is that disruptive to your practice, but you may be tempted to quit a bit early. Though it is easy to think, 'Close enough!' those last few minutes may be the most valuable ones – either because this may be the time of your deepest concentration, or because this may be the time when you are really forced to stretch your limits.

Establishing a daily practice doesn't happen overnight and may require persistence, that is, many fresh starts. The Buddha talked about *patisotha-gami* which refers to 'going against the stream'. At the outset, our practice is often beset by difficulties because of the force and momentum of our habits. This is the stream that we're going against – and, again, it can help to remember that it is not just our own personal habits but the habits of the society around us as well. We may not experience much support or understanding from others as we try to establish a daily meditation practice. So we need to understand from the beginning that establishing a practice – and maintaining it through the years – will involve effort and discipline. Recognising this fact, the Buddha put teachings about effective effort at the centre of the instruction he offered to his followers.

In the Buddha's very first and most essential discourse he presented his Four Noble Truths: that suffering exists, that suffering arises from causes and conditions, that suffering may be removed by removing its causes and conditions, and that there is a Path or a Way to removing these. This Path, in turn, he divided into the eight parts which English speakers know as Right View, Right Aspiration, Right Speech, Right Action, Right Livelihood, Right Effort, Right Mindfulness, and Right Concentration.

So Right Effort was a basic element of the teachings from the beginning. But it has often been pointed out that this English word 'right' is not quite right! In Pali the word is *samma* and in Sanskrit it is *samyak,*

soften into that place. As you do so, the body subtly releases, and you find that you can stretch a bit further.

But just as we might feel resistance to getting ourselves onto the yoga mat or to doing some other type of exercise, in spite of the fact that we know it will make us feel better in the long run, so waking up is something we often don't completely want to do. The process can be unpleasant, both physically and mentally. In fact, it asks us to face aspects of ourselves and truths about the world that we've put a lot of energy into avoiding. Part of what we're waking up to are the harsh realities of existence: impermanence, suffering, no-self. In Buddhism these are known as the Three Dharma Seals, and any system of teaching or instruction which does not acknowledge these three is said to be a non-Buddhist teaching. These three marks of existence are in fact things that we very naturally don't want to face; but, at the same time, we need to understand that if we are shutting ourselves down or closing our hearts in an attempt to deny these realities, we are simultaneously closing ourselves off from life's beauty and perfection. So it really does take a great effort to turn ourselves around.

As we make the commitment to sit every day, our discipline can seem dualistic: we are making ourselves do something; we are striving to achieve something. We do come to practice with all the habits that have caused suffering in our lives, so we must discover Right Effort through trial and error; and sometimes, if we're stubborn, it can be a lot of error. The Buddha himself engaged in extreme asceticism for years and years, starving himself until he was said to have been able to feel his spine when he touched his belly, and he only realised that he was on the wrong track when he was on the point of death. We human beings are complex, and have a powerful tendency to hold onto our ideas in spite of the evidence.

In the end, however, we have to accept that our errors, our wanderings, our missing the mark, are not separate from the Path. In fact, there is no other way for us to go forward. And as long as we are applying ourselves sincerely, with as much wholeheartedness as we can muster, then, as Zen Master Dogen tells us, not only are we are on the Way, but we are in fact accomplishing the Way.

TEISHO

✳ ✳ ✳

Zuigan Calls 'Master'
(2006–07–09)

In this teisho we meet a Zen master about whom little is known beyond the fact 'that he was well-liked, that he was a modest person, and that although he was deeply enlightened, he did not neglect his daily practice.' In this he set a model for his students.

For the teisho today we're going to take up a koan, Case 12 in the *Mumonkan*, Zuigan Calls 'Master'. The *Mumonkan*, called in English *The Gateless Barrier* or *The Gateless Gate*, is one of the collections of koans that are part of our Zen curriculum, and in the *Mumonkan* each koan is accompanied by a commentary and a verse written by Master Mumon (Wumen in Chinese), who assembled the collection. Today we're going to look at all three parts of Case 12: the koan itself, the commentary, and the verse.[4]

THE CASE

Every day Zuigan used to call to himself, 'O Master!' and would answer himself, 'Yes?'
'Be awake! Be awake!' he would exclaim, and then answer, 'Yes! yes!'
'Do not be deceived by others, any day, any time.'
'No, I will not.'

THE COMMENTARY

Old Zuigan himself sells and himself buys. He brings forth a lot of masks of goblins and demons and plays with them. How so? Look and see! A calling one, an answering one, an awake one, and one who will not be deceived by others. If you take these different appearances as really existing, then you are altogether mistaken. If you imitate Zuigan your understanding is that of a fox.

THE VERSE

Those who search for the Way do not realise the truth.
They only know their old discriminating consciousness.

4. The English version of this koan is from the Rochester Zen Center edition of the

This is the cause of the endless cycle of birth and death,
yet ignorant people take it for the original self.

There's just one protagonist in this particular koan, Zuigan Shigen.[5] Zuigan was a 13th-generation Chinese master, in other words, twelve generations after Bodhidharma. We don't know a lot about Zuigan and we don't have any dates for him, but from the people he worked with we can guess that he was active in the second half of the eighth century, probably dying somewhere round about the end of that century, which would be about 40 years after Master Rinzai was teaching. Zuigan was a disciple of the great master Ganto Zenkatsu. We do know that Zuigan was very well-liked, that he was a modest person, and that although he was deeply enlightened, he did not neglect his daily practice. This was central to his teaching as we'll see. There is an account of his main encounter with Ganto and the question he asked Ganto which eventually brought him to awakening:

Zuigan came to Ganto and asked him, 'What is the Eternal Truth?'
Ganto shot back, 'You've missed it.'

So he asks this sincere question, and yet he gets a very sharp response from Ganto. That's not it! Already missed it. But Zuigan doesn't leave it there; he comes back and asks another question:

'What is it when I've missed it?'

That's a good question. What is it when we've missed it? Surely the Eternal Truth is not affected by our not seeing it. If it is eternal, it is unchanging, right? But Ganto replies:

'It is no longer the eternal truth.'[6]

So Ganto's really painting him into a corner with this, saying that if you ask about the eternal truth, you've missed it, but you can't just rest in your having missed it, because then it's no longer the truth. This is very typical of koans; the whole point of a koan is to stymie us, to block our normal ways of reasoning things out, of making sense of them.

After this second response of Ganto's, Zuigan, we're told, fell silent. We

---

Mumonkan revised in 2011 and used by students when working on koans in dokusan (see Chapter 4 and Glossary for more about dokusan).

5. Ruiyan Shiyan in Chinese. See the Names appendix for more information.

6. Zenkei Shibayama, *Gateless Barrier: Zen Comments on the Mumonkan* (New York: Harper and Row, 1974), p. 92.

don't know how long he worked on this question, whether it was weeks or months or years, but at a certain point, when he met with his teacher Ganto, probably in *dokusan*, perhaps in public, we don't know, Ganto saw that he was ripe and so he threw something out to Zuigan. Ganto said:

'If you affirm it, you are not yet rid of the root of defilement. If you deny it, you are immersed in endless births and deaths.'

Probably Zuigan had come to Ganto to demonstrate his understanding of the koan and this was Ganto's catalyst for getting him to see his True Nature. And we're told that on hearing this Zuigan was enlightened. 'If you affirm it, you are not yet rid of the root of defilement. If you deny it, you are immersed in endless births and deaths.' So if you go around talking about the Eternal Truth, there's still defilement in that – there's separation, there's you and then there's the Eternal Truth. But if you deny the existence of the Eternal Truth, then you're just caught up in samsara, you're caught up in relativity – where birth and death seem very solid and real. How do we resolve this koan? For Zuigan the resolution came to be expressed through his daily calling out, 'O Master!' and answering, 'Yes!' This is where he demonstrated his intimate understanding of this question that Master Ganto had helped him to clarify.

We're told that Zuigan used to do this practice frequently – every day – and not only after his enlightenment, but also before, and that he continued doing it right up to his death. He never exhausted it. We're also told that he didn't always do it privately, just to himself. He would sometimes ascend the rostrum, take the teaching seat, and do it as a kind of a teisho before the assembled monks. Sometimes he would do it sitting on a certain flat rock at his temple.

One of the things Zuigan is pointing to with this is how important it is to maintain a daily practice, even after deep enlightenment. Not fully appreciating this necessity has led many teachers astray. Sometimes we read about teachers in various traditions who clearly have insight; they can express the Dharma well, but then at some point they go off the rails, they become corrupted in some way (usually involving sex, money or power), or their followers end up engaging in harmful practices; and one thing that may be going on here is that these teachers haven't maintained their vigilance. Even after an insight or two we can repeatedly lose sight of our True Nature because of our delusive habit-patterns. If we're just living out of our memory of an opening we've experienced then it's no longer a living thing. We have to maintain a living awareness that we *are* Buddha-nature. Each moment. Because each moment is completely new. That's why Zuigan could never exhaust this practice of his. Every time he took it up it was completely fresh — because the moment was completely fresh. And he was so fully engaging in this inner exchange that he was a completely new person.

The word that he uses when he calls to himself, 'Master,' in the Japanese is *shujinko*, and this refers to the head or the leader, the one in charge. He's really referring here to the master of his own mind, the one who sees and hears and tastes. The Thai master Ajahn Chah called this 'the one who knows.' Japanese Zen master Bassui[7] had this as his natural koan, 'Who is the master?' Who is the one who lifts an arm? … who drinks water? … who hears sounds? There are endless formulations of this question: What is it? What am I? Or, What is Mu?[8] Or, What was my face before my parents were born? There are all these different ways we approach this master because essentially she is unnamable. She is beyond anything we can say about her.

So Zuigan calls out to this one, and then this one answers, 'Yes!' Then he exclaims, 'Be awake, be awake!' Be fully aware. And he responds to himself, 'Yes, yes!' 'Do not be deceived by others!' There's a lot in this admonition, Do not be deceived by others. The word used for deceived is very closely related to the word for deluded. Don't be deluded by others, don't be led astray.

But who are these others? The master is One, there is nothing outside this master. Sekida[9] comments that we can't be deluded by others, we can only be deluded by our own delusions. This is the principle that con artists work on. They manage to get people to believe the most preposterous things by tapping into their greed, usually, or pride — some desire or aversion that they turn to their own use. But it would be wrong to understand this 'Do not be deceived by others!' as merely some kind of a daily ethical self-examination. In that sort of introspection, there's still a subject and an object.

Koun Yamada-roshi[10] in his commentary to the case, writes:

7. Great 14th-century Zen master.
8. See Glossary under Mu.
9. 20th-century Zen teacher and scholar; he wrote a commentary on the *Mumonkan*.
10. Successor to Yasutani-roshi.

When Zuigan calls, 'Master!' you may think that the one who calls is his superficial 'I' and the master called to is his true essential nature. That is a misconception. From the Zen point of view, you should know that the one calling and the one called to are both Zuigan's essential nature. It is sometimes expedient to name the superficial consciousness 'ego' but the truth is that the ego does not have substantial existence. It is merely a concept or a kind of delusion.[11]

Yamada goes on to describe ego as a glorious light thrown off by our essential-nature. Rays thrown off by Buddha nature. Not separate – though the rays may think otherwise. When the Baby Buddha emerged from Queen Maya's womb, he is said to have proclaimed, 'Above the Heavens, Below the Heavens, I alone am the Honoured One!' This is our absolute aloneness which includes everything. There is nothing that is separate from Buddha Nature.

The commentary:

> Old Zuigan himself sells and himself buys. He brings forth a lot of masks of goblins and demons and plays with them. How so? Look and see! A calling one, an answering one, an awake one, and one who will not be deceived by others. If you take these different appearances as really existing, then you are altogether mistaken. If you imitate Zuigan your understanding is that of a fox.

'Old Zuigan himself sells and himself buys.' What is Mumon saying? It's all just Zuigan, isn't it – the one who asks and the one who replies? So, Mumon is saying, it's as if Zuigan is selling himself something he already owns, and then he's buying that from himself, paying good money for it.

'He brings forth a lot of masks of goblins and demons and plays with them.' Goblins and demons are beings from the lower realms of existence, realms that we fall into if we separate ourselves from others. So in his commentary Mumon is playfully warning us not to be deceived by Zuigan's little drama. He says, 'Look and see!' The word he's using here is 'ni' in Japanese and it's a character that was believed to keep devils away. People would write it on a little piece of paper and they'd paste the piece of paper on their gate as protection against devils.

11. Kōun Yamada, *Gateless Gate* (Tucson: University of Arizona Press, 1990), p. 64.

Look and see! That's our best protection against what would possess us. Mumon wants us to see beyond the masks.

What's under the masks?

Who is the Master?

If we're doing zazen and we're just caught up in the usual internal monologue while we're sitting then it's like we're buying and selling ourselves. We're dividing ourselves into this and that and missing the One. Is that what Zuigan's doing? He certainly is dividing up the indivisible. But the difference is, he knows what he's up to. He's not thinking that these masks are real.

The truth is that we live in a world of differentiation. We don't live in some kind of soup where everything's all the same. To live is to live in a world of particulars. So to be alive, to be fully in this world, is to *always* be wearing masks. The secret is to move smoothly and freely from mask to mask. From role to role. The problem is that we get attached to certain masks that we wear and we identify with them and we think that's who we are. We get stuck. But we could say that practice is just learning to fully be each mask that we put on, and then to take it off and put on the next one. Put on the tooth-brushing mask, put on the answering-the-door mask, the filling-out-a-form mask, the driving-to-work mask. Wear it completely. Fill that role with our whole heart.

'If you take these different appearances as really existing, then you are altogether mistaken.' But when you see the masks as masks, it's a whole different thing. It may look exactly the same from the outside, but it's not.

As Zuigan plays with his masks, he is totally involved in the exchange. And there's joy in it, too! One ancient master commented, 'A dragon enjoys a pearl.' If you look at Chinese pictures of dragons, they always have a pearl between their claws and they also have this huge dragon-grin on their faces. They're inseparable from their pearl. It's like they're playing with it, they're tossing it between their claws and wrapping their bodies around it. There was an animé film a few years ago called *Spirited Away* by Hayao Miyazaki which had the most extraordinary dragon character in it whose body would whip around, dart and leap with incredible energy and dynamism. It's the same here with Zuigan and his 'O Master.' He's delighting in his true nature, savouring it, bringing it out and holding it up to the light. And sharing it, sharing it with others. This is really what teaching is based on, the urge to share this joy with others. So he's twisting and turning his pearl and sending out its light-rays in all directions.

Mumon ends his commentary by saying, 'If you imitate Zuigan your understanding is that of a fox.' A fox-like understanding is one which is cunning, deceptive, or not true. We have to find our own way in practice and in life. Nobody can tell us how to make the practice alive, how to make it true. The key thing is to put our whole being into it. If we do that, even if we did imitate Zuigan completely, it wouldn't just be a fox-like understanding.

The verse:

> *Those who search for the Way do not realise the truth.*
> *They only know their old discriminating consciousness.*
> *This is the cause of the endless cycle of birth and death,*
> *yet ignorant people take it for the original self.*

This verse was not written by Mumon. He uplifted it from another master, Chosa (Changsha in Chinese), who taught about three generations prior to Zuigan. And it's a very important verse. It really points to what blocks us in our practice. 'Those who search for the Way do not realise the truth. They only know their old discriminating consciousness.' Because we get caught in the dramas of our discriminating consciousness we miss the Way. We search for it everywhere and we don't find it. In Aitken-roshi's translation of this verse, 'their old discriminating consciousness' is translated as 'their consciousness up to now'. This is the consciousness of past, present, and future, of before and after. Ordinary consciousness is that internal monologue that we become so familiar with when we start to practice, consciousness of plans and worries, things to do, and things to say, and things to buy. I said and he said and she said. I'm this way, he's that way. We get so involved in this stream of thoughts and opinions and dramas that we think it's real. And it has a reality through our buying into it. Deceived by this stream of thoughts, we postulate an I. And out of that come all our attachments and aversions and delusions. This false notion is the source of all our suffering – it's what keeps us in the endless cycle of birth and death, because this limited 'ego-I' is what is born and dies.

*

There's a story that's a kind of sequel to Zuigan's case. This is related by Zenkei Shibayama-roshi in his commentary on this koan[12] and it's about another teacher, Master Gensha; his dates are 835–908, so he's more or less a contemporary of Zuigan. According to this story, a monk came one day to see Master Gensha and Gensha asked the newcomer in standard new-monk-coming-to-the-temple fashion, 'Where have you been recently?'

'With Master Zuigan, sir,' replied the monk.

'I see. In what manner does Master Zuigan instruct his disciples?' asked Gensha.

The monk described how Zuigan would call to himself, 'O Master,' and answer, 'Yes!' 'Be awake, be awake,' 'Yes, yes,' and so forth. Listening to the monk, Gensha asked him, 'Well, why didn't you stay longer with Zuigan to continue your training?'

And the monk answered, 'Well, Master Zuigan died.'

At this reply Gensha then shot an unexpected question to the monk: 'If you call out to him now, "O Master!" will he answer?'

Unfortunately the monk wasn't able to say a word in reply and remained silent.

Why did Gensha ask this question?

What was he pointing the monk towards?

Who is this True Master?

The monk's every move, his every heartbeat, his every breath was animated by this Master. Including his search, his search for the truth, his wandering from temple to temple, his coming before the masters in these uncomfortable exchanges. Who is the Master?

All he has to do is stop looking elsewhere.

We'll stop here and recite the four vows.

*   *

*

12. Zenkei Shibayama, *Gateless Barrier: Zen Comments on the Mumonkan* (New York: Harper and Row, 1974), p. 95.

*Throw yourself into
the house of the Buddha!*

—DOGEN ZENJI

CHAPTER 3

Sitting with a Group

SOMETIMES, after successfully establishing a home sitting practice, people may wonder why they should bother to sit with a group when it is easier to sit at home. In a city like Auckland, travel times may be considerable, and the hassle of getting to the Centre may seem to be directly at odds with the calm and simplicity one is hoping to find. Nevertheless, most people do find that sitting with a group offers a number of benefits that are simply not available when we sit on our own. As we sit together with ten, twenty, or thirty other people, a deep stillness emerges, and we generate a group energy that can help us to sit still for longer than we are able to do on our own and to concentrate more easily. Many people notice that even the zendo itself holds a residual energy that is conducive to a deep, settled practice. Besides this, of course, it can be inspiring to feel the support of others who share an aspiration to awaken, and to take advantage of the help and advice that the teacher and other senior practitioners are able to offer.

The tradition of Zen meditation is perhaps more group-centred than that found in some other forms of Buddhism. In the Buddha's time, the monastics typically went into the forest on their own each day to practice sitting or walking meditation, and in today's Theravada monasteries each monastic will generally have their own hut or cell where they will meditate. Many branches of the Tibetan tradition, too, are strongly focused on preparing people for long-term solo retreat. But in the very group-oriented cultures of East Asia where Zen was born, sitting together became the norm. Particularly in Japan, these group sittings came to follow a very formal pattern, much of which is carried on in Zen centres today. This can feel a bit intimidating at first, but it is part of what adds to the richness and grace of a group sitting. The formal choreography, so to speak, means that the sitting can be conducted entirely in silence (or, rather, without words, as musical instruments and chanting form part of the pattern), and it also means that once you have learned the 'steps', you can join the dance seamlessly and without distraction.

At the Auckland Zen Centre, sitters generally start by donning a brown sitting robe (though this is not required). Putting on the robe can help us to mark a transition from the busy, outward-oriented 'doing' of our day to the focused, centred 'being' of zazen. The half-hour before the start of the sitting is quiet time; this gives everyone a chance to enter a calm space where they can begin to turn the mind inward.

The zendo is where we do our formal practice, and there are a number of conventions that we observe when entering, leaving, or moving about this space. These help us to express our respect and gratitude for the practice we have received and for the efforts that have been made and continue to be made by our fellow-sitters. The Guidelines on pp. 59–61 give a summary of the forms observed during sittings and chanting services at the Auckland Zen Centre. If you attend a sitting at a Zen Centre that belongs to a different teaching lineage, you will find some differences in the details of the forms that are observed; however, the spirit behind the forms remains the same.

When people encounter the level of detail that is expressed in these guidelines they may worry that they will make mistakes. Of course we all do make mistakes, especially when we are beginners, and there is no problem with that. It should also not be a problem that the monitors who conduct each sitting may correct you. This is one way that we learn, and it is an excellent training opportunity to try to just take the corrections onboard without taking them personally.

ROSHI KAPLAEU ON BOWING

[I]n bowing down before Buddhas, there is actually nobody to bow down to and no one bowing. Who bows to what? In truth nobody bows to anyone, and yet there is this wonderful, free, gratitude-filled bowing down. In this subjectless, objectless wholehearted bowing, nothing is excluded. The whole world bows. All creatures – men, women, animals, insects – bow to one another in mutual greeting. Is this not true thanksgiving?

—from *Awakening to Zen* (New York: Scribner, 1997), p. 61.

Another issue that may arise is the question of *why* we observe all these forms. In particular, some people can be put off by all the bowing and by the prostrations that happen at the end of the sitting or in the course of a chanting service. Are we worshipping the figure on the altar? If you have wondered about this, it may help to see the figure on the altar as a reminder of our own Buddha-nature. When we bow to the figure or to each other, we are bowing to our own purest qualities and deepest aspirations, and recognising that these pure qualities are fundamentally present in each of us. Roshi Kapleau used to teach that in doing prostrations we are lowering the mast of our ego and raising up our True Nature (see inset above). Still, if you remain uncertain, probably the best advice about bowing and prostrating is to put aside all the explanations and just do it! Try it out, get the feel of it in your body and then you will most likely find out 'why'.

This advice applies not only to prostrations, but to all the forms that we observe in the zendo. In fact what we said in our discussion of zazen postures (Chapter 1) bears repeating here, that zazen is a way of working with both the body and the mind, and that what we do with our bodies affects our minds (and vice versa). Putting on a brown robe can have a calming effect on our mind, and seeing that everyone in the zendo is dressed in the same way can help us take the focus off of ourselves and encourage us to harmonise with the group. Making offerings, bowing, and performing prostrations are ways to embody humility and gratitude – and these embodiments are not just expressions of those mental attitudes, but can actually help to generate them. Turning clockwise whenever we sit down or get up from our cushion not only has a practical purpose (we don't bump legs with the person sitting next to us) but also connects us with a deep archetype of Buddhist tradition. Keeping our hands in *kinhin* posture (left fist clasped on the sternum and covered with the right hand)

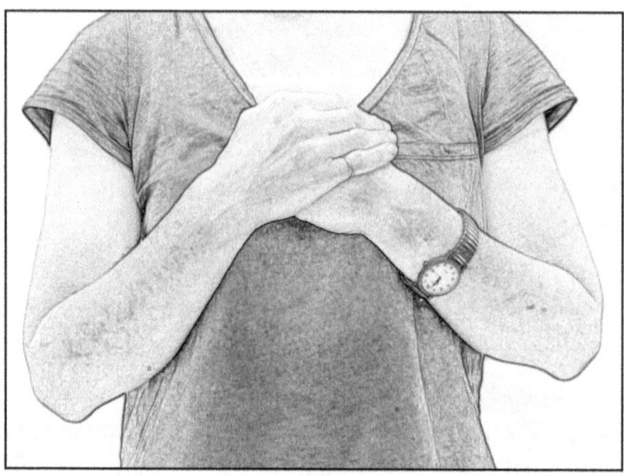

whenever we move about the zendo, rather than letting our arms dangle loosely by our sides, helps to keep us centred and to remind us that we have entered this space to focus the mind rather than let it wander in its usual unrestrained way. The clappers that mark the start of each formal round make a loud, even startling, sound and can remind us that we have come here to wake up. They are followed by the contrasting, sweet sound of three bells, and as the sound of each bell fades away, we are helped to let go of thoughts, release into the present moment, and bring our attention to the physical sensations of the body and the breath.

Though sitting together is generally the first thing that comes to mind when we think of Zen meditation, another important aspect of group practice – one that is sometimes underestimated – is the chance to practice walking meditation (*kinhin*) together. While at some centres kinhin is done at a very slow pace, in our tradition it is usually done at a normal walking pace. This is a challenging practice! The reason that we sit in stillness is because it is so much easier to observe our minds and to keep returning to an object of concentration when we are not moving and when we are facing an unchanging wall. During kinhin, the hand position that we use as well as the instruction to keep the gaze lowered offer some support for our concentration. But, nevertheless, since we are moving about at our normal walking pace, and since what we are seeing, at least peripherally, is rapidly shifting, there is a strong tendency for the mind to start moving and shifting as well. Since our goal is to bring the mind of practice as much as possible to our daily lives, kinhin offers us a bridge, a chance to work with an activity that offers more challenges than sitting still.

Because kinhin is also a chance to stretch one's legs and to use the toilet or get a drink of water if needed, we can make the mistake of thinking of this as break-time, and fall into the habit of immediately letting our mind wander without any restraint as soon as we stand up. This is really a missed opportunity. Instead, if you need to use the toilet or get some water, try to keep the mind centred on the practice while you do those things.

Like the posture that we take up on the mat or in kinhin, the zendo itself is intended to embody the qualities of mind that we seek: order, calm, and clarity. The offerings that we place before the Buddha-figure are seen as representing the four great elements of earth (fruit offering), water (flower and tea offerings), fire (candles) and air (incense offering). In other words, we are symbolically offering *everything*, and the flickering warmth of the candles, the artful arrangement of flowers and fruit, the rich smell of incense and the contrasting tones of the various musical instruments engage each of our sense faculties, encouraging us to offer all of ourselves as well.

The zendo musical instruments are employed not only to signal the start and end of rounds of sitting and walking meditation, but also to accompany the chanting service which often follows a block of formal sitting. The chance to participate in this type of devotional activity is another important reason to come along to a group sitting. Through chanting the sutras regularly, we make these ancient teachings an intimate part of ourselves; eventually we find that the words that we have repeated so many times will pop into our minds when we need them most.

Attending group sittings gives us the chance not only to practice with peers who share our aspiration, but also to learn from those who may have greater experience. In the formal tradition of Zen, you will notice that at least some of these people are identified by the garments that they don in the zendo. In particular, newcomers often wonder about the 'bib' that is worn by some practitioners. The 'bib' is actually a *rakusu*, a traditional Japanese garment that represents the Buddha's robe in abbreviated form. The sewing and wearing of a rakusu represents a commitment to the Buddhist Path and to a particular teaching lineage. In our tradition, there are different colours of rakusu for students (brown), priests and lay ordainees (black), and teachers (grey).[1] In addition, priests wear blue robes rather than the brown robes worn by everyone else.

Priests are not the same as teachers, and people often wonder what the difference is. Becoming a Zen priest in our lineage is a vocational commitment to working full-time at a Dharma Centre and to giving one's life to serve the community. Priests cut their hair short, dress at all times in plain, dark clothing, and, upon ordination, take a new Dharma name which they use publicly. On the other hand, a Zen teacher, who may or may not be a priest, has been authorised to teach Zen, to offer *dokusan* and to work with students on koans.[2] At our Centre, Amala-sensei is both a teacher (Sensei) and a priest (Amala is her Dharma name). However at our sister centres around the world, there are priests who are not teachers, as well as some teachers who are not priests (that is, they have careers outside of their Zen Centre). Besides teachers and priests, some senior students may receive lay ordination in the Three Jewels Order. Lay members of the Order, like priests, serve temples or sitting groups in our lineage, but unlike priests they do not work full-time at the temple. Rather, they commit to taking their vows out into the wider world, whether through employment, social action or other types of volunteer work.

Teachers, priests and lay members of the Order obviously have a great deal of experience in Zen practice and training and are always available to help with any questions you may have. But at our Centre an additional resource is available in the many senior students whom you will see assisting with zendo duties, such as monitoring, timing rounds, leading the chanting, playing instruments, or making offerings. The monitors in particular are charged with handling anything that arises in the course of formal rounds, as well as with supporting sitters by offering the *kyosaku* or

1. The process for becoming a formal student and for requesting a rakusu are discussed in Chapter 5, pp. 106–107.

2. See further in Chapter 4, *passim*, and in Glossary under Dokusan. Note also that a priest, while making a vocational commitment to serve a Buddhist community, is not the same as a monk or nun who has taken vows of celibacy and many other traditional vows. See in Glossary under Bhikkhu, Bhikkhuni, and Introduction, p. 4, which discusses how the tradition of non-celibate priests developed in Japan.

encouragement stick. This slender wooden paddle, unique to Zen training, is used during formal rounds to strike sitters twice on each shoulder on the trapezius muscle, the spot known in Chinese medicine as the 'triple warmer' acupuncture meridian. Skilful application of the stick can help dispel sleepiness and rouse energy, and the monitors will generally offer it at least once during each round. Receiving the stick is always optional, and is requested by placing the hands palm-to-palm. After receiving the stick the sitter again places the hands palm-to-palm while the monitor bows to the sitter. This ritual is a way of acknowledging the efforts of both participants.

In this chapter we have tried to orient you to some of what to expect during formal Zen sittings as well as to the various people who stand ready to assist you. But, though this information is intended to be useful, there is also the risk that reading about all of these forms and rituals can make the whole thing seem more complicated than it is. Essentially, when you come to group sittings, if you are willing to just follow along with the other sitters, you will quickly get the hang of it all, and even come to feel these forms as second nature. They have been handed down for hundreds of years by our Dharma ancestors because they have been found to work; so to some extent we need to have faith in our forebears' experience that these things can be helpful to our training. Remember that in Zen our goal is not an intellectual or philosophical understanding of the teachings, but rather to get the teachings 'in our body', to be able to act intuitively from a place of understanding and connection. These at first arbitrary-seeming forms around zendo etiquette are in fact designed to help us do just that, and many of us have had first-hand experience of their effectiveness.

AUCKLAND ZEN CENTRE ZENDO GUIDELINES

Entering the zendo:

- Pause just inside the threshold, place the hands palm-to-palm (*gassho*) and bow towards the altar.
- Do this *every* time you enter the zendo, even if you have only left for a moment, or if you are coming back from dokusan.

Moving around the zendo (for example, when taking your seat):

- Keep the hands in the kinhin posture (left fist clasped on the sternum; right hand covering the left).
- Maintain silence in the zendo.

Exiting the zendo:

- Pause just inside the threshold, turn around to face the altar, place the hands in gassho and bow.
- Two situations where this bow is not performed:

  When leaving the zendo for dokusan (see Chapter 4).

  At the end of a sitting when everyone is leaving the zendo together. In this second case, the bow is omitted for practical reasons: it would cause a traffic jam for everyone to turn around and face the altar. Instead, simply place the hands in gassho as you pass over the threshold. Don't bow with your back to the altar, which may cause others to bump into you.

Beginning of formal sitting or round:

- 5 minutes before sitting: Big bell in the foyer struck 3 times.
- 1 minute before sitting: Han (wooden block hanging outside zendo door) begins to play.
- Beginning of each round: Clappers struck inside the zendo by the timer followed by 3 strikes of the inkin bell. By the 3rd bell you should be in the posture that you will hold for this round.

  No moving during the round. 'No moving' means no changing posture and no gross movements of the arms or legs. If something itches, just ride it out. However, it is fine to adjust your upper-body alignment as you sit if you find yourself slumping over or needing to re-energise your posture.

End of round and kinhin:

- Single strike of the inkin bell:

  Place your hands palm-to-palm (gassho) and make a small seated bow.

  Turn clockwise on your cushion, come to standing, and place your hands in gassho.
- Second strike of the inkin bell:

  Bow to each other, turn to the left and begin the kinhin (walking meditation), generally 5–7 minutes. Hands in kinhin posture.
- Third strike of the inkin bell:

  Kinhin is over; stand in front of your mat when you reach it
- Fourth strike of the inkin bell:

Sit down on your cushion, turning clockwise, and get ready for the next
round

End of sitting:

- Single strike of the inkin bell:
  Place the hands in gassho for the Four Vows (repeated 3 times)
- Accelerando on inkin bell:
  Rise for the three prostrations. Prostrations are signaled by bells and
  deadbeats (lower hands on deadbeat)
  Prostrations are followed by a bow to the Buddha, and a bow to each
  other, signaled by bells
- Deadbeat on inkin bell:
  End of sitting; leave zendo according to instructions above

Chanting service:

- Some formal sittings are immediately followed by a chanting service. A
  chanting service normally begins with the Three Treasures (I take refuge
  in Buddha, I take refuge in Dharma, I take refuge in Sangha). Each refuge
  is followed by a prostration.
- At the end of a chanting service, the Four Vows are chanted from the
  kneeling posture with hands in gassho.

Note on gassho:

- The fingers should be together (not splayed) and palms should be pressed
  firmly against each other, elbows out just slightly.

Note that some sittings are informal. For these, there are no bells (except to mark
the end of the sitting), no chanting, and no *kyosaku*. You may change your
posture or leave the zendo and return as needed.

TEISHO

* * *

Devotion

(2011–07–31)

This teisho takes a brief look at some of the more overtly religious or devotional aspects of Buddhist practice. While these can be immensely helpful for some people, they can be a stumbling block for others. How can we offer opportunities for devotional practice without getting overly attached to the forms? At the end of her talk, Sensei opens up the topic for discussion by the group.

Today I thought I'd talk a little bit about devotion and then open up for discussion after that. Yesterday Sally and I were at the New Zealand Buddhist Council Annual General Meeting. It was held at a Sri Lankan temple, and we were there from about half past nine in the morning until after two in the afternoon. The AGM was in the morning, then we had lunch, and in the afternoon we had a tour of the temple and finally there was an executive committee meeting — so it was quite a long day. But one of the things that really impressed me about the day was how well we were taken care of. There was a whole team of temple members there, dressed in white, who served us lunch and brought us cups of tea, and there was a very beautiful spirit in which they did this. For lay people in the Theravadan tradition, a big part of their spiritual practice is offering food, especially to bhikkhus, and it was really beautiful to see this, this sense of devotion and service, and a sense of joy in service. Many of the people had their kids with them there as they provided us with lunch, and then the families ate, too.

Another thing that was moving to me was that the women who served lunch (it was mostly, but not all, women who were hosting us) especially asked for the three ordained women there to make dedications before the meal. In their tradition there are very few bhikkhunis (female monks)[3] so they asked each of us, a Korean bhikkhuni, a Vajrayana nun, and me to each do a prayer, a dedication, before the meal, and it was really clear

3. In Sri Lanka the order of bhikkhunis, which had died out there, has recently been revived, but it is still small.

that they enjoyed having that happen. I'd picked out this teisho topic of devotion before we attended the meeting, but, being there, I felt that what we saw was a real demonstration of devotion.

And there's a lot that could be said about it, but maybe we can think of this kind of devotion as being on a spectrum, so we can see that there are extremes that we might want to avoid, dangers that can come with devotion, but also that it is an essential part of practice. Devotion can become unhealthy if it's blind, or also if it's hollow. Devotion to a guru is strongly emphasised in some traditions and this can have positive effects. Two years ago I was invited to go and give a talk to a Hindu group whose main practice is singing *bhajans* or devotional songs. What struck me about the group was their warmth, and a kind of gentleness and openness. There was a joyful quality to the group that I'm guessing came from their chanting.

One of the dangers that some groups experience, though, when there is a really strong emphasis on devotion to their leader, is that it can turn into a kind of dependency or an attachment, where without that person your spiritual practice doesn't have strength. So it has the potential to induce a kind of spiritual immaturity. And also it can have a corrupting effect on the leader. If the teacher's not really far along in his development of non-attachment to self, he can identify with all that devotion, that worship, and it can lead to abuses. There are lots of examples of that; I'm sure everybody knows about some of them.

Closely related to this is the danger of hollow devotion. There's a Zen group in the US which prides itself on doing everything exactly the way it's done in Japan. The bells, the han (wooden block), the drum, their sesshins, the chanting, even their buildings, all these things are done in a way that is very precise, very meticulous in adhering to particular forms. But in fact they have a teacher who has broken the precepts for decades; there have been repeated cover-ups and then repetitions of the behaviour, resulting in a great deal of suffering. Perhaps the strict adherence to external forms is compensatory.

At the other extreme, there are groups where devotional aspects of the practice are simply eliminated. This is the case with quite a lot of groups, in the West in particular, groups that dispense with the more 'religious' aspects of the tradition, things like chanting and bowing, ordination, or going on pilgrimage. If you do strip away all that stuff and preserve only the meditation practice (which is the part that's left), then there can be a tendency to think that the meditation is no more than a kind of self-improvement practice. In this way the practice can become narrow and individualistic. That, in turn, can lead to a kind of aridity in people's sitting. That's not to say that this is inevitable, but it's a danger if there's not a larger context for our work. Chanting and doing prostrations are ways of expressing gratitude to Buddhas and bodhisattvas, ways of expressing our faith in our teachers and our interconnectedness with them across space and time.

We can easily get discouraged if we think of our practice too narrowly. Ultimately practice is not about individual advancement, not about getting somewhere, but about moving into an entirely different mode of being, where the self is forgotten. And doing devotional practices, where there's not so clearly a purpose, is a way of entering that mode. You can't really say that you chant for a reason. We chant in order to chant. And actually that's why we practice, too. The purpose of practice is practicing, it's not something outside of that. And it's the same with bowing; you can't really say to somebody what the meaning is. We can try to explain it a little bit, but you can't really say to somebody what the 'meaning of bowing' is because the meaning of bowing is bowing, and you understand bowing through doing it, not through what anybody tells you about it.

If you look up devotion in an etymological dictionary you'll find that the roots of it are *de-*, fully, and *votum*, a vow; so it means to fully vow – to completely vow – and to completely vow is not just to vow verbally but to actually carry out that vow. So to do your bow fully, to be fully present in that bow or in the chanting or in your zazen, just to be there, not a spectator of that process, but to be fully involved, as fully involved as you can be in that moment, that's really what devotion means. If we think again of those devotees at the temple, sometimes the Mahayanists can be disparaging of the practice of *dana* which is so central to the Theravadan tradition, this practice of preparing and donating food to monks. Sometimes we may hear it said that the people who are doing this are doing it simply to make merit. But there's another way of viewing it, which is that they're doing it because they deeply believe that the act is in itself meritorious. And that's very different, and is certainly the feeling I got yesterday – that people were taking joy in doing this because they believe it to be a wonderful thing to do, to offer food to others, to be there just fully serving. That's the devotional attitude, not expecting anything back, not trying to build their merit mountain, but just doing this offering for the sake of doing it.

This is very much the attitude that is encouraged in Zen, not just in offering food to others but in the way we make our own food, the way we wash dishes, the way we weed the garden, to do these actions for the sake of doing them. Thich Nhat Hanh talks about not washing the dishes to get the dishes clean, but just washing them to wash the dishes, and there's a lot of wisdom in that. It's not that we don't wash them carefully so that they *are* clean, but there's a sense of settling into a task rather than of needing to finish it so I can get on to the next thing. If we can just do what we're doing, then we find that there's peace in that and there's also joy.

So devotional activities, whether it's chanting or bowing or offering food, can be a way of reminding us that we're engaged in something much bigger than self-improvement. We're endeavouring to connect with a reality that's bigger than us in each moment and to rest in that, even though we don't fully 'get' it. That's an important part about devotion, it's not like you completely understand why you bow or why you chant, but even if you don't have a complete cognitive grasp of it, something in your heart connects with it. Something comes alive when you do it, something resonates, or warms up, and so you do it. It comes much more from the heart than an intellectual place.

I've been reading a wonderful book, a two-volume account of a pilgrimage that a Theravadan monk Ajahn Sucitto and a layman Nick Scott made on foot through India.[4] In the course of this pilgrimage, Ajahn Sucitto is invited to give a Dharma talk, and in it he talks about devotion. He talks about pilgrimage as a form of devotion, but he connects this to practice in general and he says something very profound about devotion — something more fundamental than simply surrendering to the guru or to an activity. He says:

> There is a kind of learning when we have the humility to recognise that really the learning point is where we go to the edge of where we know and where we control. And the nobility of our life, the nobility of our purpose, the aspiration of life says 'keep going past the area where you can't control it anymore and trust.' And for me this is the heart of devotion. That it is

4. Ajahn Sucitto and Nick Scott, *Where Are You Going? A Pilgrimage on Foot to the Buddhist Holy Places* (Chithurst, UK: Cittaviveka Monastery, 2010).

not a surrender of responsibility but a profound recognition of what the
responsibility of this being is — to live in accordance with Truth, to honour
Truth, and trust the truth of our life as it is.

'To live in accordance with Truth, to honour Truth, and trust the truth of
our life as it is.' For me this really captures the two sides of our practice,
where there is an aspiration to understand the Truth with a capital T, and
so there's a sense of questioning, of investigation, of paying attention, but
also at the same time, there is a trust in the truth of our life as it is right
now, an understanding that we don't need to be somewhere other than
where we are. It's really a matter of opening our eyes and our hearts to
this, to what's happening at this moment, and then the faith in our truth
with a small t, in what's going on right now, is what gives us the capacity,
the stable mind to live into our aspiration and into this greater Truth
that we don't fully comprehend. It is about letting go into that place of
no-control, leaping into the abyss.

Ajahn Sucitto talks about some of the reasons why pilgrimage is a
particularly fertile form of practice and devotion, how it is very much the
practice of deliberately putting yourself in a 'no-control situation'. And
this is particularly the case in India; this book really gives you a sense of
how crazy India can be, and dangerous — at one point the two men are
robbed of everything they have. Ajahn Sucitto says, 'We need to have
situations in which we can realise that the whole of life is a no-control
event. If we keep putting ourselves in situations where we can look at
this dichotomy, then gradually our relationship changes from being associated with the thinking, judging mind to being associated with truth
… Because of course in relative terms, there are control situations, there
are things we can do, but for ultimate truth and for awakening, we can't
do it. It has to happen through us.'

It's not something *we* do. It's more a matter of getting out of the way so
the universe can express itself through us. Just allowing the breath or the
koan to work on us, just surrendering to the process. Master Dogen calls
it having faith in the Way, and the Way is perhaps one of the best terms
to describe what it is that we put our faith in, because it has the sense of
being something that's ongoing. It's not a thing, it's not some fixed object
out there that we have to reach, but a process that we're part of, a path
that we're walking along, that opens before us as we walk, and that we
help to keep open by our walking along it.

Would anybody like to make a comment or ask a question?

STUDENT: I've got one question. In the West we seem to have this fear of superstition. We've been brought up to believe that a lot of superstitious beliefs come from primitive societies and we're civilised and we shouldn't bow to wooden images or things like this. This is a problem for us in the West I think.

AW: Yes, and there is some validity to our concern if we're talking about genuine superstition. For instance in New Guinea an old woman living on her own risks being labelled a witch and may have all sorts of evil projected onto her to the point where she is persecuted or even killed. New Zealand is a very secular society and it's not just a question of being worried about superstition, but about anything religious. All the Zen Centre can do is say to people, well, come and try it, come and see, and see if what we do resonates with you or not. For some people it won't resonate and for some people it will — there will be some that will find the formality helpful and freeing. One of the things we try to do here is to hold to the forms, but not to hold too tightly. So if somebody comes and they don't want to do the chanting that would be fine. It's not required, not an absolute, but it is offered and it's going to be offered. We're not going to stop doing it. So it's finding that balance of maintaining the opportunity to do devotions because they can be really liberating, without becoming too attached to them.

RvS: One way you can think of devotion in respect to the path, to being on the Way, is as an orientation. Devotion's a great way to re-orient ourselves, especially because our mind can be taken in all these different directions, so when we bow or chant it's a way of orienting ourselves back to the Buddha way, and *just* chanting or doing devotions. It is an opportunity to just become one, just doing. This 'just' is an extension of our sitting practice.

AW: From the absolute point of view, everything's already sacred, we don't have to make it sacred, but to undertake devotions is a way of reminding ourselves of our purpose. For example, the rakusu. We take care to always carry it carefully, fold it in a particular way, put it on a high shelf, because our rakusu is the Buddha's robe. These small actions are ways of cherishing the Buddhadharma.

STUDENT: I think the first thing that came to mind for me when you said you were going to talk about devotion was, I must have read somewhere, that koan work is essentially a devotional practice, and I guess sitting practice of any sort is the same. Maybe you could say a bit about that.

AW: We need to be reminded that our koan is much more than a means to an end, that it's about devoting oneself to a question that doesn't have an answer in the normal way. The question is the answer, and when we fully become the question then it will become apparent what that means. But it does take devotion, because the koan will frustrate the mind that thinks it's in control, the mind that sits there saying, Look, I did that! *That* mind gets completely stymied and in the process something else can become apparent. Working on a koan is working on an open question or a question that opens us up to another way of relating to things.

KA: When you were talking about the devotees at the temple yesterday and the joy with which they were serving it made me think of part of my experience last year in being on staff at the Rochester Center. I had volunteered there for many years, and been basically a full-time volunteer there for I don't know how many months or years, at different periods of time, and then last year for the first time I had the opportunity to actually go on staff there which meant that I was doing the same thing I had been doing for all those months and years, but I was getting paid for it, just a little bit, you know, just a little bit of money, but it turned out to be a really negative shift for me, I'm not saying it would have to, but that was my experience of it. I was really happy when I could set that down again and not be on staff, because I just felt like, I want to go here every morning because that's what I want to do, because I'm taking joy in doing this, not because I'm getting a paycheck and so I have an obligation to be here a certain number of hours. It just shifted something for me.

AW: I've heard from other people who found that there was something that shifted negatively when becoming a staff member — but in fact you're still a volunteer, it's not like you're being paid the minimum wage even. It's just that you're now a volunteer who's getting a little help to be able to stay maybe for a little longer or in a more sustained way, but actually you're still a volunteer, a volunteer with a little help, and I think if people were able to realise that, then they might be able to get around that negativity, which as you say has something to do with now feeling obliged to show up. And if the administration would also recognise it, too, that everyone's a volunteer essentially, including the teacher. And in fact that doesn't apply just to being at the Zen Center. It applies to whatever job we're in, that we're doing it because we've decided to do it in some sense. I mean there are cases where that's not so, indentured servitude and slavery and things like that, but for most of us we have some choice about what we do. A lot of the time our resistance to what we do comes about because we're telling ourselves that we don't have a choice. Years ago I had a friend who had a stepson. He was a teenager, and she felt he was unappreciative of all that she did for him, especially all the driving she did to drop him off and pick him up from sport and other activities. But everything shifted for her when she realised that she was doing this stuff for him *by choice*, and as soon as she really realised that, that she was *choosing* to take care of him, then her resentment about his lack of appreciation went away, and it wasn't the point anymore. She didn't need to have him appreciate what she was doing, she was doing it because she had decided she was going to do it, freely, because it accorded with her values. A lot of the time there'll be some unconscious voice in us saying, no, this is not what I want, this is not what I've chosen, I'd be happier if I were doing something else. But in fact in some sense we have chosen it, but we just may not be fully admitting that to ourselves.

STUDENT: I have a question and perhaps it's a little bit of a reflection of my ignorance but for me the devotion topic can sometimes be very challenging to tackle. When I look for example at the life of the Buddha, the Buddha himself was not a Buddhist, he just had a really big question, of 'What is this?', 'Why do we live life the way that we do?', and so before that moment where he just really decided I'm just going to tackle this question no matter what, and I'm not going to stop until I'm awake, before that he was very devoted to a path that he himself found brought him a lot of suffering. So I guess that sometimes when I see the acts of devotion, they kind of clash a little bit with me, because I feel that perhaps the one true devotion that I myself sometimes feel that I'm after is just the realisation of truth.

AW: The Buddha for all those years doing his ascetic practices, did them with great devotion, but that great devotion led him to the point where he had nowhere to go, and then from there he found another way. So it's a little bit like that image from the Divine Comedy of Dante. He travels down into the pit of Hell, he goes down through all the circles of Hell, and then he gets to the very bottom, the most abject, frozen, lifeless place of total disconnection from God, and then he just keeps going at that point. He actually passes through the centre of the Earth and emerges in the other hemisphere, onto the shores of Mt Purgatory somewhere here in the southern ocean. He hasn't changed direction actually, he's just stayed with his search, and that search turned from being a descent through all kinds of suffering, into an ascent towards 'God'. I think that you could say that's what it was for the Buddha, he just had to be sincere and devote himself and stick to his purpose, which was really to follow the Way, and that led ultimately to his realising self-denial was a dead end, as was his previous to self-indulgence. Both emphasized the self. But he had to plumb the depths of those extremes to go beyond them.

STUDENT: I'm a rookie to all this but I'm actually very into it because it is what I want to do. On this topic about devotion at least, the way we were raised back in my home, parents expect you to please them, because they gave you life, education, all that stuff, and then you devote yourself to things to please other people but you don't please yourself, and then if you actually do stuff that grows within you and you do it because you like it and you want to do it, you kind of get shut down, because people question it. So I don't know how to deal with it. It's tough, because I know what path I want to take, but on the other side you have your family pressure and all that.

AW: Ancient China was strongly Confucian (and much of Asia still is). There was strong pressure to perpetuate the family line, take over the family responsibilities and especially to keep making offerings to the ancestors. So to become a monk or a nun, to 'leave home' was a real break with that and often not welcomed by family members. The pressure was so intense and the mores of the society were so caught up in this value of filial piety that young men and women would sometimes have to starve themselves to get permission to enter the monastery or even cut off a finger to prove their sincerity. They would say, 'I'm doing this *for* my family, in the sense that I'm going to realise the Way for a greater good, out of love for the greater family of all sentient beings.' But, it's also important to recognise your family's needs, not completely reject them. We need to check what our motives really are — is there something we're running from? What is our true calling?

RvS: Just a quick comment on letting go. When we were on pilgrimage back in 2001 we ended up at Bukkokuji, and in dokusan with Tangen-roshi, I brought up problems I was having with practice and Zen training and he just said, 'Throw yourself into the house of the Buddha!' which I found very helpful. Throw yourself into the house of the Buddha — which is devotion, letting go. You can't do that if you're not ready, but at a certain point in practice you might find a little push coming from behind or within and you will be able fully throw yourself into the house of the Buddha; it can happen. You don't have to stand on the doorstep or knock politely. As Tengen-roshi says, talking about throwing, just throw yourself into the house of the Buddha.

AW: That's exactly what Ajahn Sucitto was talking about, that you can be standing right on the edge of life, and what you need to do is just dive in.

So if there are no more questions,

We'll stop here and recite the four vows.

*   *

*

When Shitou visited Qingyuan the Master said, 'Where have you come from?'

Shitou said, 'From Cao Xi' (where the 6th Ancestor had been teaching).

Qingyuan asked, 'What have you brought from there?'

Shitou replied, 'That which had never been lost even before I went to Cao Xi.'

Qingyuan said, 'Then why did you go there at all?'

Shitou said, 'If I had not gone there how could I have realised that it had never been lost?'

— Treasury of the Forest of Ancestors

Working with a Teacher

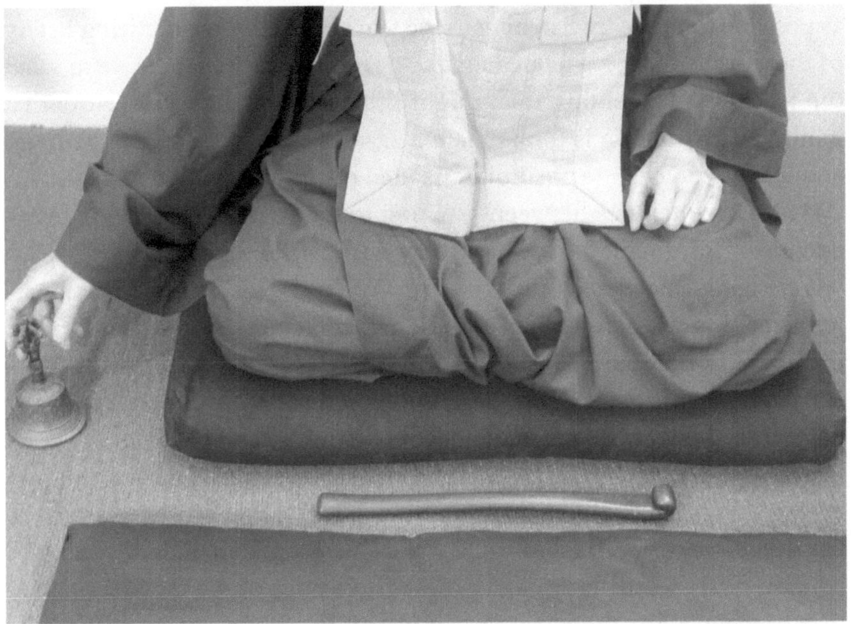

IN Chapter 3 we looked at some of the benefit and richness that can come from sitting with a group. In this chapter we'll take a closer look at one of the most important reasons for participating in group practice, namely, the chance to work with a teacher.

In Zen, points of teaching are communicated to practitioners in a variety of ways. Perhaps one of the most obvious, as well as the most culturally comfortable for Westerners, is the tradition of teisho, in which the teacher delivers a talk while the students listen. Of course, there are some important differences between a teisho and a lecture that you might hear at school or at work. From the point of view of the student, there are several things to keep in mind when listening to teisho. First of all, we are asked, while listening, to maintain a zazen posture and also, as much as possible, to continue with our practice. If we are doing a breath practice this doesn't mean that we need to count breaths while the teacher speaks, but we should try to maintain an awareness of the body and the breath and to stay as physically and mentally present as we can. If we are working on a koan, we should try to maintain awareness of that koan during the talk. If we find that it proves to be too complicated to keep our formal practice going while listening to the talk, then the instruction is to maintain the zazen posture and *just listen*, in other words to bring the attention as fully as possible to the act of listening to the teacher. Actively practicing in any of these ways during a talk can make our minds more receptive to what the teacher is presenting than might otherwise be the case. (Note that while the instruction is to maintain a zazen posture, teisho can be long, and it is fine to change position if needed during the course of a talk.)

Another difference between listening to teisho and listening to an academic or informational lecture is that with teisho we are encouraged to 'take what we need and leave the rest'. What the teacher hopes to communicate is not essentially informational, and even though a teisho may include a fair amount of information, there is no requirement that we retain it. As we listen in a state of receptivity, certain words or phrases may have a deep impact on us, may open our minds in some way or spark an insight. At the same time, listening in a state of openness means not only letting things come but also letting them go. We don't need to attach to anything that is said. Just as some words may spark an understanding or insight, other words may annoy or aggravate us, or we may feel strong disagreement. For the most part, it is best if we can just observe these feelings as they arise and let them pass, releasing them and letting them go while releasing and letting go of the teacher's words. This does not mean that we should never ask a question or bring up a problem that has arisen for us in listening to teisho. But for the most part it is best to follow the instructions to stay open, stay in the moment, and, when the teisho is over, to just forget about it, knowing that any important insights will bear fruit without the need for us to hold on to them.

Teisho and Dharma talks are only one of the ways in which Zen teachings are communicated. Paying attention to the details of posture and etiquette reviewed in the previous chapters is another important way of incorporating the teachings on an intuitive, non-verbal level. This style of learning may be not be as familiar to some of us as listening to lectures, but much can be learned by simply observing how the teacher, priests and senior students conduct themselves and by trying to harmonise with the group.

A third teaching method, perhaps the most distinctive one that has been handed down to us from our Zen ancestors, is that of *dokusan*. The Japanese word *dokusan* means to 'go alone,' and in Zen training it refers to a one-to-one meeting between a teacher and student. These meetings take place during formal rounds of zazen, and follow their own pattern of bells and bows. Once you make your way through these formalities and enter the dokusan room, you will find the teacher sitting in zazen. You take your place on the student's mat directly opposite, and just a few inches from the teacher ... and then what?

There is no way to specify exactly what will follow. The teacher is in fact sitting in zazen and most times will not have any specific question or comment for you (though sometimes she may). When students first begin going to dokusan, they will usually want to come in with a question or comment of their own. This might be a question about the practice, or a question about something that has come up in daily life, and either one is fine. If you are able to describe what is going on in your zazen and any obstacles you might be facing, then you'll have the opportunity to get individual feedback and help. Likewise if there is a persistent problem or issue in your daily life, you'll have the chance in dokusan to get a Zen perspective on it. Whatever transpires in dokusan is confidential; the teacher will not discuss it with others and neither should you, as this may cause confusion for other students, since the teaching you receive is just for you.

Gradually, as you get more used to the process of going to dokusan, you'll find that you don't need to come in with a specific problem or question each time. It is often said that you don't need a reason to go to dokusan, because dokusan is beyond reasons. Dokusan is above all an opportunity for teacher and student to work together on the Great Matter, to turn together to reality just as it reveals itself at a particular moment. So the best advice about going to dokusan is just to stay as involved as you can with your practice, and to be as open as you can to the present moment. Enter the room without any agenda. Sit and do zazen with the teacher. Perhaps some words will emerge, or perhaps a physical action. Or perhaps you will just sit and experience the moment together. This is a process which can be confusing and even frightening, but also immensely liberating; dokusan tends to crystallise everything that we believe about self and other – but it also has the hidden potential to help move us beyond that false dichotomy.

Sometimes at our Centre, *daisan* will be offered instead of dokusan. Procedurally the two are similar (though not identical), but daisan is offered by a senior practitioner, not a teacher. The main technical difference between the two is that koans are not investigated in daisan; koans may be assigned and assessed only by a teacher who has been sanctioned to do so. In addition to this technicality, however, you may find that dokusan and daisan have quite a different spirit and may function in rather different, though complementary, ways in your practice. Dokusan interviews tend to be briefer and more sharply focused on the formal practice. In daisan there may be time to talk more expansively about issues that are coming up in the course of your practice, to hear about and learn from the experiences of the person offering daisan, and just to receive encouragement. In other words, daisan can be more of a peer-to-peer experience than is generally the case with dokusan.

All of this may raise the question of exactly what it means to be a sanctioned Zen teacher who is able to assign koans and offer dokusan. A short answer would be that a sanctioned teacher is one who has been authorised by his or her own teacher to teach Zen; but a longer answer involves a look at quite a bit of history and tradition. At the Auckland Zen Centre, as at most Zen centres around the world, we regularly chant our Ancestral Line, a list of 90 names that begins with the names of seven of the many Buddhas of the past (the last of whom is Shakyamuni Buddha), before continuing with the names of 28 Indian ancestors, 22 Chinese ancestors, 32 Japanese ancestors and finally Roshi Kapleau (founder of the Rochester Zen Center). Shakyamuni, said to be the fourth Buddha of a predicted 1,000 to appear in our present world cycle, turned the Wheel of Dharma 2500 years ago, rediscovering the teachings and re-sharing them with the people of his era. This 're-' is an important traditional element: it implies that the Buddhadharma (the teaching of Buddhism) is inherently existent in the universe – that it is in fact no more than a description of the way things actually are – and is therefore readily accessible and able to be realised by anyone whose eyes are open. The six primordial Buddhas preceding Shakyamuni in the chanted lineage are a selection of the many Buddhas supposed to have lived and taught in ages almost inconceivably distant from our own.[1] They are mythical beings, but their inclusion in our chant points to the understanding that, in the unlimited expanse of beginningless time, the truth of the Dharma has been discovered again and again.

From Shakyamuni onwards, each of the ancestors named in our Ancestral Line is an historical personage and, moreover, is said to have been the student of the preceding ancestor and to have received the teachings directly from him.[2] From a scholarly point of view, this claim is questionable, and in fact the practice of declaring one's Dharma 'genealogy' emerged only in Tang dynasty China. In the Confucian social system of that time, the ability to trace one's teaching ancestors in a direct line back to the Buddha lent an important legitimacy and credibility to teachers of the Chan school, as well as providing a sort of substitute family tree for monks who, in ordaining, had left their homes, their families and their ancestors behind. Nevertheless, as Roshi Bodhin Kjolhede has written:

> The Confucian-inspired patching and back-filling of the ancestral line does nothing to diminish its spiritual value, which goes far beyond historical accuracy. This golden chain of masters points to an awe-inspiring enlightenment tradition. It reminds us of our kinship with all our awakened predecessors, both women and men, throughout the past 2,500 years. When we chant the ancestral line we breathe life into our Buddha-nature.[3]

From our modern standpoint, there are several points to take away from this discussion and from the practice of reciting a lineage. The first is to understand the importance in Zen of master-to-disciple transmission. An archetypal story about the Zen style of transmission is told about the Buddha and his disciple Mahakashyapa:

> Once when the World-Honoured One, in ancient times, was upon Vulture Peak, he held up a flower before the assembly of monks. At this all were silent. The Venerable Kashyapa [Mahakashyapa] alone broke into a smile.

1. Traditional Buddhist teaching holds that in each age a Buddha emerges to share the Dharma, which flourishes for a time (perhaps thousands of years) but eventually dies out, only to be rediscovered in another age.

2. Technically called Dharma transmission, see below.

3. https://www.rzc.org/wp-content/uploads/2012/01/Roshi-and-His-Teachers.pdf. Note that while Rochester Zen Center founder Philip Kapleau was a student of Yasutani-roshi and was authorised to teach Zen, he broke with his teacher before he was given full Dharma transmission. In the article referenced in this footnote, Roshi Kjolhede presents a thorough discussion of the various issues raised by this break.

The World-Honoured One said, 'I have the All-pervading Eye of the True
Dharma, the Secret Heart of Incomparable Nirvana, the True Aspect of
Formless Form. It does not rely on letters and is transmitted outside the
scriptures. I now hand it on to Mahakashyapa.'

—Mumonkan, Case 6

What did Mahakashyapa see when the Buddha held up the flower that the
other monks did not see? What did his smile mean? How did the Buddha
understand his smile? And what exactly did he 'hand on'? For the ancient
Chinese masters who told this story (which first appeared in the eleventh
century), the idea of mind-to-mind transmission, something beyond
words that passed between a teacher and disciple, was a defining aspect
of their teaching style and of the Zen school. Still today, the accepted way
to become a Zen teacher is by being sanctioned or certified by one's own
teacher, and thus taking one's place in this lineage stretching back to the
Buddha (or at least to Tang dynasty China). A disciple is sanctioned only
after working for many years or even decades with their teacher, and only
after the teacher feels that this person has fully and deeply grasped the
transmitted teaching and has the aptitude, spiritual maturity and upright
character required to teach others effectively.

Thus Zen remains a mentor-based process. What passes between
teacher and student is intimate and not subject to the judgement of external creeds or dogma. And, at the same time, the importance of testing
one's understanding through work with a teacher is strongly emphasised.
Though it is true that every student must do the work for themselves, and
equally true that every student is fully equipped with everything needed
to do that work, nevertheless, there is a recognised danger in just sitting
on one's own and assessing one's degree of insight for oneself. In Zen,
true spiritual confidence and stability are developed in the crucible of the
dokusan room. Additionally, while the Ancestral Line that we chant may
not be historically precise, our continued use of the chant flows out of a
conviction that what our teacher transmits to us does in fact come from the
Buddha. This Buddha may be viewed as a historical personage, or simply
as the 'awakeness' of the universe, fully available to us at any moment,
the very Buddha-mind that our teacher will work with us to realise.

In Zen, when someone is given permission to teach by their own teacher
they take the title 'Sensei' ('teacher'). The other title that you will frequently hear in Zen is 'Roshi' which means something like 'old teacher',

and is a title of great respect given to a teacher who has taught and led a community for many years. It is generally bestowed by consensus of the teacher's own students, though some teachers prefer not to accept the title 'Roshi' until their own teacher has died.

After practicing Zen for some time, you may feel that you would like to become a disciple yourself and take your place as a follower of this ancient lineage. If that is the case, then you may, in dokusan, make a request to your teacher to become a formal student. She will consider your request, and if she accepts it, a private ceremony will be arranged to mark the change in the relationship. This is an important and serious step on your spiritual journey. It expresses a conviction that you have found a spiritual home and a path to which you are willing to make a commitment. It affirms your willingness to stand by this commitment even if the path becomes rocky, steep, or narrow, as it surely will at times. Thus it is important to feel a good level of trust and confidence in the teacher and the path before taking this step. At the Auckland Zen Centre there is a minimum requirement that you should have been a Centre member for at least one year and have been coming to dokusan regularly, in order to get to know the tradition and the teacher.

Perhaps one of the trickiest areas for Western students to navigate is in finding the right degree of trust in the teacher without falling into idealisation. When we first begin to practice Zen, or when we first become a formal student, there may be a tendency to over-idealise the teacher or to view her as more-than-human. Stories we have heard about monks in ancient times becoming enlightened at a word or a blow may encourage us in false notions about what it might be possible to 'get' from a teacher. Such idealisation can be perilous, setting us up for disappointment or disillusionment down the road. And yet, for our training to be effective, we do need to have faith in the teacher and in the process – otherwise we won't take the teaching to heart.

We also need to understand from the outset that the role of Zen teacher carries a great deal of authority, and that this authority is a central part of the training tradition that we have inherited from Japan. In Zen, the teacher is responsible for making all decisions about spiritual and training matters, for example, whether someone may become a formal student, enter full-time training, ordain as a priest, move on to the next koan, and so on. Many of the rituals maintained at most Zen centres, such as bowing on entering the dokusan room, are designed to show and reinforce respect for the teacher and for the lineage that stands behind her. All of this may appear quite foreign to those of us brought up in highly egalitarian cultures. Moreover, particularly once we become formal students, we can expect that the teacher will work with us in ways that we will find demanding and that will challenge our attachments. We will need to be ready to face such challenges while maintaining our faith in the teacher's goodwill and capacity to make good decisions.

On the other hand, it is easy to see the potential for abuse in a system where there is such a powerful authority figure. While we do need to have faith in the teacher, we should never have blind faith. A brief internet search will turn up a distressing number of scandals involving Zen teachers whose misdeeds range from carrying on a secret affair with a single student to acting as serial abusers over many years. Because of the power disparity between teacher and student, and the strong emotional charge inherent in the student-teacher relationship, as with the patient-psychotherapist relationship, the student is often very vulnerable. Teachers who have sexual relations with a student are betraying the trust that has been placed in them and must be held to account by their community. Moreover, even if there is no sexual misconduct on the part of the teacher, the student may be vulnerable in other ways. If a teacher sets requirements or suggests working in ways that seem inappropriate or unhealthy, it can be difficult for the student to refuse without feeling that she is failing at the training or potentially disrupting the teaching relationship. In an interview published online the Dalai Lama speaks very clearly about such situations:

> … if a guru gives an instruction that is not in accord with the Dharma, the student should not follow it and should go to the teacher to clarify and explain why they cannot. This advice comes directly from the Buddha and is found in the scriptures. The same applies if you think the advice of your teacher is unskillful or unwise, even though it may be ethical. The purity of the teacher's motivation is not enough: the instruction must be appropriate for the situation and the culture of the place.
>
> If the guru refuses to accept your reservations about following their non-Dharmic or unskillful instructions and kicks you out, pack your bags and leave. Your guru can tell you to leave physically, but they cannot make your mind leave the Dharma.[4]

4. From notes taken during the meeting of H.H. the Dalai Lama and Western Bud-

The Auckland Zen Centre has adopted a detailed set of ethical guide-lines (available on our website under 'Governance'), covering such issues as dual relationships, sexual harassment, non-discrimination, and conflict resolution; in this we have drawn on the wisdom of a number of centres.[5] Members of the Centre are invited to familiarise themselves with these guidelines, and if conflicts or questionable situations arise in the course of participation at the Centre, they are encouraged to follow either the informal or formal procedures outlined in the document. A standing Ethics and Reconciliation (EAR) Committee has been formed to deal with any issues that may arise, from facilitating communication between two people in conflict up to and including hearing a formal grievance. Anyone seeking to join a spiritual community would do well to check if the organisation has ethics and grievance policies and, if they do, to get some sense of whether or not they are being broadly upheld.

The relationship between a Zen teacher and student is an intimate one. It is not easily compared to other relationships with which Western students are familiar. It cannot really be defined as a friendship, nor as a teach-er-student relationship in the academic sense, nor as a therapeutic rela-tionship, though it does contain some elements of each of these. Because the relationship is intimate, powerful, and yet culturally unfamiliar, it has the potential to cause a fair amount of confusion and even pain. From the point of view of Western psychology, there is no doubt that projection and transference have their part to play in what transpires between teacher and student. Old patterns from family or other relationships may assert themselves and, even if we are able to recognise what is going on, we may feel quite helpless to control it.[6] And yet, from the Zen perspective, all this is simply grist for the mill. The teacher-student relationship is not a therapeutic one in the Western psychological sense, and the teacher's job

---

dhist Teachers in Dharamsala, 1993. https://info-buddhism.com/Ethics-in-the-Teacher-Student-Relationship.html#f3

5. In particular that of the Rochester Zen Center and of Boundless Way Zen (Massa-chusetts, USA).

6. At times if personal patterns seem to be causing too much pain and obstruction, the teacher may recommend that the student work with a therapist. Many students have found that such work has not only had benefits for their personal lives, but has also freed them to focus in a new way on the work of Zen.

is not to help us analyse the patterns of our individual psyche, but rather to help us see through and beyond them. In the best of all worlds, we will stick with the teacher, and the teacher will stick with us, through the times of confusion, doubt, and pain, and this very fact will set the stage for times of joy, confidence and certainty to emerge.

DHARMA TALK
by Richard von Sturmer

* * *

Three Turning Words
(2006—07—02)

Joshu (Zhaozhou in Chinese, 778–897) is known as one of the great Zen teachers of all time. He matured slowly, studying Zen for forty years, travelling about on pilgrimage for twenty more, and only settling down to teach at his own temple at the age of 80. Perhaps because of his ability to find just the words that would be most helpful to each particular student, it was said that a golden light played about his lips when he spoke.

For this Dharma talk, we'll take up a case in the *Blue Cliff Record*. There are one hundred cases in the *Blue Cliff* and this is number 96: Joshu's Three Turning Words.

> Joshu expressed three turning words to his community: 'A clay Buddha does not pass through water; a metal Buddha does not pass through a furnace; a wooden Buddha does not pass through fire.'

And that's it. We've heard many other talks about Joshu (Zhaozhou in Chinese), because he's such a wonderful teacher, such a great master. Just a little re-cap on his life. He lived in the Tang Dynasty, the golden age of Zen, and reached the age of 119. He was born in northern China, his surname was Ho and the first record of his life is when he came to meet Master Nansen when he was 17. He stayed as a student and disciple of Nansen for forty years.

Now Joshu is a real favourite of many people, many Zen students. Zen Master Dogen in Japan used to refer to him as 'the old Buddha'. And he was old. Sensei and I visited Joshu's temple, Bailin, back in 2001. It had been rebuilt and is a flourishing Zen monastery now. Since then, we've heard reports through Andy Ferguson, who leads tours to China, that Bailin temple is becoming an international centre. Zen students from the West are training with the abbot there. When you work on Joshu's koans, you get the sense of a living presence. In some respects he's still right here, still teaching. So it's great to know that his centre is active again, after falling into ruin during the Cultural Revolution.

I want to have a look at a few brief dialogues between Joshu and some of his students. These are ones that pertain to today's case. The first one is:

A monk asked, 'What about it when all the bones are pulverised and there is one everlasting spirit?'
Joshu said, 'Hmmm, it's windy again this morning.'[7]

This morning there's a frost on the grass outside 100 Pah Road.[8]

This monk asks a very lofty question: 'What about it when all the bones are pulverised and there is one everlasting spirit?' And Joshu just brings him down to earth. Forget about the one everlasting spirit, whatever that is. It's windy again this morning. The wind's blowing.

We'll come back to this wind later on in the talk,[9] but the point here is: instead of getting caught up in concepts of one everlasting spirit or God or whatever, just get buffeted about by the wind.

Another dialogue:

Joshu was asked by a monk, 'Who is Buddha?'
'The one in the shrine,' came the answer.
'Isn't it a clay statue that sits in the shrine?' the monk went on.
'Yes, that's right,' said Joshu.
'Then who is Buddha?' the monk repeated.
'The one in the shrine,' answered Joshu.[10]

He was right. The Buddha figure's in the shrine. The way the monk asked this question, there's a kind of fixating on Buddha as being something separate from the person asking the question. Joshu goes along with that. Okay. You want to objectify Buddha? He's the one in the shrine. He brings the monk back to a reality, back to earth.

This comes out in another dialogue, which is very similar:

A monk asked, 'What is the way?'
Joshu said, 'That which lies beyond the fence.'
The monk said, 'That's not what I'm talking about.'
Joshu said, 'Which way were you talking about?'

7. From James Green, ed., *The Recorded Saying of Zen Master Joshu* (Boulder, Colo.: Shambhala, 1998), p. 78.
8. Location of Auckland Zen Centre at the time this talk was delivered.
9. See p. 94.
10. From *Original Teachings of Ch'an Buddhism*, edited by Chang Chung-Yuan (New York: Grove Press, 1969), p. 169.

The monk said, 'The Great Way.'

Joshu said, 'The Great Way leads to the capital.'[11]

The Great Way in China at that time led to the capital Xian. It's an actual path. It's a real road that you had to walk on step by step, a road that carts and donkeys and horses would go down. If you're on foot you'd get dusty and you'd get thirsty. That's the road. That's the important road. The one that you have to walk. Not some theoretical Great Way.

So this is Joshu's teaching. It's very down to earth. It's said that at the age of 60, after Master Nansen died, he spent twenty years on pilgrimage, visiting other teachers, sharpening his understanding, deepening his understanding, and it was only when he was 80 that he settled down at a temple and began to teach. And then he taught for nearly 40 years. Because he began teaching when he was so old, he relied on his great wisdom to come forth not in shouts or physical actions like some other Zen teachers, but just in words — just to say the appropriate word to the student, to open the student up — and it's said that a golden light used to play round his lips when he spoke.

This brings us to the case:

Joshu expressed three turning words to his community: 'A clay Buddha does not pass through water; a metal Buddha does not pass through a furnace; a wooden Buddha does not pass through fire.'

A turning word in Zen can be a word or a phrase given by a teacher that can open up the mind of whoever asks the question and can lead to an awakening. The turning word can be a shout, it can be just one word, Mu, or it can be a phrase, an action, a blow of the stick. Anything that precipitates an awakening experience is a turning word. One definition of turning words are words that turn over the mind of illusion and open the mind to enlightenment. So Joshu has given us these three turning words:

A clay Buddha does not pass through water, a metal Buddha does not pass through a furnace, and a wooden Buddha does not pass through fire.

I want to talk a little bit about Buddha figures, the importance of Buddha figures. Last week we had our Jukai ceremony, and behind us on the altar there's a standing Buddha figure, a Thai figure, which has a real quality

11. Yoel Hoffman, *Radical Zen: The Sayings of Joshu* (Brookline, Mass.: Autumn Press, 1978), p. 107.

of lightness to it, a noble lightness. Of course such figures are important in Buddhism for their devotional aspects. It's great to have an inspiring figure on the altar, in the zendo or in the Buddha Hall or wherever people come together to chant or to practice. And in Zen we always stress that Buddha figures are actually a reminder of our own true nature – they're not separate from us at all – so when we enter a zendo and bow to a Buddha figure or a figure of a bodhisattva, we're acknowledging our own innate, perfect enlightenment. This is what we're here to realise. Usually on the altar we have a figure of Manjushri, the Bodhisattva of Wisdom, and when we bow to Manjushri we're bowing to our own innate wisdom. When we bow to a figure of Kannon, we're bowing to our innate compassion. And with these bows there's also a sense that we're vowing to realise that compassion or wisdom.

Roshi Kapleau always stressed that it's good to refer to Buddha figures as figures, not statues. A statue is something you place in a museum or an art gallery. To say 'Buddha figure' conveys its human aspect, and it's a better way of linking that figure with ourselves. So, from a Zen perspective, when we bow we're not separate from whatever the figure is we're bowing to. In Asian Buddhism, devotion plays a very strong part, and often people pray to Buddha figures, and they do many prostrations to them. At the time when Joshu was teaching in China, it was seen that people could become overly attached to Buddha figures. They could see the Buddha as something separate, something very lofty, something that they could never attain to but only worship, and so there are many stories aimed at shaking a person out of that too-devotional mindset.

One famous story is about Danxia Tianran, a Chinese teacher whose dates are 739–824.[12] One day he was staying at Wisdom Wood temple when the weather became bitterly cold, and so he took a wooden statue of the Buddha and burned it in the fire to keep warm. The temple director got extremely upset with Tianran and yelled, 'Why are you burning my wooden Buddha?' Tianran pulled a burning ember from the fire and said, 'I'm burning this Buddha to get the sacred relics from it.'

These sacred relics, known as *sharira*, are little stones, mineral deposits, or gems that are said to be left behind when a master or a Buddha or someone of high attainment dies and is cremated. After the body is cremated, these little stones, often very beautiful, are collected and venerated. This is an ancient practice, and also one that continues in many Buddhist countries to this day. So Tianran said, 'I'm burning this Buddha to get the sacred relics from it.' And the temple director said, 'How can a wooden Buddha have sacred relics?' And Tianran said, 'Well if it doesn't have sacred relics, let's burn a couple more of them.' At that point the temple director was so upset his eyebrows and eyelashes and beard all fell out at once.

Poor temple director! However there's something wonderfully iconoclastic about this story. Clearly the temple director was too attached to the Buddha figure and that's what it boils down to. No matter how beautiful and inspirational the figures are, it's important not to get attached to them. The true Buddha is within.

12. See Andy Ferguson, *Zen's Chinese Heritage* (Boston: Wisdom, 2000), p. 111.

Let's turn now to Joshu's three turning words. First, a clay Buddha does not pass through water. There's a technique, an ancient technique in China, for making Buddha figures using clay and straw, and then once the Buddha figure is formed with the clay and straw, it's covered using a subtle paper maché technique. Tomasz Holuj, an artist and a member of the Swedish Sangha, went to California several years ago to work with a Chinese teacher at the City of Ten Thousand Buddhas in California, and while he was there he was shown this ancient technique of making Buddha figures from straw and clay. On his return he made a beautiful Manjushri figure, the Bodhisattva of Wisdom, for the Stockholm Zen Centre. If you ever visit the Stockholm zendo you may come across that Manjushri figure.

But a clay Buddha dissolves in water. The water breaks apart what is solid and unyielding. You can just imagine this clay Buddha being undone by the pressure of water, just breaking apart and dissolving and being carried away. A Mahayana sutra, the Shurangama Sutra, says this about water: 'Water is yielding but all-conquering. It never attacks, but always wins the last battle.'

All of these three turning words point to the impermanence of things, impermanence of this body, of Buddha figures, of everything. Everything is in flux, everything changes and passes away, and water is really a prime image of impermanence. There's a beautiful passage from the *Record of a Ten Foot Square Hut*, by a Japanese writer, Kamo No Chomei:

> The river flows on unceasingly, but the water is never the same as before. Bubbles that bob on the surface of the still places disappear one moment to reappear the next, but they seldom endure for long. And so it is with the people of this world and the houses they live in.[13]

Think of houses being carried away in the floods.

The next image of impermanence: A metal Buddha does not pass through a furnace. On the altar of the Rochester Zen Center is a very beautiful and mysterious metal Buddha. It's the Healing Buddha, and he has a bowl in his right hand filled with the medicine of the Dharma, which he dispenses. When we clean this Buddha once a year during the New Year's celebrations, the figure is taken down from the altar. He's not a big

---

13. Burton Watson, trans., *Four Huts: Asian Writings on the Simple Life* (Boulder, Colo.: Shambhala, 1994), p. 60.

figure, but it takes two people to lift him because he's very heavy. But even this metal Buddha has to pass through intense fire, through the furnace. It's a great image, this image of the furnace, because what is melted down can be used again — and a Buddha that's melted down can be fashioned into many different forms afterwards. This points to the Bodhisattvic spirit of Zen, that we have to melt down our own self-partiality so that we can truly be of benefit to others and of benefit to the world — this is part of Zen practice, to melt down that hard ball of ego that each one of us has, to melt it down to some degree so that our hearts become more tender and more open. That's the path of the Bodhisattva. Sometimes this melting requires quite a bit of heat. Zen Master Mumon said, 'If you wish to know true gold, see it in the midst of fire.'

Finally, a wooden Buddha does not pass through fire. There are many fine Buddha figures made of wood and polished — for example the Man-jushri figure that we usually have on our altar, a wooden figure of a young man sitting on his lion. Beautiful wooden figures like this, when they're polished, seem to glow with their own light. Over the years such a figure absorbs the concentrated energy of the zendo and radiates it back, inspiring our practice. But then again, wooden Buddhas eventually have to pass through fire, too.

It's good just to think about wooden Buddhas passing through fire, not to become attached to any of our supposed achievements in Zen practice, or at the same time, not to be attached to our innumerable failures in practice. We all fall down in practice – all of us – we fall down all the time, and when we do, we have to pick ourselves back up and return to the breath or to the koan. Not getting stuck – that's the important thing – not to get stuck on what's happened in the past, but just to give ourselves wholeheartedly to the task at hand, whatever is required of us. At a one-day sitting it's to give ourselves wholeheartedly to our practice during this one day. Shunryu Suzuki, the founder of the San Francisco Zen Center, sums this up when he says:

> When you do something, you should burn yourself up completely, like a good bonfire, leaving no trace of yourself.[14]

A wooden Buddha does not pass through fire. Completely burnt up, doing what it has to do.

Now the question arises with this koan as to why Joshu repeats the same basic message of impermanence three times: the clay Buddha, the metal Buddha, the wooden Buddha. Well, we can say that the practice of Zen is a refining process; it's the refining of our character. And this refining process involves the dissolving and melting down of our ego, and it never stops. It's particularly true during a seven-day sesshin.[15] After we come out of a seven-day sesshin and everything's so bright and light, it's like a little bit of our iron cladding has been shed. We feel a bit more free, more open to the world. This is why doing sesshin is so important; it's a shedding – each sesshin to some degree is a shedding of our carapace, the layer of protective covering or armour that each one of us has. Little by little we shed this. We realise there's nothing to defend – everything's open. That hard ball of ego begins to soften and it softens more with each sesshin. That's why in Zen we stress going to sesshin, because in sesshin transformations really begin to take place. Sesshin is like a furnace, or like a river, or like a fire. It's the place of transformation. In old times retreats,

---

14. Shunryu Suzuki, *Zen Mind, Beginner's Mind* (New York: Weatherhill, 1970), p. 62.
15. See Chapter 11.

especially seven-day retreats, were called Buddha sorting houses, because that's where Buddhas get sorted.

And I think there's an important psychological aspect to these clay Buddhas and wooden Buddhas and metal Buddhas. Joshu has chosen three different materials, and there's an acknowledgement here that people who come to practice have different temperaments and characters. This is vividly brought home to anyone who has spent time at a Zen centre or a Zen temple. It's just amazing all the different types of people you work alongside in this collective setting, everyone unique, coming from all sorts of different backgrounds. At the Rochester Zen Center people arrive from different countries: Mexico, Sweden, Poland, New Zealand, America, Canada. There are people from working class backgrounds, people who have spent many years at University, tradespeople, teachers, lawyers, even judges, all of us mixed up together, with all sorts of different quirks and tics and ways of approaching life and practice.

Some people are very soft and malleable. Some people are very retiring and others, when you first meet them, appear very stiff and unbending. But all this is really from an outside perspective. Someone might appear to you like a spiritual warrior, clad in armour, while another person when you first meet them may seem so shy that they wouldn't say boo to a goose. But you realise after a while that these are just surface appearances and they can be deceiving. The main thing is that each person is sincerely working on their practice, which means a perfecting of character, and this process is different for everyone. But whether we're introverted or extroverted, whether we're soft and watery or hard and wooden, this process of dissolving, of loosening up, of letting go, has to take place. This process of zazen is a tenderising process, letting go of what we cling to, just letting go, shedding all the time.

Take the most extreme image that Joshu uses of the iron Buddha. Someone with an iron nature may be very sure of himself, completely confident in all situations. Still, if that person sincerely wants to practice then even that iron nature will have to go into the furnace and be melted down. Roshi Kapleau said, 'To acknowledge one's limitations is hard for someone with a big ego.' And the greatest limitation is to see ourselves as separate from others. That's what we have to knock down — our sense of separation. For some people it can be a sense of our uniqueness: 'I'm special. I'm going to excel in this practice. I'm going to do really well in

this practice.' That has to be melted down. For other people, it can be a
sense of inferiority, a negative ego: 'Oh, I'm no good at this. Everyone
else is getting it, everyone else is forging ahead in their practice, but I
can't do this, it's beyond me.' That negative ego has to be melted down
as well. Washed away. Handed over to the flames. Just the process of
loosening up and letting go. That's what's important.

Setcho, the initial compiler of the *Blue Cliff Record*, has three verses to
go with each of the three Buddhas, each of the three elements. So let's
take a look at these three. [16] First, the clay Buddha:

> *A clay Buddha does not pass through water.*
> *Spiritual light illuminates Heaven and Earth.*
> *If standing in the snow were not stopped,*
> *Who would not carve an imitation?*

Now, Spiritual Light is the personal name of Huike, the second ancestor
of Zen. When Huike was born it's said that a spiritual light illuminated
the room extending into the sky. This line from the verse, 'If standing
in the snow...' refers to the famous story about Huike meeting the first
ancestor of Zen, Bodhidharma, and becoming his disciple. Huike had
heard about Bodhidharma and decided to ask him for instruction. So he
went all the way to Shaolin temple and stood outside Bodhidharma's cave
(Bodhidharma was meditating in a cave at the time) day and night, seeking instruction. But Bodhidharma would not even acknowledge Huike's
presence. He just kept on sitting:

> Huike thought to himself, 'When people of ancient times sought the Way,
> they broke their bones and took out the marrow, shed their blood to appease
> hunger, spread out their hair to cover mud, threw themselves off cliffs to
> feed tigers. Even of old were they like this. What about me?'
>
> That year on the night of the ninth of December there was a great snow.
> Huike stood by the wall. By dawn snow had piled up past his knees. Bo-
> dhidharma took pity on him and said, 'You, standing in the snow there,
> what do you seek?' Huike sighed and said, 'I only beg your compassion
> to open the gates of ambrosia and save all creatures.' Bodhidharma said,
> 'The wondrous path of all the Buddhas requires zealous work over vast
> eons, practicing what is difficult to practice, enduring the unendurable, with

16. Verses and stories from Thomas and J. C. Cleary, trans., *The Blue Cliff Record: Volume
3* (Boulder, Colo.: Shambala, 1978).

little virtue and petty knowledge, a shallow heart and a narrow mind, how can you seek to be a true vehicle?' There is no way.' Huike, hearing this admonition, was even more earnest towards the Path. He secretly took a sharp knife and cut off his own forearm and placed it before Bodhidharma. Bodhidharma knew he was a vessel of the Dharma, so he asked him, 'You stand in the snow and cut off your arm, what for?' Huike said, 'My mind is not yet at peace. Please, Master, ease my mind.' Bodhidharma said, 'Bring forth your mind and I will ease it for you.' Huike said, 'When I search for my mind, ultimately I can't find it.' Bodhidharma said, 'I have put your mind at ease.'

At that moment Huike had a great awakening. The point of this story is not so much the dramatic image of Huike presenting his arm, but of his awakening, of Bodhidharma putting his mind at ease. He unblocked Huike. He gave him the turning words that Huike needed to hear. That's the importance of 'If standing in the snow were not stopped, who would not carve an imitation?' There's a danger that if Huike just stood heroically in the snow, people of later times would take his standing in the snow as an example of great austerity and try and copy him and get nowhere, just as Shakyamuni before his great enlightenment reached a dead end after six years of great austerity. That's not the point. The point is becoming liberated, flowing with everything, becoming unblocked.

The second verse:

> *A metal Buddha does not pass through a furnace.*
> *Someone comes calling on Zihu.*
> *Several words are on the sign.*
> *Where is there no pure wind?*

Now, these verses of Setcho's are often just opportunities to tell stories and to link other stories in with the case at hand. Zihu was a disciple of Nansen, Joshu's teacher. And it's said that Master Zihu set up a sign outside his gate. On the sign were words saying, 'Zihu has a dog. Above he takes people's heads. In the middle he takes people's loins. Below he takes people's legs. If you stop to talk to him, you lose your body and your life.' And whenever Zihu saw newcomers, he would immediately shout, 'Watch out for the dog!'

This dog is just a metaphor. These are all just metaphors. It's the metaphor of dying the great death and coming back to life again. Dying the great death is seeing into our true nature. Dying to our confined, narrow, limited, ego-nature, and coming back to life, awakened. This awakening is summed up in the last line, 'Where is there no pure wind?' Pure wind abides nowhere. It's always moving, always fresh, you can't pin it down, you can't fix it, it's invisible, but it has great force. This wind's always present. It can animate us, it can fill us. Our breath connects us with this great wind.

Finally, Setcho's third verse:

> *A wooden Buddha does not pass through fire.*
> *I always think of the oven-breaker.*
> *Only when his staff suddenly struck*
> *Was the True Self liberated.*

Again, this hooks into another story — this will be our last story today. It's set in ancient times and is about the oven-breaker of Mt Sung. We don't know anything about him except that he dwelt in seclusion:

One day, leading a group of followers, he went among the mountain aborigines [the native dwellers of China at that point]. They had a shrine which was most sacred. In its hall was placed only an oven. People from far and near sacrificed to it unceasingly. They had immolated many living creatures. The Master entered the shrine and tapped the oven three times with his staff. He said, 'What humbug! You were originally made of brick and mud compounded, whence does the spirit come from, whence does the sanctity originate, that you burn living creatures to death like this?' And again he hit it three times. The oven then toppled over, broke, and collapsed of itself. Momentarily there was a man in a blue robe and a tall hat, suddenly standing in front of the Master. Bowing, he said, 'I am the god of the oven. For a long time I've been subject to retribution for my actions, but today, hearing the Master explain the truth of non-origination, I am already freed from this place and living in heaven. I have come especially to offer thanks.' The Master said, 'It is your fundamentally inherent nature, not my forced saying so.' The god again bowed, and disappeared. An attendant said, 'I and the others have been around the Master for a long time, but have never received instruction. What shortcut did the oven god find that he was immediately born in Heaven?' The Master said, 'I just said to him, "You were originally made of brick and mud put together; where does the spirit come from, whence does the sanctity emerge?" ' The attendant had no reply. The Master said, 'Do you understand?' The monk said, 'I do not understand.' The Master said, 'Bow!' The monk bowed; the Master said, 'Broken! Collapsed!' The attendant was suddenly greatly enlightened.

Broken! Collapsed!

Those were the turning words. That was what the monk needed to hear.

So the oven-breaker liberated not only the spirit of the oven, but the monk as well. The spirit of the oven was released from its fixedness, from the dead rituals that had been performed at that place. The monk was freed from his fixed notions of the teachings or what a teacher was. He was unglued as well, unfixed, liberated. That's what all the parts of this koan, all the metaphors are pointing to: to letting go, to flowing along, to melting down, to burning up, whatever it takes.

Metaphors and images and legends like these are important in Zen. They're fingers pointing to the moon – which of course is itself a metaphor. They're not the moon itself, but they can inspire us in our practice.

So, with a talk like this, if you feel you're a wooden Buddha, use that metaphor!

If you feel like you're more of a clay Buddha or a watery Buddha, work with that!

If you feel like you're an iron Buddha, stick with that!

Whatever works. Whatever it takes.

We'll stop here and recite the four vows.

*   *

*

A special transmission outside the scriptures;
Not dependent on words and letters;
Direct pointing to the human heart;
Seeing into one's nature and attaining Buddhahood.

—BODHIDHARMA

CHAPTER 5

Committing to the Path

IN A TEISHO from 2004 entitled 'Points of Entry in Zen Training,' Amala-sensei discusses various ways in which Zen students can mark their commitment to the path. One is taking the precepts in a Jukai ceremony, another is becoming a formal student, and a third is sewing a rakusu and receiving a Dharma name. In Sensei's words:

> These three are like three gates that we enter in Zen practice [and each] is a way of acknowledging, 'This is my Sangha; this is where I feel at home.' There's a lot of difference between, say, renting a house and owning a house – settling into something – and this settling is a big part of training, of finding a stable seat, a spiritual *tūrangawaewae*.[1]

In Chapter 4 we looked at becoming a formal student, and in this chapter we'll look especially at the Jukai ceremony before ending with a brief look at receiving a rakusu and Dharma name. But before getting into

---

1. A Māori word for a place to stand, a place where one feels especially empowered and connected.

the specifics of Jukai, it will be helpful to pause for a moment to get an overview of the various Buddhist teaching traditions, and to consider where the Zen school fits into the rich and varied family tree of Buddhist beliefs and practices.

From the broadest perspective, Buddhism as practiced today in different parts of the world can be divided into three main branches: Theravada ('the way of the elders'), Mahayana ('the great vehicle') and Vajrayana ('the diamond/thunderbolt vehicle'). Each of these have their origin in ancient India, where, in the centuries after the Buddha's Parinirvana, many different branches or schools of Buddhism coexisted, sometimes in the same monastery, debating with and influencing each other. But as Buddhism spread beyond India, the individuals who carried the teachings to new lands tended very naturally to present those teachings from the perspective of the school to which they belonged, and so to set the framework within which Buddhism would develop in each region. Thus Theravada teachings came to dominate in the countries of Southeast Asia, such as Sri Lanka, Myanmar, Cambodia, and Thailand – and Theravada is often referred to as the Southern School of Buddhism. In contrast, the Buddhism that made its way across the mountains into China was mostly of the Mahayana variety, while the Buddhism that came to be emphasised in Tibet (home of the youngest branch of Asian Buddhism historically) was the esoteric, or Vajrayana, tradition. Eventually Buddhism disappeared almost entirely from India itself, and so those of us who take up the Buddhist path today soon find ourselves connected through our teacher's lineage to one of the countries where Buddhism has continued to flourish down to the present day, thus aligning ourselves (perhaps somewhat willy-nilly) with one of these three great branches of the teaching. Since the Buddhist teachings that reached Japan, beginning in the sixth century C.E., came from China via Korea, Japanese Buddhism in general, including Zen Buddhism, forms part of the Mahayana. (Zen specifically reflects many native Chinese influences as well, especially from Taoism and Confucianism.)

Theravada Buddhism, as its name ('way of the elders') suggests, follows closely the practices of the Buddha's own time, including a Sangha of celibate homeleavers supported by food offerings of the laity. Doctrinally the Theravada adheres to the Pali-language canon of classical

Buddhism which includes discourses of the Buddha (the Suttas) as well as the rules and regulations for monks and nuns (the Vinaya) and various philosophical and psychological commentaries (the Abhidhamma). At around the same time that the suttas were being recorded in Pali (about four and a half centuries after the Buddha's Parinirvana), another stream of Buddhist writings began to appear, often in the Sanskrit language, which reflect a somewhat different approach. These Mahayana writings emphasise the ideal of the Bodhisattva, who vows to liberate all beings and to keep taking rebirth until everyone has attained Buddhahood; this is in contrast to the Arhat of classical Buddhism, who breaks free of the cycle of birth and death upon attaining Nirvana. The Mahayana (of which Zen forms a part) conveyed an inclusive message: that the path is open to all beings, and that all are innately Buddhas, but that with our 'minds turned upside-down by delusive thinking' we simply fail to realise that fact.[2] Scholars continue to debate the origins of the Mahayana, but, traditionally, Mahayana practitioners have claimed that their sutras,[3] too, contain the words of the Buddha, but words that were delivered only to those who were ready to hear them, and who preserved them secretly for a time. This is sometimes expressed in mythical terms; for instance one part of the Mahayana sutras, the vast Perfection of Wisdom literature, was said to have been entrusted to the Nagas — chthonic serpent deities who live under the sea. They were then retrieved by Nagarjuna (see below, p. 100) and conveyed to humanity.

If one delves even a little bit into the highly complex and sophisticated traditions of Buddhist philosophy, one will find significant differences between the many early schools of Buddhism (only one of which developed into the modern Theravada), between the various branches of the Mahayana, and even between the four major schools of Tibetan Buddhism, which are very much alive today teaching philosophy and debating techniques to their lineage descendants. This complexity and

2. 'Wonder of wonders! All beings are intrinsically Buddha, endowed with wisdom and virtue, lacking nothing, but because people's minds have been turned upside down by delusive thinking they fail to perceive this.' Kegon Sutra (called the Huayan Sutra in Chinese, or the Avatamsaka Sutra in Sanskrit), Chapter 14.

3. 'Sutra' is the Sanskrit form and 'sutta' the Pali form of the word that refers to texts containing the words of the Buddha.

diversity of belief can be surprising and even overwhelming. Where do we fit into this as newcomers to the Dharma, and how much is it important for us to know?

Of course there is no single answer to this question, and different people will have different degrees of interest in investigating Buddhist scripture and philosophy. As practitioners of the Mahayana, we are heirs to the great philosophical tradition of the Madhyamaka ('Middle-Way School') founded by the Indian scholar Nagarjuna (*c.* 150–*c.* 250 C.E.) and emphasising the teachings on Emptiness (Sunyata) and Perfection of Wisdom (Prajñaparamita). Investigating these doctrinal underpinnings of our practice can be both illuminating and helpful. Certainly, as a base-line, it is useful to know about the Three Dharma Seals: traditionally, any teachings which do not include the Three Dharma Seals cannot be considered Buddhist teachings. In other words, these are the three most fundamental points of Buddhist doctrine. Significantly enough, however, there is even disagreement among the different Buddhist schools as to exactly what these three are! But everybody agrees on two of them: *anicca* or impermanence, and *anatta* or no-self. As for the third seal, some teachers give it as *dukkha* or suffering, while others replace this with *nirvana* or the end of suffering.

Still, keeping in mind the fundamental quatrain of the Zen school, attributed to Zen lineage-founder Bodhidharma, –

> *A special transmission outside the scriptures;*
> *Not dependent on words and letters;*
> *Direct pointing to the human heart;*
> *Seeing into one's nature and attaining Buddhahood.*

– you can see that there is no requirement in Zen to master philosophy or philology. Huineng, the deeply enlightened and influential Sixth Chinese Ancestor of Zen, was supposed to have been illiterate at the time of his initial awakening.

In fact there is a criterion even more essential than that of the Three Dharma Seals for distinguishing Buddhist practice from the non-Buddhist. From earliest times and within all branches of Buddhism, the first step for those wishing to enter the Buddha Way has been to 'go for refuge', that is, to formally take refuge in Buddha, Dharma, and Sangha (the Three Treasures). In the words of Roshi Philip Kapleau, 'The foundation of

Buddhism is the Three Treasures, without trust in which and reverence for there can be no Buddhist religious life.' [4] In the context of Zen, this brings us back to our discussion of Jukai. For Zen practitioners, Jukai functions as an initiation ceremony; it is the ceremony in which we formally become Buddhists. Master Dogen saw participation in Jukai as an indispensable step on the path to Buddhahood. In the course of this ceremony we make 16 different vows or resolutions: first, the Three Refuges (I take refuge in Buddha; I take refuge in Dharma; I take refuge in Sangha), next, the Three General Resolutions (I resolve to do no harm; I resolve to do good; I resolve to liberate all living beings), and finally the Ten Cardinal Precepts (see inset overleaf).

We have already had a quick look at the Three Refuge Vows in the opening paragraphs of this book.[5] As explained by Sensei Wrightson in a 2004 teisho on The Three Treasures:

> The names [Three Treasures or Three Jewels] refer to the preciousness of Buddha, Dharma and Sangha, as well as to the quality jewels have of multiplying light, of offering illumination. Jewels are also hard and indestructible, and indestructibility is likewise a quality of Buddha, Dharma, and Sangha.

As was also mentioned before, these Three Treasures may be understood on many different levels. Mahayana teaching, for example, speaks of the Unified, the Manifested and the Abiding Three Treasures. The second of these, the Manifested Three Treasures (*genzen sambo* in Japanese), actually comes closest to the literal level of interpretation that we looked at in our Introduction (p. 3) with the word 'Manifested' referring to the way in which the Three Treasures revealed themselves in the life and person of Shakyamuni Buddha. Thus the 'manifested Buddha' means Shakyamuni himself, the 'manifested Dharma' refers to the words the Buddha actually spoke and the teachings he gave while he was alive, and the 'manifested Sangha' was the community of practitioners who gathered around him at that time.

The third category, that of the Abiding Three Treasures (*juji sambo* in Japanese) speaks to the ways in which the Three Treasures still abide in our world today. Here Buddha refers to the various forms of iconog-

---

4. Kapleau, Roshi Philip, *The Three Pillars of Zen* (New York: Anchor, 2000), p. 423.
5. See Introduction, p. 3.

raphy (figures, paintings, drawings) through which we can still see for ourselves a visual image of the Buddha, Dharma refers to the sutras (written records), through which we can still read for ourselves the words the Buddha spoke and the teachings he gave, while Sangha refers to today's community of practitioners, who continue to follow the Buddha, and who can pass along the teachings and traditions to the next generation.

It is the first category, however, the Unified Three Treasures (*ittai sambo* in Japanese), that introduces us to something much more fundamental, something not bound by notions of time. Here 'Buddha' refers to the awakened nature of the universe itself, 'Dharma' to the ways that that universe reveals its own teachings, and 'Sangha' to its essential harmony or perfection. Thus, as we have said before, the Buddha did not have to invent his teachings from scratch; rather, his task was to uncover the reality already inherent in the universe – and to teach that, by paying attention, each of us can do the same. In her teisho on the Three Treasures, Sensei Wrightson expands on the meaning of the *ittai sambo*, the Unified Three Treasures, particularly on the experiential level:

> The most basic meaning of Buddha, Dharma, and Sangha is Realisation, Truth, and Harmony. Realisation (Buddha) means an experience of the world of form-as-emptiness, of the unconditioned, when we drop discrimination and suddenly know oneness – no longer experiencing things in a fragmentary way, but as a whole, a vibrant, living, breathing whole. It may only be for a brief moment that we experience this for the first time, but it gives us great faith.
>
> The Truth (Dharma) refers to the law of the universe, the law of endless and beginningless becoming to which every atom of the universe is subject. This is the world of karma, the world of change and impermanence, the world of cause and effect. When the rain falls the ground gets wet. Dogs chase cats. If I don't have breakfast I get hungry. It's the way things interact. And we're talking also about the other meaning of the word 'dharma'. Dharma with a capital D is the Law, but dharma with a small d, often in the plural, 'dharmas', means 'things, phenomena, stuff'. And all things are subject to the law of cause and effect.
>
> And then, Harmony (Sangha) means the total interpenetration of the realm of the absolute, or oneness, and the realm of things, change, difference. Seeing these as not separate from each other. So on this level, Sangha is how you experience the world if you are awake.
>
> To put it another way, we can say that everything has Buddha Nature;

THE SIXTEEN PRECEPTS

The Three Refuges

I take refuge in Buddha, and resolve that with all beings I will understand the Great Way whereby the Buddha seed may forever thrive.

I take refuge in Dharma and resolve that with all beings I will enter deeply into the sutra treasure so that my wisdom may grow as vast as the ocean.

I take refuge in Sangha, and in its wisdom, example, and never-failing help, and resolve to live in harmony with all sentient beings.

The Three General Resolutions

I resolve to do no harm.

I resolve to do good.

I resolve to liberate all living beings.

The Ten Cardinal Precepts

I resolve not to kill but to cherish all life.

I resolve not to take what is not given, but to respect the property of others.

I resolve not to engage in harmful sexual relations, but to be faithful and responsible.

I resolve not to lie but to speak the truth.

I resolve not to cause others to take intoxicants, nor to do so myself, but to keep the mind clear.

I resolve not to gossip about the faults of others, but to acknowledge my own shortcomings.

I resolve not to praise myself (and disparage others), but to speak with humility and extol virtue.

I resolve not to withhold spiritual or material aid, but to give them freely where needed.

I resolve not to indulge in anger, but to practice forbearance.

I resolve not to revile the Three Treasures, Buddha, Dharma and Sangha, but to cherish and uphold them.

'Buddha' is the very stuff of the universe. 'Dharma' is the laws that govern this stuff, and 'Sangha' is all the beings who are sincerely endeavouring to live in harmony with the truth of this universe. So in this sense these Three Treasures are fundamental not just to Buddhist practice, but to all religious practice.

It is with these fundamental truths — with *taking refuge* in these fundamental truths — that the Jukai ceremony begins. This is followed by the Three General Resolutions, which we might view as general instructions for applying the Refuges in daily life. The Resolutions derive from a *gatha* or verse that appears in the *Dhammapada*, one of the most renowned and beloved of the Pali texts:

Renounce all evil, practice all good, keep the mind pure. Thus the Buddhas taught.

Mahayana practitioners later made a change in this three-point verse, so that the instruction to keep the mind pure was replaced by the vow to liberate all beings. This change reflects the Mahayana emphasis on including all beings in one's own awakening process, and in recognising the oneness of all humans and non-humans.

The Three General Resolutions are indeed as general and all-encompassing as possible. The Ten Cardinal Precepts, which follow the General Resolutions in the Jukai ceremony, attempt a more specific unfolding of ethical behaviour in relation to different aspects of our life. The first five of these (not to kill, not to steal, not to misuse sexuality, not to lie and not to supply or take intoxicants) have been unchanged since the time of the Buddha, and can be found as the five main lay precepts in all branches of Buddhism. With the sixth through tenth precepts, on the other hand, there is a great deal of variation between the different schools of Buddhism and for different people (lay or ordained). At the Auckland Zen Centre we take a version of the Mahayana precepts that we have inherited from the Harada-Yasutani branch of Soto Zen.[6]

Since there are ten precepts, people are often reminded of the Ten Commandments and may be tempted to think of the cardinal precepts as the Ten Commandments of Buddhism. Thus one of the first points our teachers generally make about the precepts is that they are not actually

6. For a closer look at the ten precepts of our lineage, see the next chapter, 'Upholding the Precepts.'

commandments – they have not been handed down from on high – but are rather *descriptions* of the way that we would act if we were awake – that is, if we could truly see things as they are. The central impulse that underlies all the precepts, as well as the Jukai ceremony itself, is *ahimsa* or nonviolence, the wish to do no harm. If we truly understood that we are not separate from others, if we knew in our bones that any harmful action injures ourselves as much as any presumed other, then we would easily and naturally act in the ways that the precepts describe.

On the other hand, in taking the precepts we also acknowledge that, as long as we're not fully enlightened, we will at times fail to live up to the behaviour they describe. That's a given. So it is important to view the upholding of the precepts as a process, as something we work towards. For this reason, in most Zen communities, Jukai is offered once or twice a year, and it is not a ceremony we participate in just once, but again and again. In her 'Points of Entry' teisho Sensei Wrightson comments:

> Whenever we act in a way that does not reflect a sense of harmony with all things, then for that moment we stop being a Buddhist. We're effectively not part of the Sangha at that moment. So Jukai is a chance to recommit ourselves and to re-enter the Sangha.
>
> This is why, in most precept ceremonies, the actual taking of the precepts is preceded by a brief repentance. This is a way of acknowledging how we fall down with the precepts. And so we acknowledge that, clear it away, before we rededicate ourselves, so we can make a fresh start. And of course each moment is an opportunity to make a fresh start, not just when we take Jukai. Each moment is entirely and utterly fresh and new. Just as in our zazen, over and over we notice that our mind has wandered off and we come back, it's the same with our actions. Over and over we recognise that we do something that causes ourselves or others harm, but at each moment we get a new chance, completely new. However deep that habit may be, however hard we may find it to break, each moment we have another chance to choose to act differently from the way we've acted before, to bring our understanding and our action into harmony. However long it takes. It's so important, it doesn't matter if it takes us years and years and years.

At the Auckland Zen Centre we've adopted two times during the year when we offer Jukai. One is at the stroke of midnight on the first of January, so that the first act of the New Year is to rededicate ourselves to nonharm. The fact that people all over the world are marking the New Year at this time gives the act power and resonance. The other Jukai is offered during Matariki, the midwinter Aotearoa/New Zealand New Year. In te reo Māori, Matariki refers both to the Pleiades constellation as well as to the season of its first rising. Different iwi celebrate Matariki at different times, some when Matariki rises in late May or early June and others at the first full moon or first new moon following its rising. The power of this second Jukai comes from its timing at the darkest point of the year, when the days start to lengthen once more; this marks our Southern New Year.

At some Zen Centres, taking Jukai and becoming a formal student go hand-in-hand, and a rakusu might be given in conjunction with these. At the Auckland Zen Centre, we keep each of these three as more independent gates or entry-points into the practice, and there are important reasons for doing so. For one thing, it is possible to do serious zazen without formally being a Buddhist. Some people may have had a negative experience with a particular religion or religious community and be looking for a spiritual practice free of the trappings of organised religion. Others will have a strong connection to another religion, such as Christianity or Judaism, and will come to Zen practice as a way of strengthening that faith. They may wish to practice Zen without taking Jukai, and this is fine. Ultimately the Zen experience opens us to a reality that is not Buddhist or Christian or secular or anything else, a reality beyond designations. So you can certainly take up Zen practice without identifying as a Buddhist. At the same time, it is fine to do Jukai without being or intending to become a formal student. Jukai is open to everyone, and is much too important for us to restrict participation in any way. The Bodhisattvic spirit which the precepts embody is the essential starting point for our practice. Thus the typical order of events is for people to take Jukai at least once, and perhaps several times, before becoming a formal student (see Chapter 4), and then usually to work with the teacher as a formal student for some time before requesting a Dharma name and rakusu. In this way the three different ceremonies (Jukai, formal student ceremony, rakusu ceremony) build upon each other and represent a growing level of commitment to the Buddhist path and to working within a particular lineage.

The sewing of a rakusu is itself a devotional act and it is up to the student to decide if and when they wish to take this step. The rakusu represents the Buddha's robe in miniature, and so is a concrete and public symbol of one's entry into the Sangha, and into a particular lineage family. It is mostly sewn by hand, and as one sews, one chants one of the refuges with each stitch: I take refuge in Buddha, I take refuge in Dharma, I take refuge in Sangha. Like the *kesa*, the robe that is worn by monks, nuns and Zen priests on formal occasions, a rakusu is made from small strips of fabric that are pieced together. In earliest times, it was an expression of the renunciation practiced by the monks and nuns, in that they would make their only items of clothing from discarded scraps of fabric. In fact they are said to have picked these scraps from garbage heaps or even charnel grounds. The scraps were then washed, dyed and sewn together into a single robe of uniform colour. Thus, they would take intimately to themselves the most despised refuse, or the tainted, even haunted, garments of the dead, and turn them into something sacred. This approach made for a stark contrast with widely held beliefs of the time, strongly focused on ritual purity and caste. The Buddha was well-known for rejecting caste distinctions and welcoming all into the Sangha. For our part, we can see the sewing of these small strips together into one garment as a concretisation of the process we're undertaking in our zazen, bringing together all the disparate parts of ourselves into one integral whole. It represents the healing, the making-whole, that happens through practice.

The ceremony in which one receives the rakusu is a private one with the teacher, and, in conjunction with the rakusu, the student may also receive a Dharma name which the teacher inscribes on the back of the rakusu. This is not a name that is used publicly but it is something that can inspire the student, and serve as a reminder of the vows he or she has taken. Taking on a new name offers a sense of renewal, a turning away from delusion and a turning towards awakening. In terms of choosing the name, the teacher will offer three or four suggestions that reflect qualities she sees in the student, and the student will make the final decision. The name should be something that suits the student's character, but also that expresses an aspiration, that is, something the student aspires to live up to. Sometimes a Dharma name will contain a paradoxical or oxymoronic combination of different elements, such as Earthcloud or Ironlotus. This is a way of representing our true mind which is beyond dualistic distinctions.

In the end, the sewing of a rakusu, the taking of a Dharma name and even the Jukai ceremony itself are not absolutes but skilful means, things which can help. Of course it is the actual living out of the vows that really counts. And we could just say, Okay, now I'm going to keep the precepts, and I'll do my best. But it may be we need a little more help. Participating in a ceremony, speaking the vows out loud and in public, before one's Dharma brothers and sisters, sewing a rakusu with one's own hands, chanting as one sews, wearing the rakusu whenever we sit; all of these are means of moving our resolutions out of our heads and into our bodies, where we can begin to truly manifest them in the world.

TEISHO

* * *

Faith

(2011–03–27)

In this teisho, Amala-sensei discusses the role of faith in committing to the Buddhist path. The Buddha is famous for having said, 'Come and see !' and for encouraging students to test the teachings for themselves. How does faith fit in with this ?

Today I'm going to talk a little about Faith. I've been invited by the Auckland Interfaith Council to give a talk this Wednesday, along with an imam and a bishop, on keeping and practicing faith in New Zealand today. So preparing for this talk brought up the whole question of what faith actually means in Buddhism and in Zen.

We just finished our chanting service with the Honzon Eko, the Return of Merit, which starts with this line: 'Faith in Buddha, Dharma, and Sangha brings true liberation.' So clearly faith has a role in Zen Buddhist practice, but what does it mean ? It's an interesting question because the way faith is understood in Buddhism is perhaps quite different from the way it is understood in other traditions.

The word in Sanskrit for faith is *shraddha* (*saddha* in Pali), and its meaning is closer to confidence or trust than to faith, as that word is often used in a religious context, that is, 'a strong belief in religious doctrine based on conviction.' The Buddha rejected blind faith, but he talked about rational faith (*akaravati saddha*), as being very useful. If you're a scientist and you're going to be doing research into something, you're going to pick what you think is the most reasonable and the most likely hypothesis, and then you can confidently put a lot of energy and time and money into testing that hypothesis. We can see this as analogous to how we take up practice. We may not have a huge amount of faith, but maybe enough to say, 'Well, this seems like a fairly good proposition; this teaching on the way out of suffering appears true enough to me that I'm willing to try it out.' That's what we're doing when we take up practice; we're listening to the advice of the wise (those who have gone before us) and then verifying the teachings for ourselves. Once you have done that you don't need to have faith any more. In fact in the suttas, someone who has experienced the Unborn is called *assaddho* – un-faithful – or one who has gone beyond faith.

We could say that Buddhism is a particularly non-authoritarian system of religious thought. There's a much-quoted teaching that the Buddha gave to the Kalamans (see inset pp. 116–117). The Kalamans were a community who came to him and said, We're really confused. We have all these different teachers come through our town and one teacher tells us one thing, another one teaches us something else. What are we supposed to believe? How do we sort this out? The Buddha replied that it's proper to doubt. And then he said,

> … don't go by reports, by legends, by traditions, by scripture, by logical conjecture, by inference, by analogies, by agreement through pondering views, by probability, or by the thought, 'This contemplative is our teacher.' When you know for yourselves that, 'These qualities are unskillful; these qualities are blameworthy; these qualities are criticized by the wise; these qualities, when adopted & carried out, lead to harm & to suffering' — then you should abandon them. (…) When you know for yourselves that, 'These qualities are skillful; these qualities are blameless; these qualities are praised by the wise; these qualities, when adopted & carried out, lead to welfare & to happiness' — then you should enter & remain in them.

He puts the onus back on us. We've got to listen to the wise, yes, but we must also use our own intelligence. One of the most notable things the Buddha said was, *Ehipassiko*, which means, 'Come and see.' He didn't say, 'Come and believe, believe what I'm telling you,' but, 'Come and have a look, see for yourself, see if it works for you.'

I was talking about this with the Wednesday sitting group that we run at the Auckland University of Technology and somebody said he'd realised that you don't need a lot of faith to get going in practice, but if you do practice, then your faith grows. This is true, and in fact we can go quite a long way on just a little bit of faith. It reminded me of something the American novelist E. L. Doctorow wrote: 'Writing a novel is like driving a car at night. You can only see as far as your headlights, but you can make the entire journey that way.' You don't necessarily need to know how the novel ends in order to be able to write it. You write it and out of that writing comes a conclusion. This little bit of faith that we might have can get us on the path and get us going in the right direction. If we just keep going then we'll drive into the daytime eventually. How long that takes we don't know; we don't know what our karma is, but just to keep going, headlights on, is really the important thing.

Sharon Salzburg, who has written a wonderful book about faith in Buddhism, says that the literal meaning of the word *saddha* is, 'to put the heart upon'.[7] To have faith in something is to put one's heart on it, to rely on it, to give the core of one's being to that thing or process. The Buddha Shakyamuni said faith is the beginning of all good things. The secret of life is giving from the heart. Salzburg says, 'Faith is not a commodity we either have or don't have – it is an inner quality that unfolds as we learn to trust our own deepest experience.'[8] Faith is an inner quality that *unfolds*. It's a little bit like a muscle. If you use a muscle it gets stronger, if you don't use it, it atrophies. If we practice sincerely out of that little bit of faith, really putting our heart in it, giving from the heart, then our faith will grow. It's a natural outcome, because true faith is based on experience, and practice is about paying attention to our experience.

The first of the steps on the Eightfold Path is *Samaditti*. *Ditti* means view and *sama* means whole or complete. It's usually translated as Right View but Complete View or even Perfect View are better translations. You could be wondering, how can complete view be the first step? If I'm just a beginner, how can I possibly have complete or perfect understanding? But what this means is that whatever little bit of understanding we do have is already whole and complete; in a certain sense we've already arrived. In the beginning this just means seeing that we play a part in generating suffering – our own and other beings' – just understanding that, just seeing that, is enough to want to do something about it. It is empowering. And we are naturally led to the next step, Right Aspiration. Just that little amount of faith that we can do something about our suffering is enough to get us started. We can start training the mind to pay attention to what's going on. We start with our suffering, which is exactly where the Buddha started his journey – with human suffering. Our suffering is the gateway to understanding, to insight.

In another place in the sutras the Buddha is challenged about not doing any work, and he goes into an extended metaphor about practice being like tilling the soil, ploughing, sowing, reaping. And this analogy starts

7. Sharon Salzberg, *Faith* (New York: Riverhead Books, 2002), p. 12.
8. *Ibid.*, p. xiv.

with the words, 'Faith is the seed.' So just a very small, very tiny seed is needed. But then this seed must be planted in the ground, watered, protected, cultivated until it grows and bears fruit.

Granted that we may come to practice with a little seed of insight into our own suffering, but how do we find the faith to keep watering, keep tilling, keep cultivating? In part, this faith can grow naturally; we'll see how the seed becomes a sprout, the sprout a sturdy plant and so on. But at times we won't be able to see this; the seed is slow to germinate, the seedling doesn't thrive, or, going back to our earlier analogy, it can feel like we drive and drive and our headlights only illuminate more darkness. What do we need at such times to keep on practicing? To keep going, we only need to believe one thing – that we have the potential to awaken. Master Rinzai once said, 'What is it that ails you? Lack of faith in yourself is what ails you.' Our faith has to move from being a generalised faith to being particular, the particular confidence that we can realise the truth, that we already have what it takes.

We might understand this intellectually. Sure, to practice we need to have faith in ourselves, that's pretty obvious. But it is a real turning point in our spiritual life when we recognise that that's *all* we need; that a lack of faith in ourselves is the *only* thing standing between us and awakening.

I can vividly remember the moment when I began to appreciate this after many years of practice. It was when I was on staff at the Rochester Zen Center, and we were on our week-long winter break. I had decided to use the time to do a solo retreat at a Trappist monastery, the Abbey of the Genesee, about fifty miles out of Rochester, and I was staying in one of the Abbey's houses. I was following the schedule that we use for sesshin, so I was doing many hours of sitting, and then each day during the time allotted for teisho I was listening to a recorded talk from my teacher, Roshi Kjolhede. And he happened to quote these words of Master Rinzai, and they hit me forcefully: 'What is it that ails you? Lack of faith in yourself is what ails you.' I felt that I had quite a lot of faith in Buddha, Dharma, and Sangha, but somehow that hadn't translated, up until that point, into faith in myself, bedrock faith that I could awaken because I *was* awakening. Awakened nature was all around me and through me. I couldn't take a breath without it, this Buddha nature. And yet I didn't know what it was.

Master Rinzai's words are calling on each of us to commit, to not hold back. If we really can wake up, and if we really take this teaching to heart, then suddenly what we need to do with our lives becomes very clear. How can we *not* do the work that's needed? But to really have that faith means that we put ourselves out there. We step out of our little safe world, of oh, no, maybe not this lifetime, maybe another lifetime, or, hmm, other people might be able to do it, but I can't. We're living and breathing Buddha Nature at every moment. But what is it?

After listening to this teisho I took one of my usual walks. This monastery owns quite a bit of the farmland that surrounds the cloistered abbey and they rent out the farmhouses to retreatants. It was extremely cold. In between periods of sitting I'd go out, bundled up, and walk between the fallow fields covered with snow. On this particular day, off in the distance I spotted a fox. It was far away but I could see its silhouette quite clearly. It had caught a mouse and was throwing the little corpse up in the air and catching it again, and prancing around in delight and joy at its catch. It was, I guess, sort of macabre, but at the same time it was beautiful to watch the arabesques the fox was making, leaping about, totally oblivious to everything around her, totally focused on her little mouse, a morsel of food in the midst of this barren, cold landscape. And seeing this fox at play was a wonderful teaching on the kind of application I needed to make in my practice at that time. I needed to work with joy and to bring in an element of play. I needed to play with my koan, to leap around at different angles, to explore the practice from many different points of view, and above all to treat it lightly, not getting bogged down in some kind of grim acquisitive process, which is what I had been doing up to that point — gritting my teeth, trying to wrestle the koan into submission. Of course that was creating a huge obstacle. If we approach the practice in that joyless way, then we're blocking it. We are Buddha Nature. We don't have to go anywhere or get anything.

Of course this faith in ourselves which Master Rinzai talks about is broad and vast, it's not just in our small self, but in this great self which encompasses everything — that snowy field, the fox, the mouse, the pale winter sky; everything is to be found in this Self. Master Dogen said:

> To study the way is to study the self. To study the self is to forget the self.
> To forget the self is to be enlightened by the ten thousand things.

We can only be enlightened by the ten thousand things when we forget ourselves, when we completely absorb ourselves in our practice, whatever it is. When we put ourselves into it wholeheartedly, faithfully, so there's just the breathing, or just the koan, nothing else. And when we forget ourselves, there's nothing in the way, no impediments, just vast space. We're enlightened by the 10,000 dharmas, which are teaching all the time. Like that fox, completely embodying the truth.

But, at the same time, we do need to be patient. Faith in Buddha, Dharma, and Sangha, can't be manufactured at will. Rather we cultivate it, trusting that it will unfold in its own time. It won't always be easy and, in fact, will include its uncomfortable 'opposite': doubt. In Zen faith is very often paired with doubt. And here we're not talking about sceptical doubt, the kind of doubt that makes us vacillate and holds us back, but something much more powerful. Master Daibi (1616–1673) once said:

> The ocean of the Buddhadharma can be entered only by faith. With regard to this faith, an old master laid down three essentials for training: The great root of Faith, a great ball of Doubt, and great, passionate Determination. Of these three the great root of Faith is foremost. From Faith, Doubt arises, and in order to dispel this Doubt, great passionate Determination is necessary.

If we have faith in the human potential to awaken, then the contrast between that potential and how we actually are in the world, how we respond and how our mind works, becomes painful. We find that we want to bridge that gap, to close it. And out of that pain comes the determination to do so, to do what it takes, to go from a kind of abstract faith to real confidence.

Master Dogen wrote:

> Those who believe in the Buddha Way must believe in the fact that their own self is in the midst of the way from the beginning, so there is no confusion, no delusion, no distorted viewpoint, no increase or decrease, no errors. To have such a faith and understand such a Way, and to practice in accordance with it, is the most fundamental aspect of learning the Way.

We need to have faith that fundamentally, as Roshi Kapleau used to say, we can't fall out of the universe, we can't *not* be embedded in this Way. Yasutani-roshi, when he gave introductory lectures, would sometimes talk about the two different aspects of reality, the Two Truths, as they are known in Buddhism, of the relative and the absolute points of view. The relative world is the conventional world that we live in, of time and space, here and there, past and present and so forth, and he would draw a horizontal line on the blackboard to represent this world, this aspect of reality. It's the world that most people live in most of the time and many people believe it's the only world there is. But then he would say that there's this other aspect of reality, the absolute, and he would show the way that this was related to the relative one by drawing a vertical line down through the horizontal line. And actually a vertical line exists at every single point on that horizontal line. At every point we can connect with an absolute truth that goes beyond space and time. At every point *in* space and time there is a dimension which isn't born and doesn't die.

In Zen practice we're training ourselves to be able to connect with that other aspect of reality at any given moment, without abandoning the truth of our relative existence. That dimension is always there, informing everything, as unavoidable as hitting the ground when you stamp your foot. But we don't see it. It's easy for us to be blinded, by our ideas about who we are and how things are and how they should or shouldn't be. We've got to go beyond our notions about things. We need to have the faith that that's possible. It may not happen all at once. It *won't* happen all at once. But really we only need a little bit of faith, enough faith to come back to the practice right now. We may have been off on some train of thought for the last 10 or 15 or 20 minutes. Okay. But right now, as soon as we notice that, we have a choice. We can stay caught up in our ideas about ourselves and about the world, or we can put our attention on the breath or the koan or just sitting, get out of our ideas and realise that our very own self has been in the midst of the Way from the beginningless beginning.

We'll stop here and recite the four vows.

* *

*

As they sat there, the Kalamas of Kesaputta said to the Blessed One, 'Lord, there are some brahmans & contemplatives who come to Kesaputta. They expound & glorify their own doctrines, but as for the doctrines of others, they deprecate them, revile them, show contempt for them, & disparage them. And then other brahmans & contemplatives come to Kesaputta. They expound & glorify their own doctrines, but as for the doctrines of others, they deprecate them, revile them, show contempt for them, & disparage them. They leave us absolutely uncertain & in doubt: Which of these venerable brahmans & contemplatives are speaking the truth, and which ones are lying?'

'Of course you are uncertain, Kalamas. Of course you are in doubt. When there are reasons for doubt, uncertainty is born. So in this case, Kalamas, don't go by reports, by legends, by traditions, by scripture, by logical conjecture, by inference, by analogies, by agreement through pondering views, by probability, or by the thought, "This contemplative is our teacher." When you know for yourselves that, "These qualities are unskillful; these qualities are blameworthy; these qualities are criticized by the wise; these qualities, when adopted & carried out, lead to harm & to suffering" – then you should abandon them …

'Now, Kalamas, don't go by reports, by legends, by traditions, by scripture, by logical conjecture, by inference, by analogies, by agreement through pondering views, by probability, or by the thought, "This contemplative is our teacher." When you know for yourselves that, "These qualities are skillful; these qualities are blameless; these qualities are praised by the wise; these qualities, when adopted & carried out, lead to welfare & to happiness" – then you should enter & remain in them.'

—Excerpted from the *Kalama Sutta*, translated by
Thanissaro Bhikkhu, 1994,
www.accesstoinsight.org/tipitaka/an/an03/an03.065.than.html

TRANSLATOR'S NOTE: Although this discourse is often cited as the Buddha's *carte blanche* for following one's own sense of right and wrong, it actually says something much more rigorous than that. Traditions are not to be followed simply because they are traditions. Reports (such as historical accounts or news) are not to be followed simply because the source seems reliable. One's own preferences are not to be followed simply because they seem logical or resonate with one's feelings. Instead, any view or belief must be tested by the results it yields when put into practice; and – to guard against the possibility of any bias or limitations in one's understanding of those results – they must further be checked against the experience of people who are wise. The ability to question and test one's beliefs in an appropriate way is called appropriate attention. The ability to recognize and choose wise people as mentors is called having admirable friends. According to *Itivuttaka* 16–17, these are, respectively, the most important internal and external factors for attaining the goal of the practice.

*Great becomes the fruit,
great the advantage of meditation,
when it is set around with upright conduct.*

—SHAKYAMUNI BUDDHA

* * *

Upholding the Precepts

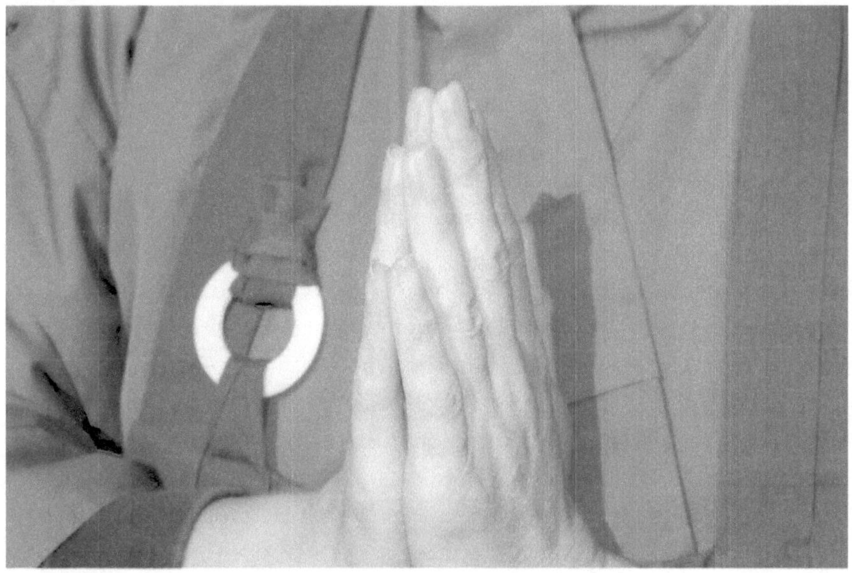

THE Ten Cardinal Precepts (see inset in the previous chapter, p. 103) that we take as part of the Jukai ceremony may, at first reading, appear to be simple statements about ethical behaviour. We soon find, however, that the more we look into them, the more multi-layered and complex they become. In this chapter we will examine some of the different ways of interpreting and working with the precepts.

From the beginning and in every branch of Buddhism, ethical behaviour has been taught as an indispensable element of practice. The path pointed out by the Buddha has traditionally been divided into three different parts, known in Sanskrit as Shila, Samadhi, and Prajña, each one building upon the others. Shila ('conduct') refers to ethical training, Samadhi ('concentration' or 'absorption') to training in meditation, and Prajña ('wisdom') can refer either to philosophical and scriptural training, or (more generally in Zen) to the awakened wisdom that transcends all dualities.

All three of these are present in the Buddha's first discourse on the Four Noble Truths. As we saw in Chapter 2, the Buddha divided the fourth of the Noble Truths, the Way out of suffering, into the eight strands of the Noble Eightfold Path: Right View, Right Aspiration, Right Speech, Right Action, Right Livelihood, Right Effort, Right Mindfulness, and Right Concentration (see inset below, p. 121). The first two of these, Right View and Right Aspiration, are concerned with the wisdom aspect of the path (Prajña), the next three, Right Speech, Action, and Livelihood, with the ethical aspect (Shila), and the last three, Right Effort, Mindfulness, and Concentration with unifying the mind through formal practice (Samadhi). If we narrow in now on the ethical strands of the Eightfold Path, we see in these the kernel of our ten precepts. Under Right Speech we can find teachings about not lying, not gossiping, and not engaging in malicious or frivolous talk; under Right Action we find the teachings on not killing, not stealing, and so on; and, finally, Right Livelihood encourages us to make our living in a way that does not put us at odds with these teachings (for example by selling intoxicants or arms).

In Zen there is often a strong focus on the Samadhi aspect of our training, and particularly on the formal meditation practices. This is not surprising as the Zen school is the 'meditation' school of Buddhism (*dhyana* being Sanskrit for meditation or absorption, closely related to the meaning of samadhi).[1] But in fact the three aspects of training are intimately interconnected. A traditional metaphor for this interdependence is that of a house, where Shila (ethics) is likened to the foundation or basement of the house, Samadhi (concentration, meditation) to the house itself, and Prajña (wisdom) to the house's furnishings. In this metaphor we see how the structure of our practice depends upon a foundation of ethical behaviour. With this foundation in place, we can, through ongoing formal practice, build a place for ourselves to live, or, perhaps better, to live out of; however, we cannot truly be comfortable or 'at home' in this place without the understanding that comes with realisation of the non-dual mind.

Upholding the precepts is seen in this metaphor as the foundation of practice because if we're causing harm, then the mind will be agitated, constricted, and unable to find a resting point. This will make for very shaky zazen. And, if our zazen is shaky, we will be unable to access the deep states of concentration required to to uncover Prajña, our wisdom mind or *bodhi* (awakened nature). But, although this metaphor presents

1. See Glossary under 'Chan'.

THE NOBLE EIGHTFOLD PATH

Based on Lama Anagarika Govinda, *The Psychological Attitude of Early Buddhist Philosophy* (New York: Samuel Weiser, Inc., 1969), p. 74.

WISDOM (*Prajña*)

1. Right View – understanding of suffering, its causes and the way out of suffering.

2. Right Aspiration – the wholesome intention to be free of suffering.

VIRTUOUS CONDUCT (*Shila*)

3. Right Speech – speaking and thinking in ways that are free from dualism.

4. Right Action – mastery of the body-mind and its senses.

5. Right Livelihood – living in harmony with our intention to be free of suffering.

MEDITATION OR MIND TRAINING (*Samadhi*)

6. Right Effort – generating wholesome and sustainable states and habits of mind and avoiding unwholesome and unsustainable ones.

7. Right Mindfulness (or Recollection) – paying attention in a way that does not get caught in craving or clinging.

8. Right Concentration – perfect concentration and unification of all creative forces.

the different aspects of our training as sequential building blocks, it is also quite possible to see how each aspect of the training supports the others in a multi-directional flow. Just as harm-producing behaviour results in shaky zazen, so our efforts at upholding the precepts will themselves remain shaky unless we have zazen to turn to as a daily place of renewal. The training of the mind that happens in zazen is crucial to the process of learning to let go of the habits that cause suffering. If we hope to change our patterns of behaviour, we must first learn to pay attention, to be very precisely aware of what is going on in our own minds at any given moment, and we must learn to *just* be aware, to observe our own internal responses without immediately moving to outward reactivity in the heat of the moment.

Further, just as Samadhi, deep concentration, allows us to access our wisdom mind, so does the unfolding of this mind begin to break down the sense of separation that gives rise to so much struggle, both in our zazen and in our lives. This sense of separation is precisely the source of our pain-producing habits; thus it is only Prajña that can cut them off at the root and that can establish Shila (ethical behaviour) as our natural way of being in the world. At that point enlightenment will no longer be something outside us that we see as a goal, but will rather be our natural function.

Finally, upholding the precepts, willingly and joyfully, is itself a way of purification, of realising our non-separation, and of expressing our complete interconnectedness with everything. Thus, Shila itself beats the path to realisation.

In his book *Shattering the Great Doubt* Chan Master Sheng Yen (1930–2009) discusses the Chinese word that is used for practice: *xiuxing*. Master Sheng Yen explains that this word connotes rectifying, correcting, or amending, and, from the relative point of view, when we practice Zen, this is what we are trying to do. If we look at this English word 'rectify', it means to straighten out, and it comes from the Latin word 'rectus' meaning right or straight. As Sensei Wrightson expressed it in a talk delivered in preparation for Jukai in 2017:

> Just as in our zazen we start with learning good posture, how to sit up straight and align the spine and the rest of the body, in our lives we are also seeking alignment; we wish to align with the truth of the universe and to learn how to live harmlessly. Of course it's not easy to rectify or straighten out our mind because we come into this life conditioned in certain ways. So the first step is one of beginning to recognise our errors, whether they're of thinking or speaking or acting. This, really, is to begin to see our suffering clearly. Our suffering can actually be a great help because it's like a big red arrow saying, Attachment here! That whatever's going on, we need to look right there. We also need to understand this universe that we are part of as a great round, so that whatever we send out, we eventually receive back.

Of course, this is because it doesn't really go out. Since we are not truly separate from the world in which we live, whatever we send 'out', we send to ourselves. This is seen in Buddhism as a natural law.

The technical term in Buddhist teachings for this law is *karma-vipaka* (often referred to simply as karma). In this word pair, *karma* means action, while *vipaka* is the result or reaction, so the two together are concerned with cause and effect. Everything, every *dharma* in this world, is the result of a previous action and can be the cause of a subsequent action. And each action we take lays down tracks in the mind. In one of the Pali suttas, the Buddha gives the classical statement of this point:[2]

> My action is my possession,
> my action is my inheritance,
> my action is the womb that bears me,
> my action is my refuge.

Most of us probably understand clearly that our actions in the world flow out of our mindstream, that any action we take must depend upon our understanding, judgement, mood and intention at any given moment. But the somewhat more subtle teaching of karma is that not only does our mindstream give rise to our actions, but equally do our actions shape our mindstream. When we willingly cause harm, we obscure our true nature and we contort our own mind. There is a popular quote (sometimes erroneously attributed to the Buddha) which expresses well the idea of karma:

> Sow a thought and reap an action, sow an act and reap a habit, sow a habit and you reap a character, sow a character and you reap a destiny.

Zen teacher and Buddhist activist David Loy, expresses it this way:

> We construct ourselves by what we choose to do. My sense of self is a precipitate of my habitual ways of thinking, feeling, and acting; just as my body is composed of the food I eat, so my character is built by my conscious decisions. According to this approach, people are 'punished' or 'rewarded' not for what they have done, but for what they have become. [3]

Thus punishment and reward are not something imposed from the outside, but grow out of our own actions. For example, if we lash out repeatedly,

2. *Anguttara Nikāya*, Section 5.

3. David Loy, *The Great Awakening: A Buddhist Social Theory* (Boston: Wisdom, 2003), p. 7.

then we will come to see the world as a hostile place, a place that we need to defend ourselves against. Our mind itself becomes the punishment. Moreover, the classical teaching on karma goes further than this and posits that what shapes our experience of the world shapes not only our minds but our actual world – that, in fact, the experience of our mind *is* our world. This is particularly applicable when we consider the effects of karma-vipaka beyond this current lifetime.

For some people such a consideration may be a sticking point. We may be able to see how karma functions in our life here and now, but, when the topic of rebirth is introduced, we may feel hesitant. And certainly we can practice Zen whether or not we are able to accept the teachings on rebirth right now. But, as rebirth is a central tenet of Buddhist teaching, it is important to at least keep an open mind and to realise that one of the reasons why this idea can be so hard for people to accept is precisely because of the mental and cultural conditioning described by the laws of karma. Though the idea of rebirth was accepted by Pythagoras and other ancient Greek philosophers, it has not been a part of the more recent cultural inheritance of the West. Adding to this is the fact that when we talk about rebirth we are necessarily talking about things that are happening in a non-material sphere. Even accepting the possibility of this can be very challenging for modern Westerners for whom materialism is such a pervasive belief system that it is often not even recognised as a belief system. This is evidence of how deeply embedded in us it is. Materialism of course proposes that matter is primary. Most people working in the field of neuroscience, for example, believe that consciousness is a kind of epiphenomenon of the brain, that at some point consciousness emerged as a result of the coming together of physical elements. But what if matter and mind arise simultaneously? To take matter as primary is a belief; it is not something that anyone has proven.

Still, if rebirth is a sticking point, there is another way to understand the birth and death talked about in the scriptures, and this is as the birth and death that is happening all the time. In each moment, by means of our sense faculties, perceptions, subconscious mental formations, thoughts and ideas we bring ourselves into existence – and in the next moment the 'self' we have created is gone and the process must be repeated. But whether we understand birth and death as something that happens continuously in this lifetime or as something that extends beyond this lifetime as well, the law of karma-vipaka can help us to understand how we got where we are right now, and also how the decisions we make right now affect our future.

It is generally not helpful, on the other hand, to ponder the karma of others, or, in particular, to blame other people for their unfortunate circumstances. Besides the fact that we simply do not have a complete picture of the causes and conditions which have brought about a particular situation, this kind of judgemental thinking works directly against the development of our own compassion, and so only introduces more negative karma into the situation. Instead, the ethical essence of the teachings on karma is to recognise that our own deeds condition our consciousness, and also that they have an effect on others' conditions. All beings seek ease. All flee from pain if they can. The precepts are meant to be protective. In keeping them we're offering others safety to the best of our ability, and if we were really able to keep the precepts 100% of the time, then we'd be offering unconditional safety to others. In return we receive a share of that safety, since an overall environment of greater safety has been created. Thus keeping the precepts functions as a kind of enlightened self-interest; but it functions also as a fundamental sort of *dana,* or giving to others.

Some people may think that all this emphasis on morality is at odds with the impression you get from reading about Zen masters. They seem so free from all kinds of convention and social custom; they do crazy things. It is true that some people can exhibit a kind of freedom that emerges out of deep understanding and wisdom — that emerges, in fact, out of intensive self-discipline and training, and out of thorough self-mastery. Such people could judge intuitively which action would be helpful or harmful in a particular situation, whether or not that action appeared to follow the letter of the precepts. But we should be very careful about attributing such a level of attainment either to ourselves or to our teachers. At a meeting in 1993 with Western Buddhist teachers, the Dalai Lama was asked about this so-called 'crazy wisdom' and said in part:

> If someone says that since everyone has Buddha mind, any kind of conduct is acceptable, or that teachers do not need to follow ethical precepts, it indicates that they do not correctly understand emptiness or cause and effect. Everyone is accountable for his or her behavior. For someone with full realization, ingesting urine, feces, alcohol, and human flesh are all the

same. But if those Buddhist teachers who ethically misbehave were to eat feces or drink urine, I doubt they would enjoy it![4]

At the other end of the spectrum, it is also possible to take an overly formal or rigid approach to the precepts. Amala-sensei tells the following story:

> When my husband, Richard, and I were traveling in Thailand, we were adopted by a young monk. He wanted to practice his English on us and he was delighted when he learned that we were Buddhists. He took us up to his classroom to meet his classmates and we talked about English words for various Buddhist teachings, such as the Three Treasures. The young monk set up a microphone and speaker so that we could be heard by the whole class, but when I said something into the microphone and then he wanted to speak, I couldn't hand him the microphone, because one of the precepts in the Vinaya is that a monk should not touch a woman, which in some countries is interpreted to include touching with any kind of utensil. And so I had to hand the microphone to Richard and then Richard would hand it to the monk. The underlying intent of the precept, to help the monk keep his vow of celibacy (the Vinaya talks about 'lustful' touching), had got lost, and the rule seemed to reinforce separation (women as impure objects), rather than breaking it down.

Ideally, the precepts can function a bit like the wooden forms used in creating concrete walls: once the walls are finished you don't need the forms anymore. You can let the external structures go because now uprightness is integral to the walls themselves. But in the meanwhile, we need to remember that the building will not be built all at once, and we need to be careful not to pull down the forms too soon. In this sense we should appreciate the efforts of the monk in Sensei's story (who, after all, was still young) to be scrupulous in his attention to the precepts he had received.

In the Zen tradition we are fortunate to be offered a variety of ways to work with the precepts we are given, making for an approach to our ethical training which can be both flexible and profound. The different approaches we consider are the Literal, the Mahayana, and the One-Mind interpretations of the precepts. Although to some extent these three interpretive approaches are sequential, moving from a simpler to a deeper un-

4. http://info-buddhism.com/Ethics-in-the-Teacher-Student-Relationship.html

derstanding, at a more fundamental level all three approaches are essential and equally valued. In this tripartite scheme, the Literal interpretation is the most straightforward one. Here we try to apply just exactly what the precept says. The Mahayana interpretation, on the other hand, looks more at the spirit of the precept. It focuses on non-harming and on considering the greatest good for the greatest number in choosing whether to follow the letter of the precept in a particular instance. Finally, the One-Mind interpretation invites us to consider each precept from the point of view of non-duality, of the essential oneness of self and other.

As an example, we might consider the issue of possums in New Zealand. An introduced species, possums wreak havoc on our native ecosystem, and various programmes have been put in place to try to control them, often by poisoning or trapping. Now consider the situation at a monastery outside Auckland which is located on many hectares of ex-farmland and regenerating native bush. This bush is home to many possums. Is it all right to kill them? The monastery community does not believe so, since the first cardinal precept clearly tells us not to kill. Because of this, the community has sought other ways to protect threatened trees, putting metal collars around their trunks so that the possums are not able to climb up and destroy the trees' new growth. Of course the number of trees that can be protected in this way is limited, but a sense of kinship with all life is preserved, kinship that includes even creatures that we humans might label 'pests'.

But we could approach the issue from another angle which considers the conflicting needs of different life-forms. Amala-sensei once discussed this issue with Professor Manuka Henare, a Māori leader who at the time was serving on ERMA (the NZ government's Environmental Risk Management Authority) and had participated in lengthy debates over the use of a very controversial poison called 1080 (sodium fluoroacetate), used to control possums and other introduced species. Dr Henare pointed out that to Māori, a tōtara tree is also a living being worthy of protection, and one unique to this land, while possums, introduced from Australia by colonists, are not threatened as a species by their elimination here. Due to a heedless human intervention, a difficult ethical dilemma arises: to kill the possum gives life to the forests and their original occupants (native birds), already severely compromised by other forms of human depredation. How do we respond? From the perspective of the Mahayana Precepts the welfare of the forests and their inhabitants might, in the balance, prevail, with the caveat that the destruction of the possums be carried out in the most humane way possible, and with sorrow and respect rather than any kind of rejoicing. The spirit of the First Precept, from the Mahayana point of view, is to refrain from killing the mind of compassion and reverence. We can use this as a guiding principle when negotiating the competing needs of different sentient beings. What is our motivation?

There is also another perspective to consider. Bodhidharma's One-Mind first precept states:

> Self-nature is inconceivably wondrous.
> In the everlasting Dharma,
> Not giving rise to the notion of extinction
> Is called the precept of refraining from taking life.

With thorough awakening we can fully uphold this aspect of the precept – seeing for ourselves that from the point of view of our essential nature nothing dies or is born. All is transformation.

In ethics things are often not black or white. The underlying question needs to be, does my action arise out of notions of self and other? What's the motivation? So even with the precepts to help us, and even with three modes of interpretation to help us, ultimately we're still on our own. We still have to look. If we're faced with a real moral dilemma, then we just have to look into our hearts, and find out what the right course of action is. Even if it's a very difficult decision, if we sit with it, connect with that reality that is deeper than our dualistic thinking, then we'll be able to make difficult choices and act in ways that may not on the surface be pleasing to others. But we can be guided by whether our decision brings a kind of peace with it. This is another example of why zazen is so indispensable.

Zen Master Dogen said that to gain a certain objective you must become a certain kind of person. But once you have become such a person, attaining that objective will no longer be a concern. What he's talking about here is that in order to see the unreality of your small mind, of your ego, and to experience the identity of self and other, you can't continue to go on acting and thinking dualistically. You have to heed what one teacher called the deeper call of the precepts. You have to listen to the still, small voice of our True Nature.

TEISHO

* * *

The Sweet Dew of Perfection Saturates All
(2006–12–17)

This teisho takes a closer look at the precepts surrounding Right Speech,
Precepts 4, 7 and 8.[5]

Today I'd like to take a look at the three cardinal precepts that deal with
speech. These are not to lie, not to discuss the faults of others, and not
to praise oneself.

These precepts have their origins in the Buddha's very first turning
of the wheel, the Four Noble Truths (see Chapter 2 inset, p. 41). In the
Fourth Noble Truth, the way out of suffering, the Buddha expounds the
Eightfold Path, and one of its strands is Right Speech. If we wish to free
ourselves from suffering we must bring our speech into harmony with
that aspiration. We must work towards speaking in ways that do not
cause harm to others or ourselves. In these early teachings Right Speech
is presented as having five different aspects: abstention from lying, from
slander, from abusive speech, from harsh speech, and from idle chatter
or gossip. So there are different ways of parsing Right Speech, but the
broad points covered are the same; any form of dissembling, aggressive
or divisive use of words, and superficial or meaningless speech, are all
seen as unwholesome.

This word un*whole*some is to the point. Words by their very nature
enable us to distinguish one thing from another and from the whole—
they divide the One into many. As well, they can be separated from the
things they refer to—we can talk about a tiger without it actually being
in front of us—much safer! These two properties are what make words
so useful, and at the same time what make them so dangerous—when
we speak there is always the potential to forget the whole picture or the
actual picture. We can even speak about what does not exist—to say 'the
horns of a rabbit' breaks no laws of language.

5. This chapter's teisho originally appeared in *Zen Bow* (the journal of the Rochester Zen
Center) Vol. 30, No. 1 & 2, 'The Critical Mind: Precepts 6 & 7,' © 2007 Rochester Zen
Center. Reprinted by permission. It has been edited slightly for this publication.

We must also keep in mind the intimate connections that exist between how we speak, how we think, and what we experience. Because these three are so closely related we get them all mixed up. The thing itself often gets obscured by the mental and verbal formations that arise around it. Language is a major factor in our ability to disconnect, to live inside a virtual world of ideas and stories which are no longer in tune with reality. Any evolutionary step the psyche takes, as Jung pointed out, creates new perils. A peril inherent in our highly evolved use of language (as compared with other animals) is that we are equipped with subtle powers of deception. We often mistake our thoughts and words for the truth — we don't see how tenuous their relationship to reality has become.

Roshi Robert Aitken in *The Mind of Clover* talks about the etymological background to the Fourth Precept, not to lie:

> The Chinese ideographs wang-yü (Japanese mōgo) are found in combination in the title of the Fourth Precept, and not commonly elsewhere. The etymological meaning is 'forgetful or neglectful words'. Deriving from this root meaning, the Buddhist and secular dictionaries offer 'a lie, a deliberate lie, wild statements, to tell a lie'. Nakagawa Sōen Roshi used to paraphrase Dōgen Zenji, saying, 'Don't use rootless words.' That's a very good way of understanding all the precepts on Right Speech: 'Don't use rootless words' (p. 49).

'Don't use rootless words.' Don't let your words be severed from reality, don't let them be severed from that which goes beyond words. Aitken-roshi continues:

> Thus we are cautioned to be loyal to the essence and not so much to be true to others. The by-product of such loyalty is that we are true to others, but the inspiration is Buddhanature.
>
> When this is clear, then the various social and psychological virtues of truth-telling are illumined. Self-deception, deception of others, cheating, gossip, and carelessness with language are all disloyal to peace in our heart of hearts. Words expressive of that peace are true. Silence expressive of that peace is true.

Later he points out that when we don't hear the silence in somebody's words, we can be pretty sure that they're not telling the truth. When you hear noise, you know something's off.

There are a number of different angles from which we take up each of the precepts. The first is known as the Literal perspective – the black-and-white view, we could say. This precept then is simply about not speaking falsely in any way: not exaggerating, not embellishing, not telling half the story. When we do this, we diminish ourselves, we obscure our lives, and we also complicate them. Somebody once said that when you start to lie, you really have to have a good memory, otherwise you get into trouble. Repeated lying also diminishes our ability to communicate because we get more and more out of touch with ourselves, as well as more alienated from others. We will tend to be more mistrustful because we assume that others are also devious. So we generate mistrust in our hearts, and of course we generate it in other people's hearts as well.

But there are occasions when lying might be necessary or compassionate. Here we move from the Literal understanding to the Mahayana, or 'great vehicle' perspective. From the Mahayana standpoint we take into account the greatest good for the greatest number – compassion comes into play because things are not always black and white. Here's a story that illustrates this principle:

A soldier was rushed back home from the front because his father was dying. An exception was made for him because he was all the family his father had. When he walked into the intensive care ward he suddenly saw that this semi-conscious old man with tubes coming out of him wasn't his father. Someone had made a colossal mistake and rushed back the wrong man.

'How much longer does he have to live?' he asked the doctor.

'Not more than a few hours. You've only just made it.'

The soldier thought of this dying man's son, fighting God-knew-where thousands of miles away. He thought of the old man holding on to life in the hope of being with his son one last time before he died. Then he made up his mind. He leaned forward, held the old man's hand softly, and said, 'Dad. I'm here. I'm back.'

The dying man clutched at the hand offered to him. His unseeing eyes opened to scan the surroundings. A contented smile spread over his face and remained there until he died about an hour later.

So was this soldier lying? On the surface of it he was. But he was doing so in the service of a deeper truth. He was the catalyst for this man's letting go, and he was embodying the truth that really we're all related, deeply related. In those last minutes, for this dying man, the soldier was his son.

The third way of looking at these precepts is from the perspective of

Buddha Nature, the view that goes beyond lying and not-lying. And this story illustrates that perspective as well, because when he took the old man's hand, we can be fairly sure that the soldier didn't have any thought in his mind about lying or not lying; he was just connecting with another human being. If we can act out of a place where there is truly no thought, then there's no one lying. We have to be very careful here and not use this teaching to justify any kind of self-serving deception (in which case of course there would be a thought of self in the mind, however unconscious).

When we work on the precepts in dokusan, there are two teachings we explore, known as Bodhidharma's One Mind Precepts, and Dogen's Master Rujing's Teaching on the Precepts (Master Rujing was Dogen's own teacher). Bodhidharma's verse is as follows:

Self-nature is inconceivably wondrous.
In the Dharma that is beyond all expression,
Not speaking even a single dead word
Is called the precept of refraining from not speaking the truth.

'In the Dharma that is beyond all expression...' We can't ever fully express this inconceivably wondrous Dharma. Any attempt to describe it will limit it. One of the enduring frustrations of being a teacher is having to talk about the inconceivable. So in effect the teacher is always lying. Always the words fall short. That's the nature of words and the nature of the job.

One of my favorite stories about this is told by Master Xuedou. Once there was a teacher who didn't give a single teisho for a whole sesshin. One of the monks complained that he had wasted his time, saying 'I don't expect the teacher to explain Buddhism; it would be enough to hear the two words "Absolute Truth."' The teacher heard of this and said, 'Don't be so quick to complain. There's not even a single word to say about "Absolute Truth."' Then he gnashed his teeth and said, 'It was pointless to say that!' Another adept overheard him and said, 'A fine pot of soup befouled by two rat droppings!' Master Xuedou then adds his own comment, 'Whose soup doesn't have one or two droppings in it?'

An alternative translation for the third line of Bodhidharma's verse is, 'Not preaching a single word is called the precept of refraining from not speaking the truth.' This is something the Buddha actually said about his own teaching career. He said that in all his forty-nine years of teaching, he had not uttered a single word. He had not said a single word because there was no thought of self or other in his mind when he spoke. It was just an outpouring. There were of course also times when he taught by remaining silent.

Master Rujing's teaching is as follows:

From the beginning the Dharma-wheel has turned, with nothing in excess and nothing lacking. The sweet dew [of perfection] saturates all. Everything is true, everything is real.

Here Rujing presents the other side. Bodhidharma was reminding us that this Dharma is beyond all expression. But at the same time the Dharma is expressing itself all the time. Everything is proclaiming the Dharma. The hum of the traffic. The squawking of the birds. The wind rattling the zendo windows. We can open our ears to these teishos that are happening all the time. To really hear them is to drink sweet dew. Even our lying and dissembling are the truth. When we lie we reveal our duplicity, our divided mind. We can learn to hear that too.

While the case against lying is fairly straightforward, we may feel a little more doubtful about Precepts Six and Seven, gossiping and boasting—how much harm do they really do? In Buddhism, ethical choices are not just based on whether a thought, word or action harms other beings, though that's certainly very important, but also on whether or not they disturb the mind's essential peace, which in turn affects whether they help or hinder us in seeing things as they are. The primary false notions we have are thinking that we live in a world that is permanent – relying on conditioned phenomena for our happiness – and imagining that we have a separate self. Breaking these two precepts reinforces in particular our sense of a separate self, and prevents our seeing that from the very beginning the Dharma wheel has turned perfectly, with nothing that shouldn't be there and nothing missing.

Another criterion for judging whether an action is wholesome or not is to look at our motives. The Buddha once said, 'O bhikkhus, I call the motive to be the deed.' What is the mind state out of which an impulse comes? The analogy given is the contrast between the way a surgeon uses a knife and the way a murderer does. Both individuals cut, but with very different results due to different motives. There are two aspects to this difference. The surgeon's desire is to help, to heal the person, but that desire is also backed up by years of training in how to do that effectively—in other words, a great deal of skill. Contrast that with the murderer, where there's both the desire to harm, and a lot of delusive thinking. The killer may well think that killing is going to be of benefit him in some way but it is in fact unskillful in the extreme.

We can apply this test to the precept against speaking of others' faults. What is the intention? There are many times in our work, in family situations, in Zen training, in the world of legal affairs, when we do have to talk about somebody's faults. But if that speech is coming out of an impulse to help or protect then we're not breaking the precept. We apply the Mahayana yardstick of the greatest good for the greatest number. But if our talk comes out of self-aggrandizement, spite, or other types of ill-will, then the precept is being broken and the results will be harmful. As Head of Zendo in Rochester I saw over and over again the corrosive effect of people talking to third parties about someone's 'faults'—in other words, things they didn't like in the other person. So often the information would get back to the person talked about, and even if it were true the manner of hearing the criticism would block communication with the person who had the complaint. Paradoxically, a fairly common motive for minor forms of speaking of others' faults can be as a substitute for real intimacy. If you share your aversions with someone it can create a false sense of togetherness, a kind of fake community. A lot of gossip comes out of that place, but it actually undermines community.

It is important to understand that the law of karma, the law of cause and effect on the moral plane, is essentially a psychological law. Causes shape their effects, so if you have thoughts that are greedy or hateful or delusive, they're going to generate words and actions that bear the stamp of those states of mind. And those actions and words will tend to reinforce the three poisons in you and in others, and generate more of them. And, as long as our thoughts are based on a sense of self and other, then they are also going to generate insecurity, fear, anxiety, tension, and so forth. Repeated over time the thoughts become habits of mind. The deep unconscious thought/feeling complexes that underlie the habits are reinforced. I came across a statement in an article about neuroscience that puts this very clearly: 'Neurons that fire together wire together.' This is akin to the teaching of Buddhism; we lay down pathways in the brain, and these pathways are what shape our character. This teaching is set out in the very first verses of the Dhammapada:

> Our life is shaped by our mind; we become what we think. Suffering follows an evil thought as the wheels of a cart follow the oxen that draw it.

> Our life is shaped by our mind; we become what we think. Joy follows a pure thought like a shadow that never leaves.[6]

So we can generate vicious cycles through our greed, anger, and delusion. But equally we can generate virtuous cycles. Since all of this is conditioned, it can be turned around, and through our generosity, and love and wisdom, we can generate positive actions and words, which then generate peace and joy, and the benefits that come from them. If we understand all of this then we'll come to see why we have to be so careful about our speech even when on the surface it may not seem to cause any direct harm.

Not discussing the faults of others and not praising oneself and disparaging others are really two sides of the same coin. The first puts the emphasis on other, on our judgmentalism, while the second puts the emphasis on self, on our tendency to favour ourselves and to look more kindly on ourselves, but the key thing here is the same delusion of self and other.

From a psychological point of view, you could say that what these two precepts are pointing to is the problem of the shadow. As we form a self-image, which we all do, there are parts of ourselves that we reject and try to push into the background. That's part of the mechanism of creating an 'I'; we identify with the bits about ourselves that we like, and we try to distance ourselves from the bits we don't like. A shadow is the perfect image for this process. Just as our solid body casts a shadow on the ground, so our solid ego-image, which requires that we view ourselves narrowly from a certain angle, casts this dark doppelganger made up precisely of what we don't see, of what we don't care to shed a light on. But just like our physical shadow, we can't get rid of it by fleeing it—it has this annoying habit of following us wherever we go, however hard we try to run away. However much we would like it to not be part of ourselves, it is, and it bears the exact shape of our ignorance.

6. *The Dhammapada*, 1:1–2, trans. Eknath Easwaran.

One of the primary ways we keep the shadow at bay is by projecting it onto others. That way we can maintain a conversation with it while imagining that it isn't a part of who we are. Jungian psychologist Robert A. Johnson said, 'To honor and accept one's shadow is a profound spiritual discipline.' Ironically the breaking of these two precepts around gossip and boasting is pretty common among people who have taken up a spiritual discipline. It's understandable. We take up a spiritual practice because we want to be better than we think we are. We want to be good people, good Zen students, and that can make us feel bad. We feel unhappy with certain parts of our personality, and so we end up focusing on the faults of others as a way of avoiding that acute discomfort with ourselves.

Vietnamese teacher Thich Nhat Hanh points out that the other side of Right Speech is Deep Listening, Compassionate Listening—learning to really listen to what other people are saying, even if they might be saying it angrily. The archetype for this is Kannon, the Bodhisattva of Compassion, whose Sanskrit name, Avolokiteshvara, means, 'Hearer of the Cries of the World'. To truly be heard is itself healing. Just that; to really be heard. Certainly I've seen this many times. Someone may start off relating something, full of agitation and tension and pain, and if they can really be heard, at a certain point, there will be a sudden shift, and all that tension will drop away, and they'll see a way forward that they hadn't seen before. Thich Nhat Hanh comments that when somebody is not listened to, when they have no avenue for being heard, then they're like a bomb ready to go off. He was saying this in the mid-eighties, but how relevant this point is to us today. It can help us to understand why there are so many suicide bombers in our world—literally, bombs ready to go off. It points to a failure in our world to listen to the pain of others, to hear that pain. Alexander Solzhenitsyn said, 'If only it were so simple: If only there were evil people somewhere insidiously committing evil deeds, if it were necessary only to separate them from the rest of us and destroy them. But the line between good and evil cuts through the heart of every human being. And who is willing to destroy a piece of his own heart?' Actually this notion that we have to destroy a piece of our own heart is the problem. We don't. All we have to do is recognize in others that other side, the so-called 'good', and to own in ourselves the 'evil'. To keep it together, to hold both sides, that's our job; to hold both sides. When we do that we won't feel the need to go on and on about other people's faults, or to trumpet our own good deeds at every opportunity. Master Dogen put it very succinctly in the *Tenzo Kyokun* (*Instructions for the Cook*): 'A fool sees himself as another, but a wise man sees others as himself.' When we allow the critical mind free rein we regard even ourselves as an 'other' chronically at fault, eternally lacking. This habit is deeply painful and clouds all our relationships. But we can overcome that split and practice radical acceptance of ourselves and others just as we are. When we do that we are drenched in the sweet dew of perfection.

We'll stop here and recite the four vows.

*   *

*

Thus have I heard. On one occasion the Blessed One was dwelling among the Sakyans where there was a town of the Sakyans named Nagaraka. Then the Venerable Ananda approached the Blessed One. Having approached, he paid homage to the Blessed One, sat down to one side, and said to him:

'Venerable sir, this is half of the holy life, that is, good friendship, good companionship, good comradeship.'

'Not so, Ananda! Not so, Ananda! This is the entire holy life, Ananda, that is, good friendship, good companionship, good comradeship.'

—*Samyutta Nikaya* 45, trans. by Bhikkhu Bodhi

* * *

CHAPTER 7

Building Community

ON the homepage of our website, the Auckland Zen Centre is described as 'a Buddhist community supporting authentic Zen practice and training in Auckland City, New Zealand'. Up to this point we have focused for the most part on various aspects of practice and training, but in this chapter we will take a look at the community that supports that training. In fact, it is impossible to have one without the other. The support that we receive from the community comes in many forms, and often, perhaps paradoxically, from the energy we put into it. This is is not well understood in societies where consumer values dominate. A person may come to a Centre expecting to be able to pay her money, receive a certain type of instruction, and then depart with a set of skills as a sort of acquisition. But in fact we need to see participation in community as an important part of the training method itself. Monastics have traditionally trained extensively in the context of a residential community before undertaking solitary practice, while lay supporters have belonged to particular village or neighbourhood communities; moreover, there has been a vital symbiosis between the two groups, each dependent on the other for material or spiritual support. For Western practitioners, too, as our commitment to making Zen a central element of our lives deepens, we soon become aware of how hard it is to do this alone; each of us needs the spiritual guidance that can be offered by the teacher as well as the friendship of other like-minded individuals. The Buddha spoke often of the importance of working together with companions on the path.

In our modern, urban environment we can often feel isolated, and in fact there are many obstacles that contribute to keeping us feeling that way. Even if we love the idea of being part of a Buddhist community, to make this a reality calls for a considerable amount of energy and commitment, often of both time and money, the two things which we may feel chronically short of already. And while we can say that a deepening practice gives us the opportunity to thoroughly reassess our priorities and to simplify our lives, this may not be so easy for those of us with family members who don't necessarily share our enthusiasm for the project. In addition to such practical obstacles, there are internal obstacles to be overcome as well. Ours is a very individualistic society, and it can often require a conscious and ongoing effort to find and nurture the willingness to function in and as community.

Perhaps the most straightforward way both to contribute to and to begin to feel part of a religious community is simply to show up. Though it can sometimes feel less complicated to practice on our own, we may also begin to notice how the efforts that each one of us makes in getting to the centre help to support the efforts of the group as a whole. At the Auckland Zen Centre, as at many Zen centres, this applies not only to attendance at formal sittings but also at the various ceremonies and celebrations that highlight important times in the Buddhist year (see inset pp. 142–143). On many of these occasions the Centre is decorated with special altars, appropriate artworks and other trimmings, and helping with these preparations is a meaningful way to get involved. Special ceremonies can serve to build not only a sense of community but also a sense of confidence in the teachings. The backbone of the ceremonies themselves is sutra chanting. Chanting is a powerful way in which we function together as a group, each one lending their voice to create a full, whole-hearted sound that is more than the sum of its parts. Chanting ancient sutras also connects us across space and time to people all over the world chanting the same words and to the 2500-year-old tradition of which we are a part. At the Auckland Zen Centre, some ceremonies also involve community action. For example, on Kannon Day, dedicated to the Bodhisattva of Compassion, we meet after the ceremony to write letters for Amnesty International. On Earth Day we take local action, such as planting trees. Here, too, acting as a group can feel more effective than acting on one's own.

Children celebrating Vesak (Buddha's Birthday)

Festive meals, either at the Centre or at a local eatery, are also often part of these special occasions. If thinking about social events makes your stomach go into a knot, you should know you are not alone. Zen practice no doubt attracts a large proportion of introverts. In sitting together in silence we act as social beings, but without the direct interaction of conversation. Not only can this be very supportive for the introverted among us, but we also come to discover that communication and bonding does take place between people in silence, and, in fact, that it takes place on a very deep level. Once we have experienced the love and support of the

Cleaning the Temple

As a precursor to our New Year's Eve celebrations we give the whole Centre a thorough clean, getting into all the nooks and crannies that are usually overlooked.

New Year's Eve Ceremonies

Each December 31 we bring in the new year with zazen and ceremonies designed to help us let go of painful habits and start the year on a positive note. Close to midnight we circumambulate the zendo in a noise-making ceremony, intended to clear out negative energies, and at midnight, we take the Sixteen Precepts and read out a special new year prayer. We end by sharing festive food together.

Parinirvana Day

Celebrated each year in early February, this ceremony honours the day of the Buddha's death or final nirvana. After zazen, there is chanting and a reading from the Mahaparinirvana Sutra. There is also an opportunity to remember family and friends who have died, either recently or in the more distant past.

Earth Day

The Zen Centre marks Earth Day each autumn with zazen, chanting, prostrations, and a monetary offering to be passed on to an environmental cause chosen each year. After the ceremony we take on a community project, such as tree-planting or gardening.

Founder's Day

Each May we mark the death day of Roshi Philip Zentetsu Kapleau (1912–2004), the founder of our lineage. Following the usual sitting there is a special chanting service and a short talk about his life and contribution to Western Zen.

Vesak (Buddha's Birthday)

Celebrated each year on a Sunday in May, this festival honouring the birth of the Buddha includes games and crafts, and is an enjoyable way to introduce children to the story of the Buddha. This is our most popular family event of the year.

Matariki Jukai

Jukai is the Mahayana Taking-the-Precepts Ceremony, in which students receive the ethical precepts, and commit to putting them into practice to the best of their ability. Matariki Jukai is held near the time of the winter solstice, the Southern New Year. During the ceremony, the Heart Sutra is chanted, and we recite a repentance gatha (verse) as a means of purification prior to receiving the Sixteen Precepts.

Kannon Day

Each year we pay our respects to the Bodhisattva of Compassion with a ceremony and an opportunity to serve others. We chant the Ten-Verse Kannon Sutra 108 times as we do prostrations. There is an opportunity to make a monetary donation at the altar to Amnesty International and, after the sitting, to take part in letter-writing for prisoners of conscience.

Bodhidharma Day

Each October we celebrate the Death Day of the founder of the Zen School, Bodhidharma. Sent by his teacher Prajnatara, Bodhidharma made the long and dangerous journey from Southern India to China in the 5th Century CE., where he sat facing a wall for nine years. He is regarded with great reverence and affection by Zen followers everywhere.

Buddha's Enlightenment Ceremony

Celebrated each year in early December, this beautiful ceremony commemorates 'the reopening of the Way' by Shakyamuni, the Buddha of our world cycle, with readings from the sutras and chanting. Following the ceremony a special dessert of sweetened milk-rice (*kheer*) is served; this is the first nourishment that the Buddha took to gain strength after his period of extreme ascetic practice and before accomplishing anuttara samyak sambodhi (complete perfect enlightenment).

group in deep silence, we may find the confidence to show up to a shared meal or to come to the table for post-sitting tea. We may suddenly find it easy to talk to the people we have sat alongside in the zendo. And we can also feel assured that, in the environment of the Zen Centre, no one will be bothered if we find we don't have anything to say; our silent presence is always acceptable and welcome.

Besides regular attendance at sittings and special events, taking part in the Term Intensives which are offered twice each year at the Auckland Zen Centre is another way to support and experience community. A Term Intensive is a practice period of a few weeks during which we can examine our spiritual lives, intensify our Dharma practice, and bring the practice to a more central place in our daily lives. This often involves commitments to add something into our lives or to take something away. People frequently start with a commitment to sit more than they have been doing; then, various mindfulness practices may be taken on, or we may pledge to cut down on some habit that feels addictive, time-wasting, or hurtful to others. What makes these practice periods work, and what keeps people coming back to them again and again, is the group element. We make our pledges publicly, and we report back to each other each week. This is what gives the Term Intensive some fibre: we are each accountable to the whole group, and our efforts support and encourage others in their commitments. A Term Intensive can give participants a sense of what is possible, with a little help from our friends. And, in being willing to open ourselves and share our struggles with others, new bonds of friendship are formed which may last beyond the few weeks of the Term Intensive.

Sometimes two or three people will specifically enter into a 'Dharma friendship' which can last for a longer period than that offered by the Term Intensive. Such a friendship may involve sharing commitments, or perhaps agreeing to sit together at specific times. For example, there were two women practicing at the Rochester Zen Center several years ago who agreed to rise at 4:00 AM each morning in order to do an extra hour of sitting before the formal rounds began. They carried on with this for more than a year, and both felt that it was something that they could never have done on their own.

Beyond the daily round of sitting, the special ceremonies, and the special commitments of a Term Intensive, much work of a more mundane type is needed to keep any Zen centre running. *Samu*, or work-practice, is offered at the Auckland Zen Centre from time to time in the form of working bees or gardening days, or as part of one-day sittings. In samu we take the idea of practice-in-motion, which we may have first encountered in the form of walking meditation (kinhin), one step further. In samu we are engaged in normal, though generally simple, activity, such as cleaning, cooking, or gardening. In engaging in such work we adopt no special physical posture; thus the only support for our concentration is the instruction to maintain silence as much as possible outside of communication directly needed for getting the work done. Samu is in many ways the central practice of Zen monasteries. How can we make the simple – or even not-so-simple – tasks and duties that we perform every day, from sweeping the floor to preparing a meal to answering our email, an expression of our practice and of our awakened mind? Though this is a practice that any of us can take up at home or at work, it is much easier to take it up with the support of fellow practitioners, all committed to maintaining silence to the extent possible, and to using the work at hand as a support for practice and for focusing the mind.

Working in this way is what the residential Zen training offered at many large Zen Centres is all about. At the Auckland Centre, we don't have the facilities to house people, but we are nevertheless committed to offering a residential-style work day. Trainees accepted into the programme, in addition to attending all Centre sittings, participate in four full work days and one half-day each week. Moreover, all members of the Zen Centre community are invited to take advantage of this programme, as their schedule permits, by participating in the work day as volunteers, attending the mid-day sitting, or joining the staff and trainees for breakfast or lunch. Breakfast is an informal meal and a good opportunity for conversation with fellow practitioners; lunch is a formal meal which includes chanting and silent, mindful eating. Though when we think of giving generously to support the community (*dana,* see below pp. 149–150), we may think first of making a financial contribution, giving of one's time is of at least equal importance. Certainly the Auckland Centre is almost entirely dependent for its functioning on the many hours offered each week by volunteers who help out in a whole variety of areas including (but not limited to) clerical, communication and IT tasks, cleaning, sewing, repair and maintenance, bookkeeping, and gardening. Ordinary tasks, undertaken unobtrusively and wholeheartedly are seen as a form of practice in which distinctions of 'giver' and 'receiver' are dissolved and in which community is given form.

On the other hand, we should not expect, if we come along to work or volunteer at a Zen centre, that every task and interaction will flow with perfect clarity and harmony. No human community has ever been perfect. In fact it is a given that wherever there is community there will at times be conflict. The crucial thing, then, and an equally important part of our training in community, is how we work with the conflicts that will inevitably arise, from interacting with people who may happen to rub us the wrong way, to working with decisions of the Centre's board or teacher with which we may disagree, to dealing with situations that may actually feel unethical to us, and where we may feel called upon to speak out. All of this provides us with opportunities to work with the precepts (see Chapters 5 and 6), and, beyond the precepts, with the *paramitas* of the Mahayana tradition (see inset opposite).

The paramitas (the 'perfections') are sometimes called the bodhisattva trainings; they are qualities which are to be perfected on the path to re-alisation, and which in fact are seen as essential elements of realisation. Master Sheng Yen[1] has this to say about the paramitas:

> In Sanskrit 'paramita' literally means 'having reached the other shore'. It also means 'transcendence,' or 'perfection'. If we exist on the shore of suffering, reaching the other shore would mean leaving suffering behind and becoming enlightened. Hence, transcendence means to become free from mental afflictions (the causes of suffering) and from suffering itself. The true practice of the paramitas is to be free from self-attachment and self-cherishing.

The path to freedom from self-attachment and self-cherishing, as the list of the paramitas (p. 147) makes clear, begins with our relationships to others. The first three paramitas (Giving, Ethical Behaviour and Forbearance) cannot be practiced in isolation. Rather, it is in the context of our human interactions that our bodhisattva training takes place. In other words, development of the qualities listed is seen as necessary for realisation, *and* there is no way to develop these qualities on our own.

The third paramita, Kshanti Paramita, most directly works with the ability to function within a community as a requisite along the path. This

---

1. Renowned teacher of Chan Buddhism, lived 1931–2009. The quotation may be found at http://chancenter.org/cmc/wp-content/uploads/2010/09/TheSixParamitas.pdf p. 4

THE SIX PARAMITAS

The Mahayana tradition most often lists six perfections, as follows:

1. Dāna Pāramitā (perfection of giving) – offering the teaching freely and supporting it generously.

2. Śīla Pāramitā (perfection of ethical behaviour) – abstaining from harmful behaviour and engaging in helpful behaviour.

3. Kṣānti Pāramitā (perfection of patience or forbearance) – being tolerant of differences and difficulties and solving conflicts peacefully.

4. Vīrya Pāramitā (perfection of effort) – practicing the Dharma with energy, consistency and commitment.

5. Dhyāna Pāramitā (perfection of meditation) – developing concentration through formal sitting practice as well as engaging wholeheartedly in whatever one is doing.

6. Prajñā Pāramitā (perfection of wisdom) – seeing things as they are.

is what Zen teacher Norman Fischer calls 'the discipline of relationship.' So often, when conflict arises, our natural tendency is to put the blame on the other person, just as we blame unfavourable circumstances or 'things out there' for our suffering in general. But bodhisattva training asks us to investigate. The possibility of a different viewpoint is beautifully suggested by the 8th-century Indian teacher Shantideva in this well-known verse from *The Way of the Bodhisattva*:

To cover all the earth with sheets of hide –
Where could such amounts of skin be found?
But simply wrap some leather round your feet,
And it's as if the whole earth had been covered![2]

2. Shantideva, *The Way of the Bodhisattva*, translated by the Padmakara Translation Group (Boston, Mass.: Shambhala, 2003), Section 5.13, p. 64.

As Zen teacher Fischer writes:

> We need others so much, and yet nothing is more troublesome than others... From spousal to international relations, people-to-people exchanges seem so difficult, nearly impossible... We might consider ourselves to be kind and reasonable people, but others seem not to be so reasonable. Or maybe we are not so kind and reasonable: maybe we have a hard time figuring out what we want and how to act toward others. Since they are the same way, dealing with ourselves and them at the same time is daunting indeed... Dealing with others isn't just dealing with others. We think of it that way, but that's a mistake. Dealing with others is dealing with ourselves dealing with others. There are no others apart from us, and there is no us apart from them. Our problems with others are our problems with ourselves and vice versa. Recognizing this is the first principle.[3]

A Zen community is in many ways like any other human group, with its conflicts and disagreements, as well as its moments of connection and joy. In some ways, however, it may feel quite unlike any other group we have been involved in. Much of the time we spend together is spent in silence and stillness. Even when we are involved in work or other non-sitting activities together we are encouraged to maintain silence to the degree possible. Each of us is 'shining the light inward' and working on ourselves, so that what we are asked to do, above all, is to support with our own silence and inward attention the inward-directed work of the person next to us. This is not the average experience of 'getting to know you'. Instead, we are learning to approach, and helping others to approach, a much deeper level, a place below our surface hang-ups and feelings of self-consciousness, where self and other, subject and object, drop away.

3. Norman Fischer, *Training in Compassion: Zen Teachings on the Practice of Lojong* (Boulder, Colo.: Shambhala, 2013), pp. 97–98.

TEISHO

* * *

Giving, Gratitude and Saying Thank You
(2010–02–07)

To thank or not to thank? Amala-sensei looks at some of the ways that Zen communities conventionally function, and some of the ways we can encourage each other both within and outside of those conventions.

This is the first teisho for this year, and the first teisho in our new zendo.[4] Since before Christmas, when I began gathering material for the January newsletter, I've been thinking about the whole question of giving and gratitude and saying thank you, and I thought that this teisho would be a good opportunity to explore these things which are so central to practice.

Periodically in newsletters we've been thanking people for various things that they've donated or done for the Centre, and so, before Christmas, I was getting ready to do that again. And as I tried to remember and write down all the things that people had offered over the year, I was really quite staggered by what a huge list it was and how the Centre really is completely reliant on people's generosity. So, deep feelings of gratitude. But at the same time I've always had mixed feelings about thanking people by name in the newsletter. Sometimes people don't want to be named; they want to be able to carry out their acts of generosity anonymously. Naming people can also generate feelings of competitiveness or inadequacy. And it's very easy to leave somebody out which can cause hurt feelings. So this talk will be a way of exploring some of these issues, and looking more generally both at giving and at saying thank you for what is given.

Giving (*dana* in Sanskrit) is the first of the Six Paramitas, or perfections, which are essential factors of enlightenment. One of the meanings of *paramita* is 'crossing over to the other shore,' and the shore referred to here is the shore of liberation, the shore where we are free from what binds us, free from fear and anger and craving and delusion. So giving or *dana* is one of the ways in which we cross over. It's a very basic way in which we leave behind 'I, me, and mine'. And it is a way of practicing

---

4. Delivered just after the move from Pah Road to Church Street. The current zendo is in Princes Street (Onehunga).

non-separation and loving-kindness, of overcoming in a concrete way our sense of being separate; and this sense of separation is seen as the source of our suffering. Thus giving is really putting into practice the Buddha's basic teaching of *pratityasamutpada*, or interdependence. The way we express the truth of mutual interdependence is by mutual intersupport, as Roshi Robert Aitken puts it.[5] We can recall here, too, the etymology of the English word 'kindness' which is related to the word kin. Kindness is an expression of kinship.

Gratitude is very closely related to giving. One way of understanding gratitude is as the enjoyment that we get from receiving others' generosity. In *The Lost Art of Compassion* Lorne Ladner has this to say about gratitude:

> As we think of others' kindness and grow grateful, our feelings of fullness allow our compulsive desires and ego defences to relax. We become more open to others, and only when we acknowledge what is good and great in ourselves do we become capable of consciously sharing it with others.[6]

So there's a kind of positive feedback loop here, and we can see how giving and receiving and gratitude are all intimately related.

Saying thank you is of course very intimately connected to our feelings of gratitude. It's really a natural impulse and something that we don't do just once but over and over. It's very much part of our ritual in Zen. The most obvious expression of this is in our bowing: our bows at the end of chanting or at the end of a sitting when we bow to the Buddha and to each other — this is a way of expressing our gratitude for the teaching and for having a Sangha to practice with.

But giving and receiving and thanking are not just aspects of Buddhist teaching; they're universal. Aitken-roshi in his book on the paramitas quotes Emerson: 'The wind sows the seed. The sun evaporates the sea. The wind blows the vapour to the field ... the rain feeds the plant, the plant feeds the animal.' and he adds, 'The very stars hold themselves on course through a mutual interchange of energy.'[7] This is the natural cycle of giving and receiving, what Emerson calls the endless circulation of the divine charity. And here this word 'charity', this Christian term, is very much akin to the Buddhist understanding of loving-kindness. It

5. Robert Aitken, *The Practice of Perfection* (New York: Pantheon, 1994), p. 5.

6. Lorne Ladner, *The Lost Art of Compassion* (San Francisco: Harper, 2004), p. 166.

7. Robert Aitken, *The Practice of Perfection* (New York: Pantheon, 1994), p. 5.

is the source of giving. So this cycle of giving, receiving and gratitude is not something doctrinal. It's much more basic than that: it's the way the world works.

This is one of the reasons why thanking Centre volunteers can walk a bit of a fine line, because really to give to one's Centre, to help it to run, is just in the natural order of things. The Centre belongs to the Centre's members, and people just do what needs to be done. And certainly when I do thank volunteers, in newsletters or otherwise, it's not a personal thanks from me so much as an expression of thanks on behalf of the Sangha.

But thanking, too much thanking, can actually emphasise self and other. When I was training in Rochester, my teacher, Roshi Kjolhede, once brought up the topic of signs. He had noticed the sort of sign you'll sometimes see at an institution, where it ends with 'Thank you'. So residents had put up signs at the Centre, for instance, 'Please place dirty cups in the dishwasher. Thank you.' And he was basically expressing his distaste for this type of sign because he felt it was emphasising self and other. To place dirty cups in the dishwasher is just to do what's necessary; why do you need to thank somebody for it? It's almost implying that there's some annoyance in there: 'Oh, thank you, at least you've put the dirty dishes in the dishwasher, not like those stupid people who don't do it.' There's a kind of intimacy that we reach with people we live with, family or others we're very close to, where we don't have to be so careful about saying thank you. And one of the reasons is that there is an understanding that we aren't separate, we are one.

On the other hand, in many situations, thanks can be really important. In fact there are always these two sides: yes, we are one, but we are also giver and receiver in our relationships. In terms of Centre volunteers, I've decided to adopt a middle way, one that will hopefully express both sides, both the basic oneness, the basic sense that people are simply doing what what they need and wish to do as members of the Centre, as well as the sense of gratitude for the giving and receiving that takes place. So I've decided that, starting from the next newsletter, I'm going to mention what people have done, yes, but I'm not going to identify people by name. This way people's anonymity will be preserved, but at the same time, we can be reminded of just how much people *are* doing and how the whole Centre functions on that basis.

There is a fine line to be walked here, because there is no doubt that we are all to various degrees attached to praise or approval and, especially when there is naming, we may be giving out of that attachment rather than just giving freely — and this is something we need to work with in our practice. In the sutras the Buddha talks about the highest or most mature kinds of giving containing no expectation of reward of any kind, no need for recognition or repayment or thanks. So wanting approval or praise is seen as a less mature motivation. This doesn't mean that we need to feel bad about giving with some expectation of reward, but we can understand that if we really fully comprehend the nature of giving, we will see that it is its own reward: giving is receiving. The satisfaction we get from giving is completely sufficient.

I heard indirectly from my teacher Roshi Kjolhede that Roshi Kapleau, his teacher, used to say, 'Praise is poison.' Roshi Kapleau felt strongly that to lavish praise on Zen students was unhelpful because it was likely to inflate the ego, and that, because it would give them satisfaction, they would attach to it. And certainly if you look at the way the masters operate in the old stories, they seem to work on this principle. Very little praise. A lot of harsh admonishment.

But this is a steep attitude. And sometimes the most helpful thing can actually be to acknowledge people's contributions. Some appreciation may be just what a person needs in order to really see the value of that contribution and keep going. This all depends on where that person is at in their training. They may need to know that they are valued. This is a razor's edge, really, for a teacher. When to praise and when to not say anything.

We also need to understand that thanking people can be an important practice for the one who receives, and that there needs to be at least mental gratitude even if there isn't expressed gratitude. I've heard that in some countries, monks do not bow to lay people when they receive something. And the idea behind this is that for them to thank the person would be to reduce the amount of merit that that person would receive from their giving. And so, out of their wanting the lay people to get as much merit as possible from their giving, they don't offer thanks. In our tradition, we don't follow this rule; we really go the other way and express our interdependence and our mutual receiving and giving through bowing to each other a lot.

The classical suttas are full of teachings on the nature of *dana*, the nature of giving. In one, the King of Kosala asks the Buddha to whom alms should be given, and the Buddha replies that one should give to those to whom it makes you happy to give.[8] Very interesting that he would emphasise this: just give to those you like to give to, who it gives you joy to give to. Another teaching says, 'Giving brings happiness at every stage of its expression. We experience joy in forming the intention to be generous. We experience joy in the actual act of giving something, and we experience joy in remembering the fact that we have given.' So to find ways to give that really help us to experience this joy.

Another emphasis in classical teachings is on the importance of motivation. The essential nature of giving is that it's done freely, that there is no coercion involved, but that it is a simple giving up, a letting go of something, with happiness, willingly. Really the essence of true giving is freedom. In one sutta the Buddha lists various motives for giving, and these include a whole range, including some which are less pure, like giving because you think that you have to, but the one that he holds up as being the most exalted is to give with the motivation that 'this is an ornament for the mind, a support for the mind.' In other words, to give because we understand that it helps to free us from samsara. Or, as one writer puts it, because it helps to rid us of the ugliness of selfishness. And it can be giving a tiny little thing, or giving something very large, but it's really the motivation, the thought behind it, that shapes the benefits or the merits that come from our giving.

The Buddha said that even somebody who throws the rinsings from their bowl or cup and thinks, 'May whatever animals live here feed on this,' receives merit. So even something as insignificant as the little bits of food that are rinsed out from your bowl, if that is given with this spirit of, 'May this bring nourishment to some small being,' that's positive. And we can take this up as a practice, especially with our food, by taking care of our food, not wasting it, and then what is left, what we're not going to eat, to think carefully about how we dispose of it. This isn't just a Buddhist thing, either. In Christian countries it is or was very common to find this spirit in regard to bread. Bread is called the staff of life, and is sacred. If you have stale bread crusts, you don't throw them in the bin, but give them to the birds.

8. *Samyutta Nikaya*, 3:24.

In another sutta[9] the Buddha offers instructions on how to give, and he lists five different qualities that are possible in our giving, and these are: to give with a sense of conviction, to give attentively, to give in season, to give with an empathetic heart and to give without adversely affecting others. Let's take a look at each of these:

'To give with a sense of conviction' is to give sincerely and whole-heartedly. For this we need to get in touch with our hearts and find what feels right for us, so that when we give we can give sincerely, without regrets. And that means being honest about where we're at. If some occasion comes along where we're asked to volunteer and we just feel too tired or there are other things we need to do, then we need to be able to take care of ourselves and not fall into a pattern of burnout. When we are rested, then we can give. And, in terms of material resources, we should give what we feel we can afford, not more.

'To give attentively' can be understood in different ways. It can relate to the sense of conviction mentioned in the first instruction, in other words not just going through the motions or giving because we feel we have to, but really putting ourselves into it. But we can also understand it as giving appropriately. In other words, paying attention to a situation so that we give what's actually needed, what's really useful. So we could even include here the harshness of the old masters as giving. Or giving feedback to an organisation which may not be popular feedback. Really being willing to stick your neck out if you feel you see something that needs to be looked at. Giving may not always just be nice-nice.

'To give in season' means to give at the right time. This is an important one. We can miss an opportunity to give. An example here may be that if somebody is depressed and you give them a call, it can make a huge difference. But if you get that little impulse and you don't follow it, then you can really be regretful later. A couple of people I've met since my mother died have expressed their regret that they were thinking of her and wanted to come and see her, but somehow there was so much busyness before Christmas, and so they didn't. And now they feel sad about that. So it's always just a matter of paying attention to those impulses and just following them when we have them. Because people do die, and moments of opportunity do pass. People do need us more at some times than at

9. *Sappurisadana Sutta*, https://www.accesstoinsight.org/tipitaka/an/ano5/ano5.148.than.html

other times. If someone's moving house, they may need your help that day, not another day. An encouraging word may really save somebody from much anguish if it's given at the right moment. Just as a word of criticism at the right moment can also be helpful.

'To give with an empathetic heart' means to give lovingly. In another sutta, the instruction is given that one must be very careful about not giving in a way that could embarrass somebody or make them feel humiliated. This is not just about material things but about generating of a sense of warmth and friendliness and of valuing a person.

Then the last one is also important: 'to give without adversely affecting others'. In other words, our giving has to be holistic and we have to consider all its effects. The needs of spouses and children must be considered.

There are also teachings in the suttas and in the Zen tradition about how to express gratitude, in other words, how to give thanks. Saying thank you, using words, can be important, but it really doesn't do justice to our deepest feelings of gratitude. Really the way that we give thanks that is more satisfying is with our body, with our body-mind. And this is where we see how the whole process is circular. The ways in which we most effectively express our gratitude for what we have received are the ways in which we give. One teacher, Ajahn Sumedho, when asked how he could possibly be repaid for his teachings would say, 'You repay me through your giving yourself to your practice, through your dedication to realising the Buddhadhamma.' Master Dogen put it this way:

> The true way of expressing gratitude for coming into contact with the Dharma is not to be found in anything other than our daily Buddhist practice itself; that is to say, we should practice selflessly, esteeming each day of life.[10]

We should practice selflessly, esteeming each day of life. The way we make a cup of tea. The way we pay for our vegetables at the greengrocer. The way we talk to somebody. All these can be expressions of gratitude. Meister Eckhart, the great Christian mystic said:

> If the only prayer you said in your whole life was 'Thank you,' that would suffice.

10. Yūhō Yokoi and Daizen Victoria, 'Shushō-gi: The meaning of Practice-Enlightenment' in *Zen Master Dogen* (Tokyo: Weatherhill, 1976), p. 63.

Really the religious attitude, whether you have a religion or not, is an attitude of gratitude, of openness to, and appreciation of, life's gifts. So often our craving or our ideas about what we think we should get or what we think we should have obscures this openness. The modern-day Christian mystic, Brother David Steindl-Rast once said:

> All is a gift. We are to accept the given until it becomes a gift.

We are to accept what we are given until we can appreciate that it is in fact a gift. And when we find this attitude of open gratitude, then we will likewise find ourselves able to give in the most open, fundamental sense. Dogen says:

> When one learns well, being born and dying are both giving. All productive labour is fundamentally giving, and trusting flowers to the wind, birds to the season, also must be meritorious acts of giving.[11]

Ultimately, giving is the act of freely giving up the self, forgetting it. Just doing what needs to be done. The most natural thing in the world. Just taking care of things. Master Fayan said:

> What is the mind of the ancient Buddhas? It is that from which flow compassion and joyful giving.[12]

We'll stop here and recite the four vows.

*   *

*

11. Master Dōgen, 'Bodaisatta shishōhō' in *Shōbōgenzō Zen Essays by Dōgen*, trans. Thomas Cleary (Honolulu: University of Hawaii Press, 1986), p. 118.
12. John C. H. Wu, *The Golden Age of Zen* (New York: Doubleday), p. 177.

Ungan asked Dogo, 'What use does the great Bodhisattva of Compassion make of all those hands and eyes?'

Dogo said, 'It is like someone reaching back, groping for a pillow with outstretched hand in the middle of the night.'

— Hekiganroku, CASE 89

CHAPTER 8

Being in the World

IN THE YEAR before the 2003 American invasion of Iraq, Amala-sensei was training at the Rochester Zen Center and was assisting the abbot, Roshi Kjolhede, while he was on sabbatical. One of her tasks was to screen posts from an American Zen Teachers' Association Listserv, which, in the run-up to the invasion, was consumed by intense debate about the impending war. According to Amala-sensei, at a certain point in the debate one of the Zen teachers recounted a story of going to a peace rally and striking up a conversation with a Quaker woman there. As the woman became aware that she was speaking with a Zen teacher, she remarked, 'Oh! I didn't know that you Buddhists stood for anything in the real world!'

This is perhaps a common misunderstanding about Buddhism. But what especially surprised Amala-sensei at the time was not that a Quaker might have such a misconception, but that some of the teachers posting to the ListServ seemed uncertain about this as well. One suggested that standing for something 'in the real world' was perhaps a bit of a koan for Zen practitioners.

PHOTO: Amala-sensei and Ven. Hanya Gallagher participating in a Greenpeace blockade of a New Zealand Petroleum Industry Conference at Sky City Casino in 2016.

Roshi Robert Aitken, a Zen teacher who, in the course of his life, frequently took strong public stands on various issues, had this to say in the introduction to *The Mind of Clover*, the book he wrote about the Buddhist precepts:

> Without the precepts as guidelines, Zen Buddhism tends to become a hobby, made to fit the needs of the ego. Selflessness, as taught in the Zen center, conflicts with the indulgence that is encouraged by society. The student is drawn back and forth, from outside to within the Zen center, tending to use the center as a sanctuary from the difficulties experienced in the world. In my view, the true Zen Buddhist center is not a mere sanctuary, but a source from which ethically motivated people move outward to engage in the larger community.[1]

If we just take up zazen as a way of creating a little bit of ease and stillness in our lives, but don't sooner or later move outward to bring our practice into our interactions, we're missing something essential. In fact, Zen practice *is* about being in the world; it is about being right here in the present moment, and if we truly are present, and if we are able to see clearly what is going on, then we will be able to respond wisely and compassionately to suffering, and take stands if necessary. So, in this chapter, we will examine some of the teachings from Mahayana scripture and philosophy which serve to keep us firmly grounded in this world, with all of its messiness and struggle. In the following chapter (Chapter 9) we will look at one example of how we have tried, at the Auckland Zen Centre, to put our understanding into practice.

To begin, let us ask where this notion of Buddhists not standing for anything 'in the real world' might have come from? It can be traced back, at least in part, to a historical misunderstanding. When Buddhism first started filtering into the West, it was seen by nineteenth-century Western thinkers as nihilistic and world-denying. And today, even though we understand the teachings to a degree, we may still unconsciously hold our culture's bias in this regard. In Western thinking there is a strongly dualistic split between body and mind, between matter and spirit, going all the way back to Plato. If we approach the Dharma while still interpreting our experience through such dichotomies, we may assume that Buddhism's emphasis on Mind implies a devaluation of physical reality or 'the world'. We hear statements like the one in the Lankavatara Sutra

1. Robert Aitken, *Mind of Clover* (New York: North Point Press, 1984), p. 3.

that 'the external world is nothing but a manifestation of mind', and we think that this somehow means that the 'external' world is not real. But in fact, the statement that everything is mind means that the world is not external at all, it is us! Such an understanding keeps us *in* this world. Master Dogen poetically brings mind and things together over and over in his writings. Here are just two examples:

> You think that your mind is thoughts and concepts, but it is really trees and grasses and pebbles and tiles.[2]

and:

> Grasses and trees, fences and walls demonstrate and exalt the Dharma for the sake of living beings, both ordinary and sage; and in turn, living beings, both ordinary and sage, express and unfold the Dharma for the sake of grasses and trees, fences and walls.[3]

This same point is approached from a philosophical perspective by Robert Thurman in the introduction to his translation of the Vimalakirti Sutra. The story of the enlightened layman, Vimalakirti, forms one of the most beloved and influential of the Mahayana sutras, and in introducing the story, Thurman speaks about the teaching of emptiness as expressed in the Heart Sutra, where we chant that 'form here is only emptiness; emptiness only form' (see inset overleaf):

> The fact that matter [form] is voidness [emptiness] is absolutely affirmative of matter, not negative of matter. Indeed, of all theories it is the *only one* that is thus affirmative. How is this so? There are basically two kinds of theory about ultimate reality: nihilism and 'absolutism'. Of course, intellectual history abounds in theories vastly different in detail, but all share one or the other of these basic postulates about reality. They either deny it altogether or else they posit some sort of ultimate entity, substratum, or superstratum that serves as foundation, essence, container, or whatever, of the immediate reality. And this absolutism, while appearing to affirm something ultimately, actually negates the immediate reality in favour of the hypostatized ultimate reality.[4]

2. Master Dōgen, *Shōbōgenzō Zuimonki*, Chapter 4, Part 7 – but have not located the reference for this translation.

3. *Bendōwa: Shōbōgenzō*, Vol. I, Kosen Nishiyama and John Stevens (Tokyo: Daihokkaikaku, 1975), p. 150 – but have not located the reference for this translation.

4. Robert A. F. Thurman, *The Holy Teaching of Vimalakirti* (University Park, Pa.: Penn State University Press, 1975), p. 3.

This chant, perhaps the most well-known and frequently recited chant of Mahayana Buddhism, is said to encapsulate the essence of the Madhyamaka teachings on Emptiness and of the vast Perfection of Wisdom literature (see Chapter 5, p. 100). It is included in most chanting services at the Auckland Zen Centre.

The Bodhisattva of Compassion
from the depths of prajñā wisdom
saw the emptiness of all five skandhas
and sundered the bonds that cause all suffering.

Know then:
Form here is only emptiness;
emptiness only form.
Form is no other than emptiness;
emptiness no other than form.
Feeling, thought, and choice —
consciousness itself —
are the same as this.

Dharmas here are empty;
all are the primal void.
None are born or die,
nor are they stained or pure,
nor do they wax or wane.

So in emptiness no form,
no feeling, thought, or choice,
nor is there consciousness.
No eye, ear, nose, tongue, body, mind,
no colour, sound, smell, taste, touch,
or what the mind takes hold of,
nor even act of sensing.
No ignorance or end of it,
nor all that comes of ignorance:
No withering, no death, no end of them.

Nor is there pain, or cause of pain,
or cease in pain,
or noble path to lead from pain;
not even wisdom to attain:
Attainment too is emptiness.

So know that the Bodhisattva,
holding to nothing whatever,
but dwelling in prajñā wisdom,
is freed of delusive hindrance,
rid of the fear bred by it,
and reaches clearest nirvana.

All buddhas of past and present,
buddhas of future time,
through faith in prajñā wisdom,
come to full enlightenment.
Know then the great dharani,
the radiant, peerless mantra,
the supreme, unfailing mantra,
the Prajñā Pāramitā,
whose words allay all pain.
This is highest wisdom,
true beyond all doubt;
know and proclaim its truth:

Gate, gate
pāragate
pārasamgate
bodhi, svāhā!

He goes on to say that it doesn't matter what you call this ultimate reality, whether God or Brahman, or even Nirvana or True Nature imperfectly understood; in each case we are presented with a world in which the spiritual seeker must strive to escape the imperfection of immediate reality in order to reach a state of 'ultimate and eternal well-being'. Nihilism, on the other hand, accepts *only* our immediate, physical reality, while relegating consciousness, our experience of that reality, to a role as an accidental, non-continuous, and finally meaningless product of the material world.

But Buddhism is the Middle Way: not nihilist and not absolutist either. Buddhists may talk about life as a dream, but it is not a dream from which we try to escape. Rather, it is a dream that we endeavour to see clearly and respond to compassionately. To do so means to first accept life as it is and *then* work with it, because it is not set in stone – it is empty of a fixed self. We can engage in and support life-sustaining activity and say no to behaviour and social structures that cause suffering to victims, and eventually to perpetrators as well.

In Buddhist teaching the sufferings of this world arise from what are termed the Three Poisons, namely greed, hatred and delusive thinking. At the most basic level, this teaching refers to the fact that all of us try hard to get what we want (greed) and to avoid what we don't want (hatred), while acting out of the basic assumption that we are separate from the things 'out there' that are the objects of our greed or hatred (delusion). As long as these Three Poisons inform our actions, the result will be suffering. Therefore any response, if it is to be effective, must come from a place of generosity, benevolence and wisdom, where the walls of self versus other have broken down to some degree. So when we say that 'form is emptiness and emptiness is form', we are describing what is seen when these walls have come down, and when we can see that our familiar world of relativity and the world of the eternal and transcendent are one. And when we chant in the Heart Sutra 'no eye, ear, nose, tongue, body, mind' we are not negating everything. We are affirming every *thing* as inseparable from every other thing; in seeing, there is no eye separate from what is seen or from the act of seeing itself. It all arises together. We can experience this directly.

At a certain point in the Vimalakirti Sutra, Manjushri, the Bodhisattva of Wisdom, asks Vimalakirti a series of questions. Vimalakirti is sick and

Manjushri, who has gone to visit him, asks, 'Householder, how should a bodhisattva console another bodhisattva who is sick?' Vimalakirti says:

> He should tell him that the body is impermanent but should not exhort him to renunciation or disgust. He should tell him that the body is miserable, but should not encourage him to find solace in liberation; that the body is selfless but that living beings should be developed; that the body is peaceful, but not to seek any ultimate calm.[5]

This is a beautiful description of the Middle Way. We understand the impermanence of the body, but we do not renounce it. We do not regard the body with disgust, but rather as the site of our Awakening. And we can widen the meaning of this passage by substituting 'body' with 'world':

> He should tell him that the world is impermanent but should not exhort him to renunciation or disgust. He should tell him that the world is miserable but should not encourage him to find solace in liberation; that the world is selfless [i.e., without a fixed self] but that living beings should be developed; that the world is peaceful, but not to seek any ultimate calm.[5]

In other words, the impermanence of the world does not lead us to renounce it, to look for a way out. Vimalakirti is the great model; in explaining to Manjushri why he is sick he says, 'the bodhisattva loves all living beings as if each were his only child. He becomes sick when they are sick and is cured when they are cured.' As long as there is suffering in our world, we are all afflicted. Without falling into utopianism we must engage in efforts to build a world in which all beings have the opportunity to evolve – in which they are not held back through lack of food, or poor education, or war, or destruction of their habitat.

As Zen practitioners we take a vow each day to 'liberate all beings'.[6] And many people, when they first hear this vow, think, 'How can I possibly liberate all beings? I can't even liberate myself; how can I even begin?' But as the motto of the Sarvodaya Movement, a village-based self-help organization in Sri Lanka, has it, 'We build the road and the road builds us.' It is a mistake to think that we must wait until we are fully enlightened to act; and, in fact, it is a mistake even to think that we *can* wait until we are fully enlightened to act. Rather our actions are an essential part of our path to enlightenment.

5. *Ibid.*, p. 44.
6. See Glossary under Four Vows.

Sincere zazen helps us to uncover our deepest aspirations, our innate *bodhicitta*,[7] and so does compassionate action. In both, we forget ourselves in the service of something greater than us. And, in both, this self-forgetfulness is the key. In the the words of Japanese Zen Master Muso Kokushi (1275–1351):

> Those who seek liberation for themselves alone cannot become fully enlightened. Though it may be said that one who is not already liberated cannot liberate others, the very process of forgetting oneself to help others is in itself liberating.[8]

7. 'Mind of awakening', see Glossary.

8. Musō Kokushi, *Dream Conversations,* translated by Thomas Cleary (Boston: Shambhala, 1994), p. 1.

TEISHO

* * *

The Hands and Eyes of the Bodhisattva of Compassion
(2014–09–23)

How can we most truly be helpful in this world?

Next week we have our annual Kannon Day ceremony,[9] so today we're going to take up a koan, Case 89 in the *Hekiganroku* (*Blue Cliff Record*), which is about Kannon, the Bodhisattva of Great Compassion. The name of the koan is 'The Hands and Eyes of the Bodhisattva of Great Compassion'. Here's the case:

> Ungan asked Dogo, 'What use does the great Bodhisattva of Compassion make of all those hands and eyes?'
> Dogo said, 'It is like someone reaching back, groping for a pillow with outstretched hand in the middle of the night.'
> Ungan said, 'I understand.'
> Dogo said, 'How do you understand it?'
> Ungan said, 'The whole body is hands and eyes.'
> Dogo said, 'You have had your say, but you have only said 80% of it.'
> Ungan said, 'How would you put it?'
> Dogo said, 'The outside is hands, the inside is eyes.'

Before we get into the koan, a little bit about the characters in this story. Ungan lived from 780–841 which puts him right at the heart of the Golden Age of Zen in the Tang Dynasty. He was in the tenth generation after Bodhidharma and was a disciple of Yaoshan Weiyan, called Yakusan in Japanese. Prior to that he also trained for twenty years under the great Baizhang Huaihai (see Introduction, p. 4), known in Japanese as Hyakujo. He started training under Hyakujo at the age of twelve, so he became a monk very early in his life, but he did not come to awakening under Hyakujo. One writer describes him as being slow in maturing. After Hyakujo died, he traveled around to other teachers and finally settled down with Yakusan — and ripened with him. The other character in the koan here, Dogo, was his fellow student, another disciple of Yakusan, and also his close friend. They were actually friends for forty years, and

9. At the Auckland Zen Centre this ceremony includes an opportunity for compassionate action as we participate in writing letters for Amnesty International.

there are many, many stories of exchanges between these two friends that have been handed down to us and that are still greatly admired today. The name Ungan (Yunyan in Chinese) was the name of the mountain where the master finally settled down to teach after he'd completed his training; it means Cloud-Cliff. Among Ungan's Dharma heirs was Dongshan Liang-jie who was the cofounder of the Caodong school in China, which came to be known as the Soto school in Japan. Both Dongshan and Yunyan (Ungan) appear in our ancestral line, so they're direct ancestors for us.

Ungan's fellow student Dogo was a little bit older than him, by about eleven years, and was also his senior in the Dharma – in fact, he had guided Ungan to become a disciple of Yakusan. Besides Ungan and Dogo, we could say there's a third character in today's koan which is of course Kannon, the great Bodhisattva of Compassion. This bodhisattva was known as Avalokiteshvara in Sanskrit, meaning 'The One Who Hears the Cries of the World', and he was originally male. But in China, where she is known as Guanyin, she was often depicted as androgynous or as a woman. In Japanese, she's called Kannon, Kanzeon, or Kanjizai, and she's sometimes referred to as the mother of the Buddhas, just as the bodhisattva Manjushri is sometimes referred to as the teacher of the Buddhas. These two, Avalokiteshvara and Manjushri, represent respectively the two essential qualities of enlightenment, Compassion and Wisdom. Sometimes these qualities are called the two wings of the bird of enlightenment, since neither can function well without the other. There's a saying,

> Wisdom without compassion is bondage, compassion without wisdom is bondage.[10]

They're really two sides of a single coin. Nisargadatta Maharaj[11] expresses this beautifully when he says 'When I look inside and see that I am nothing – that is wisdom. When I look outside and see that I am everything – that is compassion.' So these two bodhisattvas, Manjushri and Avalokiteshvara, are a team,[12] and are called the teacher of the Buddhas and the mother of the Buddhas, because, you could say, they're what

10. A Tibetan saying paraphrasing a passage in the 'Inquiring About Illness' chapter of the Vimalakirti Sutra.

11. 1897–1981, Hindu guru of nondualism.

12. Sometimes Manjushri is paired with Samantabhadra, bodhisattva of skilful means – compassion in action.

Buddhahood comes out of. So they're very exalted beings, not inferior to the Buddhas themselves.

Now in today's koan we have the question, What use does the great Bodhisattva of Compassion make of all those hands and eyes? Sometimes Kannon is depicted with many, many arms and in the palm of each of the many hands at the end of those arms there is an eye. She (or he) can have 12 faces, 33 different kinds of bodies, and, it's said, 84,000 different forms. In Kyoto there's a place, Sanjusangendo, which has an extraordinary Bodhisattva Kannon with a thousand arms. The point of this iconography is that compassion needs to take countless forms in order to respond to different kinds of people and different kinds of suffering. Tolstoy once said something which can relate to this. He said, 'Happy families are all alike. Every unhappy family is unhappy in its own way.' Every person is unhappy in his or her own way. The essence of compassion is an appropriate response. A response that fits.

So, let's look further into our case:

> Ungan asked Dogo, 'What use does the great Bodhisattva of Compassion make of all those hands and eyes?'

What is he really asking? Is he talking about Buddhist iconography? There wouldn't be much to this if he was. These hands and eyes, all these hands and eyes, are pointing to the unlimited nature of compassion, to its many forms. So we could say that he's asking about the nature of compassion. What is its nature? And most importantly, how do we manifest it? How do we make it real?

This koan is really an invitation to consider our own hands and eyes. What are they really for? How do they work? What do they give rise to? We can understand the Bodhisattva's eyes as referring to how we perceive things, and her hands as referring to what we do. Remember, in these depictions of Kannon with many arms, the eyes are actually sculpted into the palms of the hands. And she's also often holding many different kinds of implements, a different implement in each hand. You could say that each tool that she holds is embodying a different kind of consciousness. Or you could even turn it round the other way and say that every kind of action, all the different ways in which we can respond, give rise to certain kinds of understanding – compassion gives rise to wisdom and vice versa.

So we can ask ourselves, What kind of hands and eyes do I have? What kinds of affinities do I have? Where have I got something to offer? We can think of many different examples of how people may be called to help in a particular way. For instance, people who have gone through addiction and recovered can often be very helpful for those who are suffering in addiction. Or somebody who's had a life-threatening illness can help those who are going through the same. Or parents whose children have this or that affliction. But it doesn't always have to be exactly the same experience; perhaps something in one's early life has given one a passion for a particular area — a desire for justice, or an affinity for working with a particular population, with prisoners for example, or refugees.

So Ungan is asking about the nature of compassion: How do I use it? How do I manifest it? And Dogo answers very directly. He says, 'It is like someone reaching back, groping for a pillow with outstretched hand in the middle of the night.'

The first thing that one might notice about this reply is that it's kind of paradoxical. We're talking about eyes and yet Dogo's saying that this is something that happens in the middle of the night, in complete darkness. This person may not even open her eyes. And yet she finds that pillow and adjusts it, gets it back under her head.

Now what does this mean, this middle of the night that's being talked about here? There's a clue to this in the introduction to this koan. The koans in the *Blue Cliff Record* were originally compiled in eleventh-century China by Xuedou Chongxian (called Setcho in Japanese), and were then commented upon, several generations later, by Yuanwu Keqin (Engo). When we take up these koans in dokusan, we just work on the case, not the commentary, but Engo's introductions can often be quite illuminating, serving as pointers which highlight the theme of each koan. For this koan Engo says, 'When the entire body is the eye, while seeing you do not see. When the entire body is the ear, while hearing, you do not hear. When the entire body is the mouth, while speaking you do not speak. When the entire body is the mind, while thinking you do not think.'

Dogo's response about what happens in the middle of the night is pointing to the kind of response in which there's no thought of being a helper, no seeing a person as being a helpless victim. There's discernment there, because we can find the pillow and put it where it needs to be, but not the kind of discriminating that we conventionally do. It's pointing to a kind of helping that embraces everybody without attachment, without aversion.

Elsewhere in his commentary Engo says, 'You must cut off emotional defilements and conceptual thinking. Become clean and naked, free and unbound. Only then will you be able to see this saying about great compassion.' Then your heart will be wide open.

And while this is a lofty state, at the same time it is something very ordinary, and the image Dogo gives is a very ordinary one: 'like reaching for a pillow at night.' Like taking a tissue when you need to blow your nose. Like putting a raincoat on when it's wet.

Probably most of us have met nurse aides in hospitals or rest homes, perhaps when we've been ill or when we've been visiting an elderly parent or relative; people who are not well-paid, who do difficult work, but who manage to work with a spirit of love and compassion day in and out: changing a bedpan, wiping somebody's bottom. This is bodhisattva work, or at least it has the potential to be so. In doing these kinds of things, how do we see what we're doing? How do we regard urine and faeces? How do we see someone who's wet their bed? Master Dogen, commenting on this koan, says, 'There is no distinction between eyes and darkness.'

There's a kind of seeing which involves not seeing. What isn't seen are false distinctions. There's a teaching in the Mahayana tradition about the six paramitas or perfections. These are the essential ingredients in awakening for the bodhisattva, ways of waking up, and the six are: giving, ethical behaviour, patience, diligence or vigour, meditation, and wisdom.[13] And the way in which these are perfected is to be able to carry them out without any sense of there being a self or an other. In other words, to take the first one as an example, there's giving, but no seeing yourself as being a giver, a 'generous person'; no seeing the receiver as being deserving or undeserving or someone who should be grateful; and no seeing the gift as being a gift. You understand that those labels are all provisional, all empty of abiding selfhood. So there's no self-consciousness or other-consciousness there. Just the act. Just giving. And in the same way there can be just helping. It's like someone reaching back, groping for a pillow with outstretched hand in the middle of the night. Just doing what needs to be done.

13. See Chapter 7, p. 147.

Ungan then replies to this explanation by saying, 'I understand.' And Dogo comes back, 'How do you understand it?' He challenges him to show how he understands. Because it's all very well having an explanation like this, an image, even a beautiful one, an apt one, but we have to make it real, especially in the case of compassion.

So Ungan responds, 'The whole body is hands and eyes.' Complete involvement. No room for self-consciousness. Master Dogen comments on Dogo's 'I understand' by saying that it is not just words, but, as he puts it, the movement of his own hands and eyes. And one of the points of the koan is to present this in another way, without using words. So we can ask ourselves, What would this look like in my life? How would this look at work? In my marriage? Or when I'm with an elderly parent? Or a child having a tantrum?

Next Dogo says, 'You have had your say, but you have only said 80% of it.' Why does he say 80%? Ungan's response seems pretty good. Even Master Dogen, commenting on this, says that Ungan didn't leave anything unsaid. Master Dogen also remarks that Dogo's saying that Ungan got 80% was a kind of praise. And there are two ways of understanding this. One is that words can never express 100% of anything. How could words get themselves around limitless compassion? Even if you just took all the compassionate acts of a single day. But there's another meaning here that is probably even more important. Really as bodhisattvas we can't ever think of anything as being completely finished. Yasutani-roshi used to say about this story that this 80% was pointing to the fact that we could always do better. I was looking at the Vimalakirti Sutra recently and there was a striking statement in it:

> Causes and conditions are the place of practice. For none of the links in the chain of causation from ignorance to old age and death ever come to an end.[14]

The sutra is referring here to the twelve links of dependent co-arising that map how suffering comes into existence.[15] And it's saying, these links *never* come to an end. There's *always* going to be suffering. Which means there's always suffering to respond to.

14. Burton Watson, trans., *Vimalakirti Sutra* (New York: Columbia University Press, 1996), p. 56.

15. See Glossary under Pratītyasamutpāda.

Master Dogen also once said, 'When the Dharma fills your body and mind, you understand that something is missing.' Since there's no end to life, that means that there really is no end to practice. To think in terms of completion just doesn't really fit here. The Bodhisattva of Great Compassion just responds, not evaluating, not counting, not thinking of percentages, but just responding. Issan Dorsey, founder of Maitri hospice, said that being a true bodhisattva was 'nothing more than being an impeccable housewife.' A bodhisattva's work is never done.

But Ungan is not fazed when Dogo seems to be saying to him that he hasn't completely got it. He asks, 'How would *you* put it?' He's challenging Dogo to say more. And Dogo says, 'The outside is hands, the inside is eyes.' Outside, compassionate action, inside clear seeing.

One of the points of the koan is to understand whether this is deeper than Ungan's statement. Is this one more than 80%? Master Setcho, the original compiler of the *Blue Cliff Record*, says, 'Don't you see? The net of jewels reflect each other. Where does the eye of the staff come from? I cry, Tut, tut!'

This needs a little bit of unpacking. First of all, the net of jewels. This refers to the Diamond Net of Indra. It's an image that comes from Huayan literature, the writing of the Avatamsaka Sutra school, and in those writings the Diamond Net of Indra is presented as a model of the universe. Imagine a great three-dimensional net and at every intersection of the strands of this vast net there is a jewel, and each jewel reflects every other jewel in the net, so if you look into one jewel, you see the jewel next to it, and in that you see the reflection of the one next to it and so forth. So every single jewel contains infinite, nested images of every other jewel in the net. You could say that this is a formulation of a holographic universe that was imagined long before anybody knew about holograms. It is a teaching about our profound interconnectedness. We are each of us the whole universe, each of us a jewel in the vast net, containing every other jewel.

Setcho then asks, 'Where does the eye of the staff come from?' There's a story behind this image that would have been known to people in the Tang Dynasty. There was a blind mountain man who would come down to the village market to sell fortunes. He would descend each week and the road that went down to the village from his hut was very muddy, and yet he would wear white cloth shoes to walk it. One day somebody asked

him, 'How come your shoes don't get dirty, old man, when you're blind?'
And the old man raised his staff and said, 'There's an eye on the staff.'
In Zen literature a staff is often used as a symbol for our True Nature.
Commenting on a koan called Basho's staff Mumon says, 'It helps you
cross the river when the bridge is broken down. It accompanies you to
the village on a moonless night.' It's there even when the way forward
seems impossible, when we can't find our way home.

Today's koan about the Bodhisattva of Great Compassion appears not
just in the *Blue Cliff Record*, but also in the *Shoyoroku* or *Book of Equanimity*, and there Wansong, the compiler of the collection, comments on
this eye in the staff by saying:

> When reaching for a pillow at night, there's an eye in the hand. When
> eating, there's an eye on the tongue. When recognising people on hearing
> them speak, there's an eye in the ears. Su Zizhan conversing with a deaf man
> just wrote. Then he laughed and said, 'He and I are both strange people. I
> use my hands for a mouth, and he uses his eyes for ears.'[16]

Wansong's pointing to something very fluid and unobstructed here,
but at the same time very ordinary. Something that functions even when
you're deaf or blind — or both. Think of that story of Helen Keller who
was profoundly deaf and blind from a very early age. There was this
moment when her teacher Anne Sullivan held Helen's hand under the
gushing pump, and feeling the running water, she suddenly recognised
that the little taps that her teacher was making on her arm stood for that
water. That was the turning point for her, when she went from being
locked inside herself, in a 'dark chamber', to being able to finally discover
herself and communicate with others. What was it that recognised water?
What sees when we reach for a pillow in the night or stumble to the
bathroom? What is the eye of the staff as it probes? Or of our ear, or our
tongue?

This is really the core question in this koan. Can we see where this eye
comes from? Can we see that source, and the hands and eyes even in the
most helpless person, even in somebody evil or depraved?

Master Tenkei[17] said, 'Have you seen the jeweled net? The universe
wherein there is no obstruction between things is these hands and eyes.'

16. Thomas Cleary, *The Book of Serenity* (New York: Lindisfarne Press, 1990), pp. 229–30.
17. Japanese Master Tenkei Denson (1648–1735).

Crystal clear on all sides, open and unobstructed in all directions, emanating light and making the earth tremble in all places.

How is this manifested?

If there's any life-koan to have, it's this one. How do we manifest compassion?

Master Setcho asked, 'Where does the eye of the staff come from?' And then he says, 'I cry, Tut, tut!' He recognised he had gone too far, that he couldn't possibly tell us that. We have to find it out for ourselves.

Where does the eye of the staff come from?

We'll stop here and recite the four vows.

* *

*

*A monk asked Dasui, 'When the conflagration at the
end of the kalpa sweeps through and the great cosmos
is destroyed, I wonder, is this one destroyed or not?'*

Dasui said, 'It will be destroyed.'

The monk asked, 'Will it be gone with everything else?'

Dasui replied, 'It will be gone with everything else.'

— Hekiganroku, CASE 29

CHAPTER 9

Standing On and For the Earth

IN Chapter 8 we examined how Buddhist teachings can help to keep us firmly anchored in our world and how they encourage us to actively 'build the road as the road builds us'. For those of us at the Auckland Zen Centre, a central way in which we have tried to do this has been through involvement with environmental initiatives. The core teaching of Buddhism that each thing depends on every other thing — that each

---

PHOTO : The Centre's altar on Earth Day.

thing fundamentally *is* every other thing – helps us to understand that we must care for our 'environment' in just the same way we would care for our own bodies. Moreover, this is an area where we can, and must, work on multiple levels simultaneously, that is, we must 'think globally and act locally'. This slogan is actually a wonderful expression of our Buddhist practice: training to be radically present to each detail of our lives, while holding the liberation of all beings as an underlying intention.

The interconnectedness of all life, and in fact of all phenomena, is beautifully summed up in the teachings of Vietnamese Master Thich Nhat Hahn on 'Interbeing', a term he coined to translate the Sanskrit term *pratityasamutpada*. Usually translated as Dependent Co-arising, *pratityasamutpada* is an essential element of Buddhist teaching; in fact the Buddha said, 'Whoever sees the principle of Dependent Co-arising sees the Dharma, and whoever sees the Dharma sees the Buddha.' But Dependent Co-arising is a pretty dry term and it is often taught in quite a dry, complex way – so we can be grateful to Thich Nhat Hanh for coming up with the term Interbeing which is so much more accessible and alive.

Though we can read detailed explanations of Dependent Co-arising's twelve aspects, the simplest way of understanding it is when the Buddha says, 'This being, that becomes; on the arising of this, that arises. This not being, that does not become; on the cessation of this, that ceases.' In other words, nothing stands alone, and when we start to look deeply at ourselves and our reality, the boundaries of self begin to break down, and we have a great deal of difficulty saying exactly where 'we' end and what is 'not us' begins. And the reason we have difficulty is because there is no such place.

We can think of many examples of this, perhaps most obviously the way that our bodies cannot sustain themselves without a constant interchange of air with our so-called environment. Thich Nhat Hanh, when introducing the concept of Interbeing would hold up a sheet of paper:

> If you are a poet, you will see clearly that there is a cloud floating in this sheet of paper. Without a cloud, there will be no rain; without rain, the trees cannot grow; and without trees, we cannot make paper. The cloud is essential for the paper to exist. If the cloud is not here, the sheet of paper cannot be here either. We can say that the cloud and the paper inter-are….
>
> If we look into this sheet of paper even more deeply, we can see the

sunshine in it. If the sunshine is not there, the forest cannot grow. In fact, nothing can grow. Even we cannot grow without sunshine. So we know that the sunshine is also in this sheet of paper. The paper and the sunshine inter-are. And if we continue to look, we can see the logger who cut the tree and brought it to the mill to be transformed into paper. And we see the wheat. We know that the logger cannot exist without his daily bread, and therefore the wheat that became his bread is also in this sheet of paper. And the logger's father and mother are in it too. When we look in this way, we see that without all of these things, this sheet of paper cannot exist.

Looking even more deeply, we can see we are in it too. This is not difficult to see, because when we look at a sheet of paper, the sheet of paper is part of our perception. Your mind is in here and mine is also, so we can say that everything is in here in this sheet of paper. You cannot point out one thing that is not here—time, space, the earth, the rain, the minerals in the soil, the sunshine, the cloud, the river, the heat. Everything coexists with this sheet of paper.[1]

It is easy to see the applicability of such teachings to our current environmental crisis. On the macro-level, we know that we have entered an era of mass extinction of species, of climate crisis, and of chemical and plastic pollution, all brought about by our human activity. We also know that, as a nation, New Zealand's level of per capita greenhouse gas emissions is one of the highest in the world, and that, in contrast to other countries, a large portion of this pollution is produced by the dairy industry. At the Auckland Zen Centre, we have responded to this knowledge through work with global political organisations such as 350.org, with community groups engaged in such projects as tree planting and organic gardening, and most personally through adopting a vegan diet at the Centre.

Changing our eating habits gives us a means to care for the environment on the most intimate level. It has long been a standard practice in Asian Zen temples not to cook or serve flesh foods, and this practice has been adopted also at the Rochester and Auckland Zen Centres. Roshi Kapleau was an early proponent of vegetarianism as part of the Western Buddhist path, and by 1981 had published his book, *To Cherish All Life: A Buddhist Case for Becoming Vegetarian*. Thus we have always been a vegetarian centre, but to make the move to an entirely plant-based diet, as we did in 2016, was a new step. As Amala-sensei wrote at the time:

1. https://www.lionsroar.com/the-fullness-of-emptiness/

BODHISATTVA'S VOW

by Torei Zenji (1621–1692)

I am only a simple disciple, but I offer these respectful words.

When I regard the true nature of the many dharmas, I find them all to be sacred forms of the Tathagata's never-failing essence. Each particle of matter, each moment, is no other than the Tathagata's inexpressible radiance.

With this realization, our virtuous ancestors gave tender care to beasts and birds with compassionate minds and hearts. Among us, in our own daily lives, who is not reverently grateful for the protections of life: food, drink, and clothing! Though they are inanimate things, they are none-theless the warm flesh and blood, the merciful incarnations of Buddha.

—Excerpt from the version used by the Diamond Sangha
    http://diamondsangha.com/wp-content/uploads/2014/06/
    Sutra-Book-New-final.pdf

Of course it is up to each person to decide what to eat, and people's needs vary greatly, but choosing [a plant-based diet] can be a powerful way of cultivating a heart of compassion, and of strengthening the habit of non-harm …

In addition to adopting a plant-based diet, we have worked towards growing for ourselves as many of those plants as possible, both in the home gardens of Centre members and also through our involvement with the Dig It! Royal Oak Organic Garden. This community garden is a thriving venture that includes local schools, community groups and residents. Everyone is welcome, but the garden makes extra effort to ensure that people who identify as having an impairment or who experience mental illness are at home in the garden. At the Dig It! Garden we have not only cultivated a plot but have also been able to support organic gardening workshops for the general public. Of course any food that we can grow ourselves, or encourage other urban dwellers to grow, means that much reduction in the carbon footprint involved in the production and transport of industrially farmed produce. As we shop for food as well as for non-food items, we try to buy local products as much as possible, and to minimise and reuse plastic and packaging. We make our own cleaning products, refilling reusable containers with bulk supplies available at a shop around the corner from the Centre, and we are happy to offer information and encouragement to others. Even simply remembering to take one's own reusable bags each time one goes out to the shops can be a meaningful mindfulness practice that helps us to embody our care for the planet.

We have further expressed our care for our neighbourhood through the creation of another garden quite different to the one in Royal Oak. The back of the Centre's zendo is separated from a council-owned carpark by a strip of steep slope, which, at the time that we took possession of our building, was a forlorn, sun-baked wasteland, sprouting only weeds and rubbish. With assistance from a local government grant, our Sangha have cleared the litter and weeds, mulched the ground, and planted over 100 hardy native plants that now draw native birds and insects into this tiny oasis. We have also installed bench seats so locals can enjoy the garden and have planted the area around the benches with flowers that create a blaze of colour over the summer months.

More recently, in February of 2019, Amala-sensei organised a series of discussions about the climate crisis that were held at the Centre. Sangha members with direct personal experience of climate change activism, fossil fuel divestment, lifestyle simplification and political advocacy were invited to give presentations on responding to the climate crisis, on both the practical and emotional level. As a result of the sessions a Green Network was set up to help inform members about climate issues, research and actions, and to look into ways the Centre might reduce its own carbon footprint and encourage others to do so.

The work of the Green Network emphasizes a further dimension to our climate crisis efforts as well. We must acknowledge that the 'rapid, far-reaching and unprecedented changes in all aspects of society' called for by the IPCC (Intergovernmental Panel on Climate Change) may not happen fast enough to prevent ecological and social collapse within our lifetimes. Given this human-generated catastrophe, how must we live?

We come back to the existential questions about birth and death which are at the heart of Zen. George Monbiot has said that we have two tasks, throwing ourselves into the effort to avert collapse, and preparing ourselves for the likely failure of these efforts. He says, 'Both tasks require a complete revision of our relationship with the living planet.' And with ourselves.

Our actions on behalf of the planet, from the most broadly political to the most quotidian, are informed not just by traditional Buddhist teachings, but also by those of twenty-first century science, and by a desire to bring these two traditions into dialogue with each other. In one of her earliest Dharma talks, delivered in 2004, Amala-sensei spoke of being deeply inspired by the work of Brian Swimme, a mathematical cosmologist who had undertaken the project of communicating the wonder of scientific discoveries to the general public, and of trying to heal the split that we have in our culture between science and art, and between science and religion. Delivering her talk just days after Roshi Kapleau's death, Amala-sensei said that, in presenting Swimme's work to the Sangha, she felt that she was carrying on Roshi Kapleau's project as well:

> One of [Philip Kapleau's] great passions was adapting Buddhism to Western culture, finding ways to make it come alive for us as Westerners. And the scientific project is so much a part of who and what we are as Westerners that there needs to be a way of bringing this whole aspect of the human enterprise into our religious practice, and this is what I've found so exciting about the work of Brian Swimme — that he is showing us how we might do just that. As Swimme sees it, science has made wonderful discoveries, but the scientists themselves haven't been transformed by those discoveries. He says scientists get so impressed with the mathematics of their research area that they lose sight of the marvels of a fern or an ant. That's the way he puts it. This reminded me of the well-known line from Walt Whitman's Song of Myself:
>
> *And a mouse is miracle enough to stagger sextillions of infidels.*
>
> And yet how many human beings when they see a mouse truly see it? Do we truly comprehend its force, its power, its overwhelming miraculousness?
>
> Swimme points out that just as the discoveries of science have remained abstract and haven't been incorporated by human beings into their world view, the teachings of religion, too, can become abstract. We may read,

for instance, in the Bible, about the 'water of life', and yet, Swimme asks, how does this relate, for example, to the hydrology of the Mississippi river? There's a kind of disconnect between the religious symbol and *actual* water, water that we might experience as a sacred thing in itself. And of course this is where the great strength of Zen lies, that it trains us simply to apprehend things directly, as they are.

Nevertheless, Sensei points out, most of us in the modern world live in cities, where the earth is paved and the stars are obliterated by bright lights, and where we and our children spend many hours in front of screens, which gives us a completely mediated experience rather than a direct experience of the world. She goes on to say:

There are people of middle age and older who were not exposed to television right from an early age. I know in our family we didn't get a television until I was five or six. A friend who used to live in Pittsburgh (USA) remarked that when he went back to visit his parents he noticed the forest behind his parents' house had changed. He said that when he was growing up the woods were criss-crossed with little paths made by the neighbourhood kids who played there. When he went back to see his parents he discovered that there weren't any paths in the forest anymore – because the children weren't playing outside. It's a huge sea-change … to imagine there are children growing up not experiencing the outdoors!

Besides the fact that lives spent in front of a screen are cut off from the direct experience of the outdoors, there is the further problem that much of our mediated screen-world is saturated in the assumptions and mechanisms of a consumer society. Amala-sensei quotes Swimme as saying that 'consumerism is based on the assumption that the universe is a collection of dead objects.' She then comments:

A collection of dead objects. How untrue this is! What a delusion! Through zazen we can come to experience the vibrancy of every moment, of every tiny little object, of every object's living presence. But instead we live with a kind of disconnect where we're not really at home in our own world. How else could we be so wantonly destroying our habitats and species except that we're not really living in the world that we're living in?

The fact is that we live in a throw-away society, yet both science and Buddhism teach us that there is really no 'away' into which we can throw things. Our rubbish, our carbon emissions, our plastic all remain here with

us and continue to affect our ecosystem. This is a concrete example of
what the Buddhist teachings on karma-vipaka have always maintained;
we do indeed reap what we sow.

Just before Siddhartha achieved Buddhahood, the story goes that Mara
(the Buddhist embodiment of evil and death) appeared and said, 'Are you
sure you are the one? Are you sure *you* have this Buddha nature? Do you
really believe *you* are worthy of coming to Supreme Enlightenment?' The
future Buddha touched the ground lightly with his hand and asked the
Earth herself to bear witness. And the Earth replied 'He is worthy! He is
worthy! There is not one spot where he has not offered himself totally,
selflessly, for the welfare of all beings.'[2] This is a wonderful scene and a
beautiful affirmation of the Buddha's being a child of this Earth. Where
else could he be but here? Where else can we humans be, except here on
the Earth? This is where the Buddha perfected himself and this is where
our work is too.

2. From the Buddha's Enlightenment story told on 8 December in Zen centres in the
Kapleau-Yasutani lineage.

TEISHO

* * *

It Goes Along with Everything Else
(2018–12–11)

Anxieties about the end of the world are not particular to the modern world, but in our era of climate crisis and nuclear weaponry, they have taken on a new force and urgency.

Tonight we are going to take up a koan from the *Hekiganroku*, Number 29, Dasui's 'It Goes Along with Everything Else'. Here is the case:

> A monk asked Dasui, 'When the conflagration at the end of the kalpa sweeps through and the great cosmos is destroyed, I wonder, is this one destroyed or not?'
> Dasui said, 'It will be destroyed.'
> The monk asked, 'Will it be gone with everything else?'
> Dasui replied, 'It will be gone with everything else.'

This koan, which deals with mass destruction, has particular relevance for us because of the predicament, the moral emergency, we are now in as a species.

Because our enormous technological power is not matched by our spiritual development we have reached a crisis-point unlike any other in the history of humankind, one in which all other sentient beings and so-called inanimate things are irrevocably caught up. Human activity is now the dominant force on the planet (a staggering 96% of the planet's mammal biomass consists of us humans and our livestock), and it is not only proving deadly for many non-humans but unjust and unworkable for a large part of humanity as well. Either we make a transition to a new life-sustaining civilisation that is no longer fiercely armoured against and antagonistic towards nature (and to whatever else we deem 'other'), or we condemn ourselves and future generations of sentient beings to a more and more diminished and impoverished world, if not to extinction. Our present consumer society measures success in terms of corporate profits – 'how fast materials can be extracted from the Earth and turned into consumer products, weapons and waste' as Joanna Macy puts it, and very few of the world's leaders are brave enough to abandon the industrial growth model, even if they mouth support of sustainability.

We are in the midst of the sixth period of mass extinction in the history of the Earth, losing 30,000 species a year. All previous mass extinctions were caused by natural processes; the present one is caused by us. Humans are causing such vast physical changes to the planet that Dr. Niles Eldredge, a paleontologist at the American Museum of Natural History, likens the chaos we are wreaking to that caused by the asteroid that plummeted into the Gulf of Mexico at the end of the Cretaceous, killing off the dinosaurs. Not even the deepest oceans or highest mountains are untouched by the consequences of human activity. As a paleontologist, Eldredge brings a long view to this urgent problem, proposing that Phase One of this particular bout of mass extinction began not with the industrial revolution a couple of hundred years ago, but 100,000 years ago, with human beings' dispersal beyond Africa! Everywhere we early humans went we over-hunted, to extinction, the large (and naively trusting) animals we found there. Only in Africa, where the large animals had a chance to evolve along with us, did they survive. Phase Two began 10,000 years ago with the advent of agriculture, when humans started to transform large tracts of the landscape. The exploitation of fossil fuels has merely allowed the speed of that transformation to go exponential. From the point of view of many other species, human beings have been crashing around the world like a bull in a china shop for a very long time. But now that bull is very, very large.

We human beings have been wreaking havoc because of our limited world-picture, and the climate crisis is our wake-up call. Because of our years of denial and inaction, the situation is urgent and possibly already at tipping point. The IPCC (Intergovernmental Panel on Climate Change) said earlier this year that, 'Unless we make rapid, far-reaching and unprecedented changes in all aspects of society' we are going to reach catastrophic levels of overheating by 2030. That's less than twelve years away. 'Catastrophic' means not enough food, massive displacement of people as sea levels rise, an increase in conflict and wars, societal breakdown. The end of our world as we know it.

Of course anxieties about the end of the world are not unique to modern times. In today's koan a monk comes to Master Dasui and asks, 'When the conflagration at the end of the kalpa sweeps through and the great cosmos is destroyed, I wonder, is this one destroyed or not?'

The master in this story is Dasui Fazhen (878–963). He was a disciple of Changqing Da'an and took his name from Mt Dasui in Sichuan province where he taught. A kalpa is an eon, the period between the creation of one universe and the re-creation of another universe. It's an extremely long period of time, and also an expression of the cyclical nature of things in Buddhist cosmology, where everything is part of a beginningless and endless process of creation and destruction. In Buddhism a kalpa is divided into four phases: Formation, where the universe comes into existence; Abiding, where it endures for a certain time; Destruction, where it all collapses; and a final phase of Emptiness. Out of this emptiness the whole process begins again. This mythical formulation ties in loosely with the theories of some contemporary cosmologists who propose a cyclical big bang/big crunch model of the universe.

So the monk has probably read in the sutras about the end of the kalpa, when everything is consumed by a great fire, and this has raised doubts and fears in his mind. He is confronted with death on a cosmic scale. We perhaps find some consolation regarding our individual deaths; we may die but life goes on, we will leave behind a legacy in our children, or in our good works. But in regards to the annihilation of the universe itself, there's no room for that. So the monk asks his burning question, 'Is this one destroyed or not?'

When he says 'this one' he is not referring here to his small self, but rather to our unborn and undying Buddha Nature. Won't that at least survive? But Dasui says, 'It will be destroyed.' The monk can't stomach this and asks for clarification, 'Will it be gone with everything else?' And Dasui says, 'It will be gone with everything else.'

Teachers always tailor their responses to the mind-state of the student. The monk wants some reassurance and some certainty – 'Tell me that *something* will survive!' And his question springs from a dualistic mind, an 'either-or' mind (is this one destroyed, or not?). This is similar to the koan Mu, where a monk asked Master Joshu, 'Does a dog have the Buddha Nature or not?' and Joshu says, 'Mu!' which means '[has] not'. Of course, the teaching is that everything has the Buddha Nature. Why then does Joshu say 'has not'? The sutras also say that Buddha Nature is unborn and undying. So what does Dasui mean when he says, 'It will be destroyed'?

In the Samyutta Nikaya the Buddha says, 'Is and is-not are the twin barbs on which all humanity is impaled.' Students have to find out for themselves what Joshu meant when he said 'Mu!' It's the same here. Dasui is giving a teaching here that relates perfectly to the monk's state of mind (the monk is clinging to an idea, and whatever we cling to is subject to birth and death), and is at the same time an expression of an absolute truth. Buddha Nature 'goes along with everything else' because you can't somehow separate it out from what is destroyed.

But in the verse to Case 23 in the *Mumonkan*, Think Neither Good Nor Evil, Master Mumon writes about Buddha Nature:

> *You describe it in vain, you picture it to no avail;*
> *You can never praise it fully; stop all your groping and manoeuvring.*
> *There is nowhere to hide your True-self.*
> *When the world is annihilated, 'it' remains, indestructible.*

This is the other side of the coin. The monk wants to be told that some 'thing', some entity will survive when everything is destroyed, but Dasui's response goes beyond concepts of destroyed and not-destroyed. Our longing for an 'is or is-not' type of answer comes out of a desire for a safe, secure place where we can rest. Of course, this longing is the cause of our suffering. We suffer because we cling to a notion of some underlying 'me' and the need to protect that 'me' against the slings and arrows of the world.

For 21st-century human beings this koan takes on new resonances, because we are now, as a species, agents, and not mere victims, of mass destruction. This knowledge has hung over us since the industrial-scale efficiency of Hitler's death camps and of the atomic bombs that the US dropped on Hiroshima and Nagasaki, and is now intensified as the planet overheats, the ice sheets melt, and floods, fires, droughts and famines become more and more frequent. Thus this question about the end of the world has become an immediate one, pressing in on all of us, at some level in our minds. The terror that this monk felt is our terror.

The possibility of a nuclear catastrophe was one of the things that initially brought me to practice. Back in the 1980s, as the Cold War entered its fourth decade, the United States and Soviet Union had about 40,000 nuclear warheads between them, and all these weapons were ready to be fired off, pointed at each other. At that time it seemed quite possible that a nuclear war could be started – possibly by accident – a war that would kill hundreds of thousands if not millions of people, contaminate vast areas, spark an unprecedented refugee crisis and perhaps cause what was known then as a nuclear winter.[3] Contemplating this possibility, a question would come up strongly. How would I respond? Would I rise to the occasion and be able to help others or would I just be a coward? I really couldn't answer this question, but it motivated me to practice. In 1984, working with these issues, I had a series of dreams in which I would witness the start of nuclear war. In one, after the first mushroom cloud has sent everyone underground, I discover a small Buddha figure in the hospital basement where I have taken shelter, and tearfully suggest to those around me that we do zazen together.

In his book, *The Fate of the Earth*, Jonathan Schnell explores how humankind's ballooning power to destroy has changed things:

> Such imponderables as the sum of human life, the integrity of the terrestrial creation, and the meaning of time, of history, and of the development of life on earth, which were once left to contemplation and spiritual understanding, are now at stake in the political realm and demand a political response from every person. As political actors we must, like contemplatives before us, delve to the bottom of the world, and Atlas-like we must take the world on our shoulders.

As Carl Jung said, the world hangs by a thread and that thread is the human psyche. The ecological catastrophe unfolding around us demands that we all become contemplatives *and* political actors. How can we respond adequately to life-and-death issues without delving into our minds and plumbing the depths of our own aggression, our own deepest fears, our own profound separation from our world and from the billions of people who suffer under our current system? Philosophical answers are in themselves not enough – they must be urgently put into practice in the ways we interact with others – the way we vote, how we participate

---

3. The theory was that if a large amount of material went up into the atmosphere it would block out the sun and have a similar cooling effect to a massive volcanic eruption.

in the democratic process, the groups we support, how we earn a living, what we eat and what we do with our leisure time.

Tenkei Denson (1648–1735), a Japanese Soto master, commenting on Dasui's 'It Goes Along with Everything Else', says:

> The underlying meaning is that the fire that consumes the universe at the end of the eon is already upon you all. So everyone should urgently make a thorough investigation. If you waste time hanging around, you will lose your life.[4]

The truth of annihilation that is brought into our consciousness so violently by the presence of nuclear weapons, and by our overheating planet, is not a new truth. But it is present in our world in a way that is clamouring to be recognised, to be seen and heard. The fire that consumes the universe is already upon us all, but also now, in our hands! The Italian poet and social reformer, Danilo Dolci, asked to comment on the apocalyptic world that we live in, said:

> It has been astutely observed that apocalypse contains the sense of unveiling or revelation, as well as that of ending. Yet what should we think of this complex of intuitions and nightmares, of desires, dreams and catastrophic fears? I believe that, for a person who is aware, every day has its own apocalypse, every day unveils itself, every day goes into dust. I find one remark of Jung's very telling: each one of us can discover and defuse our most secret traumas in order to set in motion an alternative way of life.[5]

Each of us is a human bomb that must be defused. If we are honest we can perhaps begin to see that the rise of the suicide bomber is not an aberration but a twisted expression of our collective human karma. In family systems theory the suicide bomber would be called the 'identified patient' – the family member who most obviously shows the pathology of the system. May our apocalypse be not a literal end, but one that reveals human society's pathology, the particular shape and flavour of its *dukkha* right here, right now. Because then healing can happen.

The flipside of realizing our destructive potential as human beings is the awareness that what we do *matters*. When our activities send a whole

4. Thomas Cleary, trans., *Secrets of the Blue Cliff Record: Zen Comments by Hakuin and Tenkei* (Boston: Shambhala, 2000), p. 92.

5. Danilo Dolci in *Facing Apocalypse* (Washington, D.C: Spring Publications, 1987), p. 110.

species into extinction, or cause an ecosystem or traditional culture to collapse, 'it' goes along with them. We lose our very life. But if we can take off our armour and defuse our most secret traumas, there is the possibility that we can come back into harmony with the rest of nature. Instead of letting the world overheat, can we throw our attachments on the pyre?

'The fire that consumes the universe at the end of the eon is already upon us all.' It is through allowing ourselves to be totally burnt up in our zazen, in our efforts to protect sentient beings, and in honestly facing global suffering, that we discover that which is indestructible. How can 'it' possibly be destroyed? It is not that we can go to some secure place called Buddha Nature and find safety there. There is no such place. There is no such thing as 'Buddha Nature', because if it's a thing then it can be destroyed. Rather, we can burn up in each moment, in our difficulties and conflicts and daily struggles. We can completely burn up so there is no residue. This is our refuge.

There is a coda to today's koan that doesn't appear in the case itself. After his exchange with Dasui, the monk didn't accept the answer he had received and went to visit another Zen master, probably hoping that this master would say that Dasui had got it wrong. So when he arrived he related the whole exchange. After listening, the second master lit a stick of incense, turned in the direction of Dasui's temple, and offered it, praising Dasui's response. He then urged the monk to go back and make his apologies to Dasui for not valuing his fine teaching. The monk followed the second master's instructions and returned to Dasui. The journey may have taken a long time, because when he got back he found that Dasui had died. The monk couldn't make his apologies and was even more perplexed. So he made the journey back to the second master again, perhaps in the hope that the second master would elaborate on why he found Dasui's answer to be so exceptional. But when he reached his destination he found that the second master had also died.

In this second half of the story the fact of destruction/impermanence is brought into the personal realm. In the first part the monk asks his cosmic question about the destruction of the universe, but now he is faced with something much more intimate — the passing away of his teachers. It is really a parable about missed opportunities; the monk had the chance to learn from these two masters, but he wasn't ready to hear their teachings; he was caught up in trying to pin down 'is or is-not'. Meanwhile life kept flowing on.

The Earth has survived five previous periods of mass extinction, each time remaking herself over a period of 10 to 30 million years. The Earth will bounce back, and, though we humans and many of our fellow sentient beings may not survive, 'the force that through the green fuse drives the flower' will bloom once more. But this does not mean that we should just fatalistically participate in the destruction of our biosphere. Not at all. We must do everything we can to avert collapse. We can take on the prospect of the destruction of our biosphere, and our part in it, as a way of waking up to both our own fragility and that of the world. The old dream is the human-centric one, a nightmare of separation from the rest of nature and from much of humanity as well. We need to see ourselves as sustainers, not consumers; as upholders of the Dharma living in a Mahasangha that excludes no one and no thing. If not, we will be like the monk in the koan, missing our chance to wake up, and then finding that our teachers – the penguin, the cheetah, the coral reef and all the rest – have gone.

We'll stop here and recite the four vows.

*   *

*

Great is the matter of birth and death.
Life flows swiftly by; time waits for no one.
Wake up! Wake up!
Don't waste a moment.

—VERSE OF THE HAN

* * *

CHAPTER 10

Investigating the Great Matter

IN encouraging us to take up the practice of zazen, Master Dogen tells us to 'take the backward step and turn the light inward.' Zazen is based on the faith that answers to our deepest questions about the Great Matter of Birth and Death can only be found by looking within, and that within ourselves we will find all that we truly need. But, as has become increasingly clear with each chapter of this book, this inner-directed search will, if conducted with clarity and sincerity, take us in some unexpected directions. We find that we cannot take on this search in isolation; not only do we benefit from the support of Sangha and teacher, but we benefit as well from offering our support to Sangha and teacher, and, as best as we are able, to all beings. This is inevitable, of course, because our True Nature does not exist in isolation, and the further we go with our inward search, the more we discover our dependence on and interconnectedness with everything else. Thus, like ripples in a pool, the topics of successive chapters in this book have moved progressively outwards: from the first decision to attend a group sitting or to start working with a teacher, through committing to ethical behaviour in our interactions with others, to bringing our work out into society at large.

But as our practice draws us outwards into personal and social engagement, we need to be sure that it continues on its inward course as well. Sometimes these two movements, inwards and outwards, will support each other in a harmonious equilibrium; but often we can feel pulled between them. Where should we best direct our energy and time?

For many people the initial impulse to practice zazen is triggered by questions about life and its meaning. Who am I and how did I get here? What does it mean to be a human being and how should I use my life? What are birth and death? Sometimes the questions have arisen with acute force following a loss or trauma: the death of a loved one, the break-up of a relationship, even the loss of a job or a relocation. In the natural course of events, time has a tendency to heal our wounds, and to dull the strength of our questioning. But Zen practice leads us in the opposite direction. Zen asks us to resist the impulse to brush our fundamental questions aside; instead of avoiding the discomfort and existential angst to which such questions may give rise, we are encouraged as we move forward in practice to concentrate and intensify our questioning. Instead of letting the mind's energy disperse as we ponder our various problems from a philosophical or psychological point of view, we work with our teacher to find the 'right question'. Then, focusing the energy of all our doubts, confusions, and perplexity into the one practice that we have been assigned, we use this single practice much as we would use a magnifying glass to start a fire.

As our questioning deepens, it can also become more and more continuous. We all need some time each day to simply do the formal practice, to dive deeply into silence as we hone our one-pointed concentration. But as we learn to be more single-minded, we can begin to see everything through the lens of practice. Thus whatever we encounter in our daily life becomes not so much a distraction *from* practice as a reminder *to* practice. Anything that comes up can be used to reawaken our wonder, reignite our investigation and nurture our compassion. Moreover, the issues that we encounter through our engagement with the world at large can serve as strong catalysts for some of our deepest questions. The crisis faced by humanity on a planetary level that we delved into in our last chapter is a prime example of this. Or consider the experience of Roshi Kapleau, who served as a court recorder at the war crimes tribunals held in Germany and Japan after World War II. Months of listening to accounts of the most heinous crimes against humanity led directly to his intense interest in Zen practice.

We might also remember the example of the Buddha himself. The well-known story of the Four Sights relates how Prince Siddhartha, having been brought up in the most luxurious and protected of environments, gained permission from his father to leave the palace grounds for the first time when he was 29 years old and on the cusp of taking on some of the responsibility for the governance of his kingdom. With his charioteer Channa, the future Buddha made several journeys into the city, each time seeing a sight he had never seen before: an old person, a sick person, a corpse, and a monk in meditation. Each sight had to be explained to him by Channa, and Siddhartha, for the first time, had to grapple with the fact that sickness, old age and death come to each of us — including even himself, his young wife, and his newborn baby son. Upon seeing the fourth sight, Siddhartha realised that he, too, must discover for himself the peace which radiated from the monk in meditation.

Of course it may seem highly fantastical that an intelligent, well-educated young man of 29 had never seen, experienced, or even heard of sickness, old age or death. But this story is pointing to the fact that although each of us may have heard of these things, we have not truly taken them on board. In the Samyuktagama Sutra, the Buddha taught that there are four types of people: those who hear of a death in a neighbouring village and thereupon realise the truth of impermanence and the need to practice; those who realise this truth upon hearing of a death in their own village; those who do so after experiencing a death in their own family; and those who only realise the truth of impermanence when on their own death bed.

A traditional verse inscribed on the wooden block (*han*) that hangs outside the zendo of most monasteries and Zen centres refers to the Great Matter of Birth and Death that is at the root of our search:

> *Great is the matter of birth and death.*
> *Life flows swiftly by; time waits for no one.*
> *Wake up! Wake up!*
> *Don't waste a moment.*

In describing her own call to practice, Zen teacher Blanche Hartman begins by quoting this verse of the *han*, and then tells us that the great Indian ancestor Nagarjuna said that *bodhicitta*, the desire for awakening in order to awaken others, is above all aroused by seeing the impermanence of our world of birth and death. Hartman says:

This was very true for me. This is what turned me toward practice. I was going along, living my life, when one day my best friend had a really bad headache. She went to the doctor the next day, was diagnosed with an inoperable brain tumor, went into a coma and died. Whoosh! Just like that. I was stunned.

Often we don't think so much about birth and death until someone close to us – particularly a contemporary – or even someone younger than us, is suddenly dying, and then we get it that we are also impermanent. In that great Indian classic, the Mahabarata, there's a passage where a great sage is asked: 'Sir, of all of the things you've observed in life, what is the most amazing?' And he responds: 'That a man seeing all around him die, never thinks that he will die.' That's certainly the way I was until my friend Pat died.[1]

On the other hand, it is not always difficult circumstances or personal tragedies that give rise to the sudden pressure of questions, but sometimes just the opposite. Co-author Kathryn reports:

As a young adult, I had found myself thoroughly caught up in the busyness of pursuing a career, being a wife, raising children, and trying to establish the financial stability to make it all work. In my mid-forties, as my children approached adolescence, I suddenly felt that I had a moment to come up for air and look around me. My marriage was happy; my children were wonderful. We were all in good health, we had just bought a new house, and I had a job I really enjoyed. But ... was this it, then? Was there no

1. http://www.chzc.org/hartman5.htm

more to life? What did it all mean? Why did I still so often feel unhappy and unsettled? And why was there so much suffering in the world, and what could I, with all my good fortune, possibly do about it? Stumbling upon the Rochester Zen Center at this moment in my life, I soon found myself working on the koan 'Mu' as a way to focus my questioning.

In Zen training, koan work is often offered for this purpose. But working with a koan is not the only way to approach the Great Matter. Not only do we bring our own circumstances to the practice, but we bring our own temperaments as well, and the practice that our teacher helps us to choose – in the Zen tradition this will generally be either breath practice, koan work, or shikantaza ('just sitting') – should match both our temperament and our circumstances. If one is gripped by existential doubts and feels that one simply 'has to know', then koan work may be the best choice. If one has confidence that 'from the very beginning all beings are Buddha' and that whenever we sit in zazen we are expressing and unveiling our Buddha-nature, then breath practice or shikantaza may be more appropriate. Breath practice in particular may also be assigned as a means to calm and settle the body-mind.

But even more important than the choice one makes is knowing that no choice is really the wrong one; it is rather as if the different practices highlight different facets of the same work. In fact, whatever practice we have been assigned, we really need to cultivate simultaneously an attitude of exploration as well as an attitude of faith. If we are working on a koan, our approach will emphasise such qualities as questioning and meticulous investigation, but we need to guard against becoming overwrought, overly tight or focussed on attainment. A strong underlying sense of trust in our innate perfection will help us move our questioning away from being a source of tension and more towards a kind of wonderment. If we are working with the breath, on the other hand, or doing shikantaza, our approach will focus on being present, being without goals, and letting go of any thoughts or feelings that arise. But here, the danger is one of falling into 'dead sitting', a kind of quietism which may be enjoyable, but where there is dullness rather than awareness. Remembering that we have come to practice in order to wake up, to see things as they are, and to work for the liberation of all beings, can help to energize the practice and keep our minds open and alert.

Sometimes people come to the practice with pressing questions and they may wonder 'how long it will take'. At what point will they find the answers they are looking for and be done with the tedious practice of sitting still? Particularly if we are working on a koan we may be impatient to find 'the right answer'. But as the 'answers' offered by Zen practice begin to emerge, it is rather the intrinsic worth of the practice itself that is revealed more and more clearly. In sitting zazen we give expression both to our own enlightened nature and to our determination to work for the enlightenment of all beings. The practice involves great patience, but at the same time our patience and our potential are increasingly revealed to us through the process of practice itself. So if we find ourselves struggling with a koan, it may help to remember that for most people the work on an initial koan is a long and multi-faceted process, one which may be marked by sudden breakthroughs, or which may, on the other hand, more closely resemble the process of flowing water gradually wearing away a stone. But either way, letting go of our preconceptions about that process is essential, as is recognising that each person's process is unique.

Whatever our practice, we each of us bring our own habits and experiences – our own karma – to the work, and as the practice reveals those habits and our own particular karmic formations more and more clearly, they can eventually begin to shift. Any single shift may be more or less powerful, and more or less transformative, but there is always further to go – while, at the same time, there has never been anywhere to go from the very beginning.

Zen takes courage and commitment. Investigating the Great Matter can at times be scary, disorienting, frustrating and confusing, and it has been said that the single main job of a Zen teacher is simply to find ways to encourage the student to keep going through all of this. Zen practice does not, fundamentally, take place on an intellectual or discursive level, and the answers that we seek will not come on a discursive level either. This investigation is a process without beginning or end in the conventional sense, as Master Dogen so famously said:

> There is no beginning to practice nor end to enlightenment, there is no beginning to enlightenment nor end to practice.

Zazen is not a difficult task. Just free yourself from all incoming thoughts and hold your mind like a great iron wall. Think of your own room as the whole world, and that all sentient beings are sitting there with you, as one.

Make a searching examination of yourself. Realise that your body is not your body. It is part of the body of sentient beings. Your mind is not your mind. It is but a constituent of all mind. Your eyes, your ears, your nose, your tongue, your hands and your feet are not merely your individual belongings but are in joint ownership with all sentient beings. You simply call them yours — and others'. You cling to your own being and consider others separate from you. It is nothing but a baseless delusion of yours.

Just free yourself from all incoming complications and hold your mind like a great iron wall. No matter what sort of contending thoughts arise in you, ignore them and they will soon perish and disappear of themselves. And just as soon as your thought expands and unites with the universe, you are free from your stubborn ego.

You will then enter into where there is no relativity, no absoluteness. You are now transcendent, far above both discrimination and equality. You have nothing to receive and there is nothing to receive you. There is no time, no space. There is no past, no future, but one eternal present.

This is not the true realisation, but you are walking near the palace. Just free yourself of all incoming disturbances and hold your mind like a great iron wall. Then one day you will meet your true self as if you had awakened from a dream, and will have the happiness you could never have derived otherwise. Zazen is not a difficult task. It is a way to lead you to your long-lost home.

— Soyen Shaku (1860–1919), adapted from the translation by Nyogen Senzaki that appears in *Like a Dream, Like a Fantasy*, edited by Eido Shimano (Japan Publications, 1978), pp. 100–101.

TEISHO

* * *

Tsunami

(2005–01–09)

In this teisho, Amala-sensei brings together the teachings of Buddhism and of science to grapple with the Great Matter of Birth and Death.

Today, we're going to talk about the tsunami which happened two weeks ago in the Indian Ocean.[2] What can we learn from it? Such catastrophic events always raise questions for people. There was an article in the Herald by a journalist who put the words 'God' and 'Tsunami' into Google and came up with 800,000 hits. So clearly it has inspired a lot of people to question, perhaps more so this time because of its timing, the day after Christmas. And the kind of question that comes up for believers in God, is, what kind of a God could allow such a thing to happen?

In Buddhism we don't have a God-concept; we don't posit an all-merciful, all-powerful deity to whom we look for protection. But this still doesn't let us off the hook in coming to terms with such violent cataclysms, where there is so much suffering. So in this talk I want to look at this particular cataclysm and see what we can learn from it. But I'd like to preface this investigation by saying that what we talk about this morning is not meant for the victims, it's meant for us, who are regarding this event at some distance from it. Victims don't need words. They need concrete help. Shelter, food, comforting arms. They have to do their own work of coming to terms with an event such as this, that completely turns their lives upside-down. But we're called upon to face such events as well, and that's what this talk is going to be about.

We'll start by looking at what happened.

On the 26th of December at about 8:00 am local time, an earthquake occurred along the thousand-kilometre faultline off the coastline of Sumatra, where the Eurasian and the Australian tectonic plates meet. It was a massive quake, nine on the Richter scale. The sea floor ruptured, and the sea bed was vertically jolted. One scientist said it was as if there was a big paddle on the ocean floor that had suddenly been pushed up. This

2. 26 December, 2004. 275,000 people were killed in 14 countries.

upheaval displaced hundreds of cubic kilometres of water, and huge waves fanned out in two directions across the Indian Ocean, pretty much along a north-south axis, and these waves created destruction for the next seven hours as they intersected land.

It took only 15 minutes for the waves to reach Sumatra. These waves were going at 800 kilometres an hour, an incredible speed. After 30 minutes, the waves hit the Andaman Islands, after 90 minutes Sri Lanka, in two hours they reached Thailand, in three the Maldives, and after seven hours they hit the coast of Africa. You can get some sense of what a huge global event this was from the fact that geophysicists at NASA were able to detect the earth spinning on its axis microseconds faster than it usually does. And the whole earth actually tilted 2.5 cm on its axis. It's amazing to think that we can measure such minute changes, but apparently we can.

The reason why these waves are so destructive is that out at sea they're not very high, but when they reach coastal waters they simultaneously slow down and increase in height. It's a bit like cars on a motorway. If the front car stops there's still all this energy in the cars behind, so they keep going fast and end up piling up on top of the cars in front. And what happens when the water reaches shallower areas is that the front of the wave slows down but the back of the wave keeps going fast and so it builds up; it piles up into a massive wave. There's nowhere for the water to go but up. So in some places the waves were two stories high.

Just imagine how frightening it would be to face such a wave. Ten metres, or more than 30 feet — and not just one wave, but several, at intervals between about 5 and 14 minutes. At one place in Sri Lanka the water from the waves reached a whole kilometre inland. In many places there was very, very little warning — and in most places there was actually none except for the receding of the tide, hundreds of metres out, the seabed left exposed. And at that point people had maybe 10 or 15 minutes to flee. Further inland, if you weren't right at the beach, the only warning would be an almighty roar. Some people, when they heard this thought it was a terrorist attack of some kind.

So that's the basic mechanics of this event. But for us human beings, when catastrophes like this happen, we very naturally want to know not just *what* happened but *why*. We may cast about for an explanation, even for something or someone to blame. Could better warning systems, for example, have prevented so much death? It's unlikely that much could have been done in Sumatra where there were only 15 minutes between the earthquake and the waves, but elsewhere, if there had been more timely warnings and a better-coordinated response, many, many lives could have been saved.

Geophysicists in Hawaii knew 15 minutes after the earthquake that there could be huge waves, and they actually did try to contact the countries involved. The Pacific Tsunami Warning Center sent alerts to 26 countries including Thailand and Indonesia, but struggled to reach the right people. 'We tried to do what we could,' said the Centre's director, Charles MacCreary. 'We don't have any contacts in our address book for anybody in that particular part of the world.' Just imagine what these geophysicists are going through now wondering what more could have been done, what an agonising place it must be for them, knowing now just how much devastation there has been.

On the coast of Africa where there were seven hours between the earthquake and the waves, Kenyan police cleared the beaches, but that was the exception. Everywhere else nothing was done and hundreds of people died. The worst was Somalia which is of course in the grips of civil war as well. Negative effects of natural forces are compounded by human failings.

There is a story of some men from New Zealand far from the shore off a beach in Thailand. They were diving deep and they noticed that suddenly the visibility went from about 20 metres down to about two metres, and they realised there must have been something happening, but they had no idea out there in the deep water just what was happening, and so they just kept diving for the rest of the day. When they got home, they found their wives and children were safe. And the reason they were safe was because the police had cleared that particular beach. Very little notice is being given to this, but it's quite a sobering thought, that the message must have got through in some form to these beaches on the coast of Thailand, but there was only one place where the police took the message seriously and cleared the beach. Some people have suggested that perhaps nothing was done because there was concern about what it would do to the tourist trade. So here we see how lack of awareness can turn into something more sinister.

Even if we put questions of technology and politics aside, there were warning signs in many places. One of the most interesting reports was about the Yala Wildlife Park in Sri Lanka. People going in thought that they would find huge numbers of drowned animals. But they didn't. Of 250 tourist vehicles that entered the park on that day, only 30 came back. So most of the people in the park perished. But the animals didn't. Sensing something, we don't know what — there have been speculations over what might have been the impetus for these animals to move — but at any rate, they sensed something and they moved to higher ground and were saved. And there are many other stories of similar things. Elephants in Thailand at a certain resort cried and cried until their mahouts moved away from the beaches, saving the tourists who were being given rides. The elephants who weren't working, who were chained up, broke their chains in order to flee. And in the Andaman Islands there are some very ancient tribes living in the bush. The islands are low and there were fears that these tribes would have been wiped out. But in fact they weren't. They were able to read the warning signs, perhaps the movements of animals, and they also moved away from the coasts. Apparently in their mythology there are stories of shrinking islands, so perhaps hundreds of years ago, or repeatedly over thousands of years, there may have been great waves, and the memory of them is preserved in their culture.

Unfortunately, modern industrial people have lost the sensitivity that comes from living for many generations in one place closely observing its rhythms. Instead, we tend to imagine nature as outside of ourselves, as a force to be opposed. This was illustrated beautifully during the tsunami by what has become a quite famous photograph that appeared on the cover of the Herald either on Boxing Day or maybe the day after, and it was of this surging wave with one small person floating in it — you could just see his head, it was a young man. And the caption or the title on the photo was 'One Against Nature'.

But in fact, it wasn't one against nature at all. About a week after the disaster some enterprising reporter found this young man and there was another photograph of him, now dressed and on solid ground, and one of the things he said in his interview was that he realised when he was swept up in the wave that the only way he could survive it was not by fighting it, but by going with it.

But so much of our activity in the modern world puts us at odds with the rhythms and requirements of nature. Friends of the Earth pointed out that the destruction of mangrove forests and coral reefs made the effects of the tsunami much worse in some places in Thailand. Mangrove forests and coral reefs have been replaced by hotels and highways and shrimp farms.

So we can see how the actions or inactions of human beings may have compounded the suffering caused by this tsunami. And we can see how our advanced technologies and communication systems were life-saving in some instances, but also that vast improvements are called for. But we can also see the limitations of such a discussion. It doesn't really get at our deepest *why's*. Why do such things have to happen in the first place? Why do people have to die? Why is there so much suffering?

In Zen practice, when we find ourselves caught up in questions of 'why', our teacher is apt to tell us to let go of the 'why' and just ask 'what'. This can be good advice for our meditation practice, and it can be instructive as well in the face of a catastrophe such as this one. We have already reviewed the basic mechanics of this event. But let's take a closer look. In Zen we don't separate the material and spiritual realms; there's just this one reality. And that means that the 'why' is right there already in the 'what', to some degree at least.

Earthquakes happen when the plates that make up the earth's surface suddenly move against each other. A tension builds up between these great floating pieces of the earth's crust, and something has to give. And so there's a slippage one way or the other. And tsunamis happen when the plates in question are under the sea. (Volcanic eruptions sometimes also cause tsunamis — there were big tsunamis after the great explosion of Krakatoa in Indonesia.) So these events happen because of the dynamics of our earth, because of its fundamental makeup. What we live on, the tectonic plates, are like islands floating on the surface of the earth's mantle. One scientist in explaining this held up an apple. He said, 'The earth's crust is like the skin on this apple. It's very thin. Underneath there's a seething mass of molten rock, the magma.'

We human beings and all the other sentient beings on this earth are, to use an old expression, skating on thin ice. We're living on a very thin unstable crust above a seething mass of molten rock. The analogy of boiled milk is also used. You know what it's like after you've boiled milk, you get a thin soft skin on the surface that moves around on the liquid underneath. That's how delicate and unstable this ground we live on is.

This crust is not entirely distinct from the deeper liquid layers of the earth. At the point where the tectonic plates meet, sometimes the crust, the surface plate, will sink down and be reabsorbed into the molten lava of the earth's mantle. Or at times the lava rises up through the cracks and spills out – that's volcanic activity. In Auckland we live on formations that have come out of such activity. Everything around us here in Auckland is evidence of the dynamic life process of our earth, and sometime within the next thousand years, there will be another eruption. We don't know when, but judging from the history of our land here, it will happen at some point.

This earth we live on is unstable. It's full of tension. But it's this very tension that gives life to everything. If it weren't for this instability, there would be no human beings, and no other sentient beings existing at all. We have to go a little bit further back into the history of the earth and the solar system to appreciate this. It turns out that the existence of abundant life on this planet is a function of its size. There are two different kinds of strong bonds which are active in our universe (and also two kinds of weak bonds which we don't need to discuss here). The strong ones are gravitational bonds and electromagnetic bonds. Gravitational bonds are the attraction between different masses, and electromagnetic bonds are the attraction between protons and electrons; they are also what hold atoms together to form molecules. So you have these two types of attraction working in the universe. With gravity, it gets stronger when there's more mass. I weigh less on the moon because of its smaller mass. Electromagnetic forces work differently. Positively charged protons and negatively charged electrons bind together to create atoms.

When our solar system was born, all the planets in our system began evolving. But in the end, only this planet, the Earth, has produced life as we know it. Of course we don't know everything about the other planets, and maybe we'll discover things there which we could call life, but the Earth has developed incredible complexity in its life forms in comparison with the other planets in our solar system. We can take two planets as contrasting examples which throw light on just how extraordinary it is that life exists on our particular planet at all. One example is Mars which is smaller than Earth. There all the chemical creativity got choked off fairly early on, because the bonds between atoms won out against the gravitational forces. Whereas here on Earth we have a very thin crust with lots of vitality beneath it, on Mars the crust got thicker and thicker. So Mars now is rock, solid rock, all the way through. The strength of those molecular bonds just choked off the possibilities for change. On Jupiter which is much larger than Earth, you have the opposite happening. Huge gravitational forces on Jupiter meant that molecules beyond the simplest couldn't hold together, they would just get pulled apart by gravity. So Jupiter is mostly gas. As far as we know Jupiter never even got to create rocks let alone more differentiated and complex forms of life.

But here on Earth there is a delicate balance between gravitational and electrical forces. The two are held in a creative tension. And so we have at the surface a thin solidified crust where the molecules hold together in a myriad of forms and beneath it the churning liquid mantle and beneath that a solid and incredibly hot centre. We are living on a semi-liquid Earth, a planet that is flowing and changing, vibrantly alive, not static at all.

Through this examination we can begin to see how earthquakes and upheavals in the great ocean that gave birth to us are unavoidable. We can begin to see that we live in a world that is inherently violent and unstable. Mars, which has a solid crust, without tectonic plates, is much more static. We can't say anything is entirely dead, but timeframes on Mars are slowed right down; there's not so much happening there. But here on Earth, we have abundant life. And the fact is, there can be no life without tension and instability – without impermanence. Because it's when things are unstable, when there's a tension or imbalance between two points, that things flow. So this instability is the nature of life. It is a requirement of life.

Nor is it just what life *out there* is like – it is not the case that we can stand and observe life's processes, that somehow the natural disaster is one thing, but we're something else. In fact, we *are* life, and we can't stand outside and observe this process of impermanence.

Our Earth is constantly teaching us through such devastating events as earthquakes and tsunamis. And it is constantly pointing out to us the First Noble Truth: that life is *dukkha*. This word *dukkha* is usually translated as suffering, unsatisfactoriness or sometimes misery, but if we go back to its roots, *dukkha* may refer to an axle hole which is off-centre. So another way of thinking of *dukkha* is when things feel out of kilter, out of whack. And when we examine the way our whole Earth works, we begin to understand that there can only be life when things *are* slightly out of kilter. There can only be creation, movement, development, when there is destruction, because the creation has to come out of something.

So the Buddha really meant it when he said that life is out of kilter. There's no other way to do life. And if you are living, if you have a body, then there's no way that the primal aspects of *dukkha* can be avoided. Death cannot be avoided. Loss cannot be avoided.

On the other hand, what the Buddha actually said is that all *conditioned things* are unsatisfactory, which you sometimes hear stated as '*unenlightened* life is suffering'. And certainly it's true that certain aspects of *dukkha*, of suffering, of misery, can be transcended through awakening, and through seeing clearly who and what we are. So there is loss and change, and then there is all the stuff that we add to these fundamental experiences that come with being alive. Strongly identifying with our apparent self, terrified by even the prospect of loss, often we human beings shut down, we constrict our hearts and grasp at what we imagine to be solid and reliable. This is the *dukkha* that we really can do something about. But how can we learn to do that? How do we learn to live with the awesome power of the earth and its waters and winds which can wipe us out just by flicking their tail so to speak? In his book *Living With the Devil* Stephen Batchelor says:

> The very earth that can leave you dumb with wonder as you contemplate its selfless unfolding will destroy you with neither malice nor mercy should its tectonic plates shift beneath your feet. Sublimely indifferent to our hopes and fears, life snuffs us out at death no matter how tenaciously we cling to it.[3]

We're terrified by this impersonal force that has so little regard for us as individuals. Shantideva, the great writer of *The Way of the Bodhisattva*, said:

> The untrustworthy Lord of Death waits not for things to be done or undone. Whether I am sick or healthy, this fleeting lifespan is unstable.[4]

This fleeting life cannot be trusted. We can't rely on it to be a certain way. All we can do, if we are functioning from a place of awakening, is to unite with our circumstances completely – whatever they are. When

3. Stephen Batchelor, *Living with the Devil* (New York: Riverhead, 2004), pp. 23–4.

4. Shantideva, *The Guide to the Bodhisattva's Way of Life*, translated by Stephen Batchelor (Dharamsala: Library of Tibetan Works and Archives, 1979), p. 15.

you think about it, if you're swept up by a tsunami, you don't really have any choice but to embrace it — it has embraced you.

And yet, try as we might to accept this on an intellectual level, that these disasters are an inevitable part of life, on the emotional level we still may wonder, why did so many children have to die? And why did *these* people have to die, while *those* were saved? This is something that often will come up for survivors, or parents — for parents who survived, whose children die, there may be the extreme pain of asking, why did they have to die? Why couldn't I have died? But children in a very real sense are closer to death than adults. They're more vulnerable. Their lungs are smaller. Their arms and legs don't have the same strength or their bodies the same stamina. It's less likely that they know how to swim. And so they're often the first to be gobbled up by these enormous forces.

But why is one child saved while another perishes? The most honest answer that we can give to this question is that we just don't know. Of course, as Buddhists, we could certainly say that a particular child dies because it is his or her karma to die. But what does that really mean? Karma simply means that all things have a cause. So saying that somebody dies because it's their karma is really just saying that causes and conditions led them to die. Or they survived because causes and conditions allowed them to survive. Karma is counted among the five imponderables in Buddhism, among the things that are deeply, deeply complex and mysterious. It doesn't really provide us with easy answers.

On the television there was a piece on the experiences of some of the survivors of this cataclysmic event. One was a young British tourist, she was probably about 20, who was interviewed at the airport. She was weeping because a fellow tourist, another young woman, had asked if she could hold her hand, and she refused saying she knew that if they held hands they would both be dragged down. All she could think of now was watching this other girl sink into the water and drown.

Another story was of a local woman with five children, five little children, all under about age six or seven, and her terrible dilemma as the wave approached...which one do I pick up? In the end, all five children drowned.

There's a similar story in the *Therigatha* about Patachara, one of the early disciples of the Buddha, who, to cut a long story short, was crossing a river in flood with her two children. She'd just given birth to the second child and was very weak, so she couldn't cross with both of them. She left the older child on the bank, carried her baby across the raging river, put him down on the far side, and then started to go back for the older child. As she was going back, an eagle came down and plucked up her baby off the shore. She couldn't do anything, she was in the middle of the river, and she started screaming and screaming, and her older child on the farther bank thought he was being called so he jumped into the river to go to her and was drowned. Earlier she'd found her husband dead from a snake bite. After this she returned home to find that the flood had completely destroyed her parents' home and her parents and her brother were also dead. She became crazed at all this loss, and eventually came before the Buddha, naked, and in a state of derangement. He spoke these words to her:

> The four oceans contain but a little water compared to all the tears that we have shed, smitten by sorrow, bewildered by pain. Why, O woman, are you still heedless?

All the water of these great waves that struck the coasts around the Indian Ocean, these hundreds of cubic kilometres of water, cannot be compared to the tears that have been shed over the eons by people suffering great loss. This is the nature of the world in which we live.

We'll finish with another passage from *Living with the Devil* by Stephen Batchelor:

> The infinitely poignant beauty of creation is inseparable from its diabolic destructiveness. How to live in such a turbulent world with wisdom, tolerance, empathy, care, and non-violence, is what saints and philosophers have struggled over the centuries to articulate. What is striking about the Buddhist approach is that rather than positing an immortal or transcendent self that is immune to the vicissitudes of the world, Buddha insisted that salvation lies in discarding such consoling fantasies and embracing instead the very stuff of life that will destroy you.[5]

We'll stop here and recite the four vows.

* *

*

5. *Op. cit.*, p. 10.

Layman Pang was sitting in his thatched cottage one day studying the sutras.

'Difficult! Difficult! Difficult!' he suddenly exclaimed. 'Like trying to store ten bushels of sesame seed in the top of a tree.'

'Easy! Easy! Easy!' his wife, Laywoman Pang answered. 'It's like touching your feet to the ground when you get out of bed.'

'Neither difficult nor easy,' said their daughter Lingzhao. 'It's like the teachings of the ancestors shining on the hundred grass tips.'

— The Recorded Sayings of Layman Pang

CHAPTER 11

* * *

Intensive Practice: Sesshin

Sesshin always takes us beyond ourselves. Meditation undertaken intensively over successive days becomes a journey into the Unknown. That's the nature of contemplative work — we're leaving behind what we know (or think we know) in order to make new discoveries ... Sesshin is a true adventure, with its traps and treasures, unforeseen events, and strange occurrences that we can't know beforehand, no matter how many sesshins we've attended. Every sesshin is a 'first' because not one of us is the same each time.

—Roshi Bodhin Kjolhede[1]

1. Quotations in this chapter from Roshi Kjolhede are from an unpublished manuscript on 'Sesshin.' We are very grateful for permission to draw from this work for this chapter.

FOR Zen practitioners, it is above all in sesshin, the traditional week-long Zen retreat, that we have a chance to 'shine the light inward' and single-mindedly dive into our particular practice. While a consistent routine of daily sitting is the foundation of Zen practice, it is only after attending a sesshin that many of us feel we have come to appreciate the full potential of zazen. At times daily practice can feel a bit like bailing water. In the minutes or hours that we find for our sitting each day we can counteract to some degree the busyness, over-stimulation and stress of our lives in the modern world, but when we stand up from the mat we may quickly be caught up in the maelstrom again.

Although there is no doubt that in an hour or even 30 minutes of meditation we can experience a wonderful shift in our nervous system, our consciousness and our mood, in most cases this shift is taking place at a relatively shallow level – and sesshin reveals, above all, that there are layers and layers more to be explored. Yasutani-roshi (Kapleau-roshi's main teacher) liked to describe our minds by making an analogy to a ball-point pen. In this analogy, our discursive, thinking mind represents the tip of the pen. It is important, because it is functional – we can't write without this tip. But it is just a tiny part of our vast mind, and, for most of us, this tiny bit is the only part we are truly aware of. Sesshin offers the opportunity to begin to explore the unknown territory that lies beyond our discursive thinking.

Our method for undertaking this exploration is radically simple: at all times and to the best of our ability, to stay with our practice. Before attending sesshin we may certainly have been told by our teacher, 'Just the breath!' or 'Just Mu!' But it is only in sesshin that we begin to get a sense of what it might really mean to pour our whole mind, heart and being into this one focal point, hour after hour, day after day. The beauty of sesshin is that everything, down to the most minute detail, is designed to support us in this task.

In sesshin, in stark contrast to our daily life, we have almost no decisions to make, and almost no responsibilities. Our seat in the zendo, our seat in the dining room, and our bedroom are assigned to us. We don't have to decide what to wear, as we are all dressed alike in brown robes. We don't have to decide when or what to eat as we simply file into the dining room at the sound of the gong, and the food is presented to us. There is nothing to buy, no errands to run, no calls to make. We don't even have to know what time it is, as there is a timer to sound all the bells, drums and gongs that signal for us when to get up, when to eat, when to come to the zendo, when to rest. The guidelines we have agreed to follow prohibit any kind of reading or use of a phone or other electronic device. Thus our minds are truly free to do just this one thing.

Of course that doesn't mean that doing it becomes easy! When we are placed in this rarefied atmosphere free of distractions, we may experience something similar to what many people experience when they first take up meditation: the mind, paradoxically, seems busier than ever. We may find that, instead of settling down, our mind begins to grasp at any possible internal or external stimulus in what amounts to a kind of panic at being left without any of its usual preoccupations. Little things can start to seem immense, whether slight physical discomforts that we obsess over until we convince ourselves that we must be dying, or small noises in the zendo: if only the person sitting next to me would *stop* breathing in that annoying fashion, then I would be able to concentrate and get somewhere with my practice! Sesshin can become a long parade of such 'if onlys'.

Placed in a situation where we have so few choices, we may be amazed to observe our reactivity and judgmentalism about virtually every small thing. We begin to see how much energy we put into 'picking and choosing' each day, into trying to arrange things the way we like them rather than the way we don't like them. But in sesshin, as often as not, things are *not* the way we want them to be! And once we are able not only to observe that fact, but to actually accept it and relax into it, this can be a wonderful gift. We can't change anything about sesshin, so we just have to go with it. And if we can stop assessing, stop worrying about whether we are feeling okay or doing okay, and just be present with what is, then suddenly everything opens up and becomes not just bearable but vividly alive.

A sesshin takes place over a relatively short period of time – a single week is the standard length for a full sesshin – but each hour of those seven days forms part of a precisely orchestrated schedule. As a glance at the inset overleaf (p. 217) will show, this schedule is a challenging one, involving a very early rise and many hours of formal sitting each day. Unlike retreats offered in some other traditions, in the lineage of the Auckland Zen Centre all the elements of the schedule are required unless there are medical reasons for not participating, and those accepted to sesshin sign an agreement to complete the full number of days for which they have applied. The result is that sesshin attendance effectively compels us to do much more than we would have been able to do on our own and indeed more than we would have thought possible.

The quality of our practice is likewise supported by the structure of sesshin, and in particular by the three basic guidelines which govern all of sesshin, and which compel us to patterns strikingly different than those of our daily life. The first guideline is to maintain silence. There is no talking in sesshin outside of dokusan. For many of us, it may be hard even to imagine keeping silence for a solid week; but this is an absolutely crucial part of moving beyond our surface thoughts. The purpose of the outer silence is to create a space in which inner silence can emerge, where our endless inner chatter and commentary can give up its hold on us, or at least slow down; and although, when we first dive into the near-total silence of sesshin, the surface thoughts may seem more numerous and insistent than ever, we need to have confidence that the outer silence will eventually do its job. Becoming aware of our incessant mental activity is, of course, an essential first step.

In addition to not talking, various other guidelines serve to deepen the silence of sesshin. We try to walk quietly, to open and close doors slowly and carefully rather than letting them fall shut, to eat without excessive clanking of our cutlery, and so forth. All of these are important mindfulness practices as well as supporting others by minimising distractions.

The second basic sesshin guideline after silence is to keep the eyes down. This second guideline is actually an extension of the first in that it creates a sort of visual silence. As a corollary to our verbal silence, this visual silence functions to limit communication. There are many ways that we communicate with each other nonverbally, such as through eye contact, facial expression, body language and gesture, and the instruction to keep the eyes down makes clear that we are not to engage in such forms of communication any more than we are to engage in verbal conversation. Instead, each person's attention is directed inward on their own work, and each person allows the other participants the personal space to do *their* own work without being distracted or observed. It is fascinating to learn, over the course of a sesshin, how the slightest thing that we see or attend to in our environment can set off a cascade of thoughts and judgements; and though this will inevitably happen at times, we can significantly cut down

SESSHIN SCHEDULE

4:10 Wakeup

4:30 Outdoor Kinhin

4:45 Zazen*

5:15 Chanting Service

5:45 Zazen with dokusan

7:00 Formal Breakfast

7:20 Samu (work practice)

8:30 Rest

9:30 Zazen

10:15 Teisho

11:05 Zazen

12:30 Lunch (informal), rest

1:30 Zazen with dokusan

3:30 Chanting Service

3:50 Group Exercises

4:40 Zazen

5:15 Formal Dinner, rest

7:00 Zazen with dokusan

9:30 Four Vows

---

* The standard round is 35 minutes, followed by kinhin (walking meditation).

on these flights of fancy by keeping the gaze lowered and by attempting to restrain our natural tendency to latch onto everything going on around us.

Another aspect of visual silence is the instruction not to look in mirrors, not to shave, apply makeup, spend time styling our hair, and so on. All of this speaks to getting our attention not only off others, but off ourselves as well! – and particularly off of worrying about how we appear or what impression we are making on others.

The third general sesshin guideline is to eat moderately. In part, this is simply a very practical guideline, especially in the early days of sesshin, when the early rise and long hours of sitting mean that almost all participants will struggle with sleepiness. Having a full belly increases the sleepiness exponentially. But another aspect of this has to do with self-discipline and with taking only what we need, out of respect for our food and for all beings. In sesshin, we are using our bodies and our minds in a completely different way than we normally do outside of sesshin, and, especially as sesshin progresses, we are expending much less physical and mental energy. This shift is reflected in our metabolism, which means that we simply do not need to eat the same amount of food as we do outside of sesshin; about one third to one half less is the normal guideline, though this can vary considerably among different people.

Beyond the general support of the schedule and the guidelines, a more personal and direct support for our work in sesshin comes in the form of encouragement from the teacher, who offers dokusan multiple times each day as well as a daily teisho, and from the monitors, who take responsibility for keeping the sesshin running smoothly, who keep everyone on track through announcements and instructions, and who stand ready to help out with any physical or emotional crisis that may arise. Equally, however, we are supported by our fellow sesshin participants. This is an example of a positive type of peer-pressure. When we sense the seriousness, dedication, and effort of our fellow attendees, we naturally want to give our best as well. We come to realise that the group as a whole depends upon the sincere efforts of each one of us, and that together we actually create a group mind and group energy from which we all can draw. A useful analogy for this is to think of migrating geese: by flying in a v-formation, they create an airwave to which each bird can contribute energy when flying strongly and from which it may draw energy when tired.

Drawing on this group energy is a subtle thing, since we have talked about the importance of turning the attention inward rather than outward, refraining from verbal and nonverbal communication, not getting caught up in observing others or in worrying that they may be observing us – and to this we could add, in general, not concerning ourselves with other people's practice or comparing their work to our own. In this sense each of us is very much on our own in sesshin. And yet, at the same time, sesshin manages to be a quintessentially group practice: sitting, walking, working, exercising, eating, resting – virtually everything is done together as a group, in striking contrast to the lives most of us lead outside of sesshin. Moreover the emergence as sesshin progresses of a group mind, which we can sense even though (or perhaps because) we keep our eyes down, is not a fantasy. As we troop individually into dokusan, teachers often report that from their point of view we appear to be functioning rather like a school of fish: in one round student after student reports an inability to settle, in the next round people are struggling with discouragement, in the next many people are energised and focused.

As the days of sesshin progress, the mind begins to simultaneously settle and open. Breaks in the incessant chatter of the monkey-mind may occur, bringing a deep sense of peace. But strange things may also start to happen. As we peel back the layers of the mind one by one, a kind of unloading begins to take place that may take many different forms. Long-repressed memories may well up. Sudden spikes of sadness, anger, or joy may overwhelm us for no apparent reason. We may experience visual or auditory hallucinations. Roshi Kjolhede, in an unpublished manuscript on the topic of sesshin, has written in detail about such occurrences and how to work with them:

> One of the natural effects of sitting day after day, many hours a day, is to experience a change in one's mental processing of things. There's a sense of steadily losing one's bearings. This happens as the mind begins to slip free of its mental models, the mind-fetters that reduce our perceptions. Ordinarily we see reality not as it is, in its wholeness, but through the filter of our conceptual structures. As these structures release their grip on our perceptions, the mind seems to lose its moorings. It's rather like treading water – we can't seem to get a foothold.
>
> There's nothing to worry about in this shift; it's what needs to happen if we are to broaden our vision and see beyond the ordinary world of phenomena. In order to reach a new shore, we have to be willing to let go of

terra firma and venture beyond the known and familiar. Zazen enables us to do this, safely and gradually. As a side effect of this opening process we often experience *makyo*…

Makyo (spelled the same whether singular or plural) is a Japanese term we use for lack of a suitable equivalent in English. Broadly, it refers to any unusual mental or physical phenomena that occur as a side effect of doing zazen.

The most common makyo are hallucinations. Images often appear on the wall we're facing in zazen – faces of people or animals seem to come up the most. The human faces may be familiar to us or not. Sometimes they can be remarkably clear and distinctive, but of no one we recognize! Forms of other creatures may elicit tenderness in us or provoke fear. Other common illusions are landscapes or geometric or abstract designs. And probably everyone from time to time perceives odd fluctuations of light and dark, usually in one's peripheral vision – the play of shadows, flickering lights, and elusive patterns.

The visual illusions can get laughable. For several sesshins I sat next to a monk who later reported having had a vivid makyo that had become recurrent for him: before him stood a tall, refrigerated cooler stocked with beer!

Auditory hallucinations are less common, but also well-known to sesshin veterans. They may hear bells that haven't been struck, or they mix up those that have been with other sesshin bells and gongs. They may hear brief murmurings or loud reports.

One woman reported smelling, in the middle of sesshin, the distinct aroma of her mother's fresh-baked bread. Many sitters have described feeling light pressure on their faces in the very same spot: between the eyebrows. Others report the sense of their hands, in the oval zazen position, suddenly being larger than their whole body.

Another garden-variety makyo is crying. When this happens without our knowing why, we can chalk it up as makyo, an effect of the mind-body relaxing and opening through deepening zazen. But what about when it has a story behind it? For example, crying might come from remorse elicited by memories of our having once hurt someone. Such a catharsis could happen at any time, but is especially likely when the thought-noise of the mind has been dialed down through sustained zazen.

To cry in the zendo for any reason can be discomfiting the first time it happens, especially for men. Many of us have been conditioned to deny our feelings, and see crying as weak. But what kind of 'strength' does it show to stifle this natural release of feeling – especially within an enterprise dedicated to personal authenticity? We can either relax and open ourselves to what needs to emerge or we can clench ourselves against it, but we can't have it both ways. And as for possibly disturbing others with our crying, there is too much at stake in sesshin to be concerned with that. If we were to be sobbing long enough to distract others, the monitors would gently escort us out of the zendo to settle down. But until it reaches that point, crying in sesshin is far more likely to be experienced by others as inspiring than disturbing. The sound can do much to 'water' the sometimes arid atmosphere of sesshin.

How do we deal with makyo? The first, crucial step is to identify the phenomenon as a makyo. This may be easy enough when experiencing simple hallucinations, or crying without knowing why, states that are easily recognizable as side effects of intense meditation. But there are far more subtle makyo, which can settle over us without our knowing it. In sesshin it is common, for example, to go through periods of addled thinking and other states of confusion that we don't recognize as such. And until we realize we're in a makyo, we're captive to it.

A literal translation of makyo is 'devilish phenomena.' They bedevil us when we don't see them for what they are — passing phenomena that have arisen out of conditions of concentrated sitting. Even the most spectacular makyo, though, can steal over us without our noticing them, especially late in sesshin. I once suddenly found myself having spent half a round of zazen 'at' a truck stop. It had been an immersion in a virtual reality of neon signs and tractor trailers rolling in for refueling. I had been completely syntonic with my makyo — lost in its spell!

Among extreme sesshin makyo, none could rival, for sheer dislocation, the one visited upon a young participant many years ago. On Day Five he worked himself into the conviction that he had to get to Boston, and apparently without awareness that he was violating the most basic rule of sesshin, slipped away. He found his way to the airport, bought a ticket, boarded a plane, and only when halfway to Boston snapped out of his trance.

At the other end of the continuum of makyo are the physical side effects of serious sitting. These include random shudders or starts, tingling, and inexplicable feelings of heat or cold. When in my first months of Zen practice an occasional itchy welt would break out on my face, I was concerned enough to consult a dermatologist — who could offer no explanation. But after a more experienced practitioner tossed it off as 'just a makyo,' I stopped thinking about it and sure enough, it stopped happening.

In addition to the physiological and the hallucinatory side effects of meditation, there are some that stretch the definition of makyo. Probably the most common in this gray area are the emotional states elicited through intense zazen. Anger in one of its many forms, sadness, envy, jealousy, regret – many a sesshin participant has had to ride out these states. Fear is another unwanted guest, either fear of something or someone in particular or a generalized state of anxiety. Although these states are not considered makyo in the strict sense of the word, inasmuch as they arise in the context of sustained sitting they may be considered as such. Besides, labeling them as makyo enables us to avoid taking them seriously.

What unusual physical or mental phenomena that arise during rigorous zazen should *not* be considered makyo, then? Indeed, from the standpoint of practice, every mind-body state can be regarded as makyo, since all phenomena are transitory and thus not to be clung to.

From India comes the story of a prince who went to the Royal Jeweler with a daunting order. Handing him a gold ring, he commanded, 'You shall engrave on this ring some words that will buoy me in times of misfortune and restrain me in times of fortune.' A week later the prince returned, and with a low bow the jeweler presented him with the ring. On it were these words: 'It will pass.'

Thus, Step Two in dealing with makyo, after recognizing it as makyo, is to remind ourselves that it will pass. Hallucinations pass, crying spells pass, confusion passes, fear, sorrow, discouragement, and every other emotional state passes. So do high-energy states and periods of doubt. This being so, Step Three, then, is to refrain from getting mentally involved with any mental or physical state at all. This means neither fighting, suppressing, or avoiding it, on the one hand, nor dwelling in it or wallowing in it, on the other. And how do we manage this? By directing our attention back to our practice – immediately. Just as we do with thoughts.

Letting go of anything is difficult. Our habit of clinging to our thoughts and states is deep-rooted, and it takes most of us a long time to realize how much misery we incur through our clinging even to what we view as desirable.

Some of the most bedeviling makyo are those that seem most desirable, because they are captivating. Sexual fantasies can be enticing. So can images of food and other sense pleasures. Certain participants also become ensnared in their own wit, silently weaving puns, jokes, and comical scenes. And psychic experiences, though rare, can be especially beguiling. But most alluring of all, it seems, are states of euphoria – when you find yourself in what seems like Heaven, why would you want to leave? But meditation has its own Law of Gravity, as anyone can confirm who has spent precious time floating in clouds of bliss, only to then come crashing back to earth. After all, no state is permanent.

Students who in dokusan report something unusual that has happened to them will then sometimes ask, 'Is it real?' This is a good question for philosophical debate, but an irrelevant one for actual practice. 'Real' is a construct of the mind, which is itself ungraspable. What we conventionally regard as an objectified world of 'things' is determined by our sense perceptions – sight, sound, feeling, smell, taste – which themselves depend on consciousness. In Buddhist terms, subject and object 'co-arise'; each is meaningless without the other. In one of the earliest Zen documents, 'Affirming Faith in Mind,' seventh-century Chinese Zen Master Sengcan lays this out succinctly:

> *For things are things because of mind,*
> *As mind is mind because of things.*
> *These two are merely relative,*
> *And both at source are emptiness.*

In the arena of practice, then, whether an experience is to be called real or illusory is beside the point. What matters is that we allow nothing – no thing at all – to divert our attention from the practice that is our focus. Thus, however we may define makyo, we won't go wrong by *treating* every phenomenon as such. Memories, thoughts, even insights all warrant the same response – recognizing it as makyo (or illusory inasmuch as it is transient), then directing the attention back to the breath or koan.

Over successive days of sitting, as the mind is gradually able to unload more 'stuff', and as we become more able to let go of that stuff, our energy becomes more concentrated. On the physical level, disturbances such as pain in the legs or back may dissipate, along with the sleepiness that we experienced early in sesshin. Now we will very likely find that we need far less sleep than we do outside of sesshin, and this gives us the opportunity to do *yaza*, or late-night sitting. Yaza distinguishes itself from other parts of sesshin in that it takes place outside of the required schedule and is not governed by the usual bells and gongs of the rest of the day. People may sit in the zendo, or anywhere else in the buildings, or they may sit or walk outside under the stars. In the dark, mysterious, freedom of the night we encounter ourselves and our practice in a new way. There's a Japanese Zen saying, 'Walking alone through the universe', which sums up the beauty and magic of yaza.

People are often somewhat astounded at the suggestion that they do extra night sitting after they have already completed the long hours of required zazen. And they very naturally worry that if they stay up late – or for the whole night – they will be exhausted the next day and unable to stay awake during the required rounds. This can happen. But deep in sesshin, if sesshin is working on us as it has the power to do, we will not need to worry about the next day. The only moment is the present one, and the only concern is the practice. What is the practice calling us to do right now? With what subtle language is it speaking to us? What does it want us to discover in the night? Our only task in sesshin is to follow this call. And, while we may be tired tomorrow, there is at least an equal possibility that the extra sitting will increase rather than decrease the level of our energy. Our powers of concentration build on themselves.

In the end we can't predict what is going to happen in the next day, the next hour, or even the next minute of sesshin. We cannot predict or control when things will suddenly shift – as they always do – but can only learn, with increasing sesshin experience, to ride out the shifts, whether for the better or for the worse, with as little grasping and aversion as possible. As has often been said, sesshin is a series of ups and downs. Yasutani-roshi used to say that one could accomplish as much in a strong seven-day sesshin as one could by sitting at home daily for two to three years. But what do we mean by 'accomplish'? From the Buddhist view what we are doing when we sit is purifying our karma. In sesshin we can observe this process taking place at high speed: emotional and physical obstacles may be thrown at us one after the other with alarming rapidity – but, at the same time, we may find that we can move through each obstacle just as quickly, and even experience some remarkable breakthroughs.

Though the primary way that we purify our karma and offer our support to others in sesshin is simply by focusing on our own practice to the best of our ability, another way that we accomplish this is through work. In our tradition, each sesshin participant is assigned about one hour of work each day and is trained in their job before sesshin starts so that they can spend the hour in silent focus on the task at hand. This is a wonderful opportunity to practice mindfulness and 'moving zazen'. At sesshin it is easier than it is in our daily lives to maintain a focus on our practice while engaged in activity, both because the activity is done in silence and because of the many hours of sitting that take place both before and after the work period. Even more important, however, than maintaining the mental focus is the spirit of service in which we undertake our work of helping to feed our fellow sitters or to keep things tidy for them. In giving our best to whatever tasks we have been assigned, we act as sesshin bodhisattvas.

Nor does it stop there. The interconnectedness that reveals itself day by day in sesshin extends beyond the bonds we feel towards our co-practitioners and out to our connection to all beings everywhere. We take time to formally recognize this during the chanting services which take place each morning and afternoon as well as prior to each formal meal (see the inset overleaf, pp. 226–227). But fundamentally we can see all of sesshin, not just our chanting services, as a recognition of our interconnectedness, or One Mind. We come to sesshin to purify our minds and to work on behalf of all beings; and, as the work of sesshin progresses, it becomes clear that these two are not ultimately separate tasks. Let us end this chapter as we began it, with the words of Roshi Bodhin Kjolhede, who in the course of his life as Zen student, monitor and teacher has completed many hundreds of sesshin:

> Ironically, the ultimate benefit of sesshin, beyond both the personal and social, is also beyond proof. This is the spiritual force that emanates from sesshin while it is occurring. For the power of mind is illimitable, its effects unfathomable. The thirteenth-century Japanese Zen master Dogen was speaking to this, out of his deep Enlightenment, when he declared:
>
> > When even just one person, at one time, sits in zazen, he becomes, imperceptibly, one with each and all the myriad things and permeates completely all time, so that within the limitless universe, throughout past, future, and present, he is performing the eternal and ceaseless work of guiding beings to enlightenment.
>
> If that is the power of an individual sitting alone, the collective good generated by dozens sitting together for a week is incalculable.

The Five Reflections

With all that lives
let us honour the Three Treasures.
Let us recall the exertions
of Buddhas and Bodhisattvas.
This meal is the labour of countless beings —
let us remember their toil.
Defilements are many and exertions weak —
do we deserve this offering?
Gluttony stems from greed —
let us be moderate.
Our lives are sustained by this offering —
let us be grateful.
We take this food to attain the Buddha Way.

Verse of the Main Meal

Our meal is offered
to Buddha, Dharma and Sangha.
With teachers and family,
with nations and all life,
let us equally share.
To beings throughout the six worlds
we offer this meal.

Offering to the Hungry Ghosts

All hungry ghosts!
All tortured spirits!
Now we give you this Dharma-food.
May it fill the ten directions
and satisfy hunger in realms of darkness.
All hungry ghosts!
All tortured spirits!
Abandon greed
and rouse the desire for enlightenment!

Offering to the Thirsty Spirits

To you spirits tortured by thirst
we give this liquid offering.
Many your thirst be relieved,
may your suffering diminish.
May all beings attain Buddhahood!

THE JOURNEY OF SESSHIN
Selected Excerpts from Daily Sesshin Teishos

* * *

Day 1
Baggage (excerpt)

About a week ago I watched a film by Wes Anderson called *The Darjeeling Limited*. It's the story of a train trip made by three brothers in northern India. It's a year after their father has died and they're going to visit their estranged mother. The title comes from the name of the train that they're traveling on, and it's a very eccentric train — really the product of Wes Anderson's imagination. The story follows the three brothers and their interactions both on and off the train: in the first-class sleeper they share, and also on excursions they make during the train's lengthy stops.

All three brothers have the same luggage; very fancy, matching, monogrammed, leather luggage; multiple bags in different shapes and sizes. Near the end of the film, when they are returning home, it happens that they arrive at the station when the train is already pulling away. They have all their luggage with them, and they all run as hard as they can to try to catch up with the train and get on. They have to leap up onto the very end of the moving train, the guard's van. It's a beautiful scene; they're running, running, and then one by one as they leap onto the back of the train, they drop all their fine bags, and the bags fly off in different directions. When catching the train becomes more important than anything else, their hands just open and the bags fly away. And it's implied in the story that they needed to let go of their baggage in order to complete their journey and return home.

You could say that we've all boarded the Sesshin Limited, and we're setting out on a journey together. It's a seven-day journey — most of us will be together in this sesshin for the next seven days (a few people, the part-timers, will be getting off at earlier stops). We each come with our own baggage, with our own karma, but we're all headed in the same direction. And it doesn't matter what practice we're doing, whether we're doing breath practice, or shikantaza or a koan; these are all just different ways of loosening our tight grip on our karmic baggage and engaging with the great matter, the great matter of birth and death.

At this stage of sesshin, this early stage, often we experience a lot of thoughts and a lot of restlessness and physical tension. Many of us, because of our lifestyles, are chronically over-stimulated. We're so bombarded by stimuli that we arrive on edge, in an unstable, discordant state. And so at the beginning stages of sesshin, we need to put a big emphasis on letting our restless minds settle. It's like we're unconsciously in fight-or-flight mode. Some of us will tend to be more frequently in fight mode, for others of us our default will be flight. Both are restless and unstable. If we tend to go into fight mode we'll be annoyed with all kinds of things, from our sleeping arrangements to the person next to us, resisting with our thoughts, judging. If it's flight, we'll be wanting to run, wishing we were elsewhere, mentally checking out.

The rule about no moving during a round is so helpful here, because it means we can't run, we have to turn around and face what's happening. Fighting or fleeing from what's going on will often manifest as mental and physical tension. If you notice your mind is tense then just soften around that mentally. In other words let it be as it is. Because so often we add tension on top of tension. There is a certain kind of tension in the body or the mind, and then we resist that; we actually make it worse by adding another layer of tension there – hardening, closing. Instead we need to see if we can just soften around the tension, breathing it in with the next in-breath, and out with the next out-breath. In the single inhalation and exhalation really is the whole gamut of how we need to work with what comes up in practice. Breathing it in, accepting whatever's going on as the reality of this moment, breathing out, releasing it, completely. Letting it all go so that there's room for what the next moment brings.

Day 2

Working with Hellish States of Anxiety and Aversion (excerpt)

Today on our sesshin journey we're going to visit one of the six realms of unenlightened existence: Hell. We won't be talking so much about a place of punishment as about states of mind here and now, and how we create hellish states for ourselves in sesshin.

When the Six Realms are depicted, it's usually in the form of a wheel

(see figure in Glossary under Pratityasamutpada, p. 284). At the centre
are the three animals who represent the drivers of the wheel: a green
snake for aversion, a red rooster for passionate attraction, and a black
hog for the darkness of delusion.[2] The three animals form their own
circle, biting each other's tails, pointing to their interrelatedness. The Six
Realms are then depicted in six pieces of pie around that centre, and then
around the edge of those are the twelve links of Dependent Origination,
which show all the things that co-arise along with our suffering. And
this whole wheel is usually shown in the clutches of Yamaraja, the Lord
of Death, a fanged monster who grips this whole mess in his claws. He
curls up his tail around the bottom of this Wheel of Samsara, the wheel
of unenlightened existence.

The realms are a way of teaching us about our suffering, depicting our
suffering in all its variety. Besides Hell, the other realms of unenlightened
existence contain hungry ghosts, animals, humans, jealous gods, and
heavenly beings.

In these depictions, if you look closely, you discover that in all of
the realms, all six of them, there's a little figure of a Buddha. What this
is pointing to is that each realm has its own kind of saviour and salva-
tion – its own kind of teaching – and that with wisdom and compassion,
the experience of all the realms, including Hell, can be completely turned
around. They go from being places of bondage to being the ground of
our liberation. And it's especially important to understand this in relation
to our hellish states. We tend to look upon our afflictions as our enemies,
and we try to get rid of them, and this is a big mistake. The Buddha in the
Hell realm holds a purifying flame. No one in Hell or in any of the other
realms stays there forever, and in Hell the suffering can be transformative. The Buddhist hells (and there are many) would be more accurately
described as purgatories.

In *Thoughts Without a Thinker* Mark Epstein says, 'We cannot try to
find our enlightened minds while continuing to be estranged from our
neurotic ones.' In fact for hellish states, the problem *is* our estrangement.
We push away our very painful emotions. We hold them at arm's length
in a variety of ways. And because we do this, these aspects of ourselves
remain estranged. We have not entered into their purifying fire. What this
means in our zazen is to sit with an open heart, with a kind of gentleness.

2. The Three Poisons, see Glossary.

It's hard to articulate this because it's not a verbal thing. It's more to do actually with the body, how we hold ourselves. You could say it's to do with our emotional attitude, our stance. We express this open heart in our posture: a straight back and an open chest, the shoulders dropped, the neck relaxed. But it's not enough just to have that posture; there has to be an inner attitude that goes with it. And it can take years to find this inner attitude, an attitude of kindness, honesty and patience – patience with ourselves, with our intransigence – just as it can take years to really find our seat, to find a posture that is stable and easeful. To see the old habits come up, to recognise them: 'Oh, there you are again, you old Mara.'

It can help to remember that even the Buddha Shakyamuni, with all his spiritual attainments, had to deal with Mara, the tempter that appears in the suttas, sowing doubts. We're told that just before the Buddha's great awakening, Mara came to him and whispered in his ear, 'Are you worthy? Have you really got what it takes to wake up completely?' Mara is a personification of the ego-mirage. Mara doesn't want the Buddha to come to awakening. This is deeply threatening to him. Our ego-mirage, this bundle of tensions to which we cling, is deeply threatened by the prospect of our waking up. So it sows seeds of doubt. We all experience this. But whenever Mara would appear to the Buddha, and he continued to do so after his great awakening, the saving thing for the Buddha was that he would recognise him. 'Is that you, Mara?' he would say. And of course then Mara had no power.

Day 3

Seeing into the Ghostlike Nature of our Longings (excerpt)

Yesterday in teisho we looked at hellish states of anxiety and hatred and how to work with them with patience and clear-sightedness. Somebody asked me yesterday in dokusan, because we'd been talking about opening the heart in relation to working with painful emotions and situations that come up, Can I *make* my heart open? And it was a good question because certainly we're the ones who closed our hearts, and so we should be able to open them, but it's not quite as simple as that because if we try and force something then we're falling into the trap of aversion again. So really it's more that we can invite our heart to open. Sometimes it will, sometimes it won't. But it's the invitation that sets the tone. This willingness creates a kind of energy field of goodwill which is very helpful.

Today we're going to look at another realm, the realm of Hungry Ghosts, or *pretas*. Whereas the antidote needed for the hellish states is love, a kind of holding, for this realm it's non-attachment, or letting go. The hungry ghosts are a way of vividly depicting our unhealthy attachments. They're depicted as extremely bloated, swollen-bellied creatures with very thin arms and legs, and very long, thin necks and tiny mouths. These are the beings that we offer food and drink to at our formal meals. In the meal chant we say that we're offering these beings 'Dharma food'. They need Dharma food, they need teaching, because ordinary food doesn't satisfy them. They try to eat and drink but any food they manage to get down their narrow throats burns, it's very uncomfortable, and anything they drink turns to fire. And their stomachs, we're told, can't digest anything. So it's a desperately painful existence. They want to eat; they're hungry and thirsty; they seek gratification, but they can't find it, not even momentary satisfaction, but they keep on eating and drinking the foods that they can't digest or receive nourishment from. Pretty crazy.

Any time we fall into addictive behaviour or compulsions of different kinds, we're entering the realm of hungry ghosts. This could be sexual addictions, or addictions to unhealthy relationships, or eating disorders, as well as classical kinds of substance abuse, alcohol and drug addiction. In all these cases we continue to do something which we may even be aware is harmful to us, but we can't stop ourselves.

We talked yesterday about the inner disparaging voice, the inner critic, that can arise in us, often from very early in life. And it's important to see that our addictions can be used as a way to silence that corrosive inner critic, at least temporarily silence it. Alcohol abuse would be an example. It's important to understand this because we can then see that alcoholism or other addictions can actually be coming out of a deep longing to overcome our feelings of estrangement, a longing to actually reconnect with ourselves and the world. Of course it very quickly has the opposite effect, and gives that inner critic even more ammunition to shoot at us about our failings and our lack of willpower and so on. But that spiritual dimension is there. Alcoholics Anonymous is based on the recognition that there is spiritual longing underneath our addictions and compulsions. The antidote to our compulsions is in recognising that spiritual longing.

The problem with hungry ghosts is that they don't learn. They just keep on going back to the very foods and drinks that cause them so much discomfort. They keep seeking and grasping at what can never slake their thirst or satisfy their hunger.

When hungry ghosts try to satisfy their cravings by their eating and drinking, it just makes them feel worse. This is pointing to the truth that our suffering can't ever be assuaged by indulging our cravings. This is actually like pouring oil on fire. The fire just gets bigger. Rather like those fire service kitchen safety demonstrations, we've got to remove the oxygen that makes that fire burn, to put a lid on it. The oxygen is delusion. It's imagining that the objects of our desire will, if obtained, make us happy. I mentioned yesterday that in these depictions of the Six Realms, in the corner of each realm there's a Buddha. Actually, we're told, all these different Buddhas are manifestations of the Bodhisattva of Compassion, Kannon. And in the hungry ghost realm, the Buddha that appears there carries a vessel in which there are treasures. The treasures in this vessel are not things, but Dharma treasures, treasures of the teaching. What the hungry ghosts need to see is that their longings are ghostlike, not real.

The truth is that we do bring our grasping mind, the mind that causes us so much pain, into our work on the practice. And that's wonderful, really, because then we can start to appreciate how painful that mind is. Laozi said, 'Those who would gain what is under heaven by tampering with it, I have seen that they do not succeed. For that which is under heaven is like a holy vessel, dangerous to tamper with. Those who tamper with it harm it. Those that grab at it lose it.'

It's when we stop grabbing at things that we experience our richness, our treasure. We see how we contain everything. Sometimes it helps to practice letting go on little things. It's amazing how we can allow little attachments to take over the mind. For many sesshins, I'd have a little repeating drama that would happen at dinners, at formal meals. I was monitoring, so I was sitting at the head of the table, and it would always take a while for the salad to get down to me, and I'd be thinking to myself, 'Are they going to take all the parsley? Then there won't be any for me. Are they going to take all the parsley?' So there'd be this build-up and then finally the salad would come to me and there would be some parsley and I'd think, 'Aaaah, there's parsley!' Or there wouldn't and I'd think, 'Hmmm, greedy, they took it all and didn't leave any for me.' We can make little things into a big drama. We create little habits for ourselves whether they're at meals or at other times during sesshin as a way of creating a sense of being in control of the situation. If I get my parsley fix then everything will be fine. I need the iron (or whatever it is). We can feel comfortable if we're in that groove of thinking. But it's all quite ridiculous. Seeing how silly it is, how we can get caught up in these foolish little things can help us to break the attachment. We can laugh at ourselves, see our clown-nature. The hungry ghosts are terribly humourless creatures. Completely caught up in their drama. The drama of pleasure and pain and gain and loss. Sometimes when people hear teachings about letting go, about being unattached, they can feel uneasy and wonder if that means that they have to give up everything, give up their house, and their money and their relationships — but it's not always about that. We have to be realistic about where we are spiritually and what we can and can't let go of. But at the same time we have to begin to recognise the insubstantiality of the things we want, not to mention the insubstantiality of ourselves.

There's a Vajrayana master called Chagdud Tulku who was asked about whether lamas have attachments. And he said something that really captures the subtlety of this issue. He said, 'I don't know how other lamas might answer this, but I must say yes. I recognize that my students, my family, my country have no inherent reality.... Yet I remain deeply attached to them. I recognize that my attachment has no inherent reality. Yet I cannot deny the experience of it.' And he ends by saying, 'Still, knowing the empty nature of attachment, I know my motivation to benefit sentient beings must supersede it.' [3]

Knowing the empty nature of attachment, I know my motivation to benefit sentient beings must supersede it. In our zazen, and especially in sesshin, we get a good chance to see our attachments in all their glory. We get to see our ghostlike existence again and again, and the ways in which we're not fully living this moment. Seeing this can strengthen our resolve, our aspiration to go beyond our apparent limits, beyond our fears, and let go of our self-clinging.

---

3. 'Human Nature, Buddha Nature: An interview with John Welwood,' *Tricycle* (Spring 2011).

Day 4

Jealous Gods: Powerful but Still Suffering (excerpt)

Today we're going to visit a third realm of unenlightened existence, the realm of the jealous gods or Asuras. The Asuras were thrown out of the Heaven of the Thirty-Three. We don't have to go into the cosmology here, but just to say that because of being thrown out of this heaven, the Asuras have a chip on their shoulder, and they're constantly fighting to try and get the fruit of a tree that stands between their realm and the realm of the Devas (divine beings) right next door. They're always struggling to acquire something, something that they feel is rightfully theirs, this fruit. They have a strong sense of entitlement.

The fact that they have fallen from this other higher realm is pointing to there being something divine about them. We can see that, but there's also a lot of suffering. And their suffering is really in their restless quest to acquire what they think they're lacking, to gain the upper hand, to get even with the Devas who live next door in their peaceful, beautiful land. We can recognise Asuras in the world as highly ambitious people, effective people, people who set goals and achieve them. There's a lot of energy in this. A very strong sense of self. A lot of pride. But also confidence. There's a confidence here that they can get what they want, and therefore they put a lot of energy into it. So it's their confidence in a sense that allows them to get as far as they do.

We can think here of larger-than-life characters that we read about or hear about — millionaires, people who create mega-companies, make blockbuster movies, or have great achievements in sport, such as winning the Tour de France ten times. If we look into these people's lives, then we often find that they're still not satisfied — they have all these achievements but they're still not content. They discover that really they're only as good as their last race or their last film, and they find out that all the money they've acquired has no flavour, doesn't reach what is really gnawing at them. Or, the big company they've created is boring now. Think of somebody like Donald Trump[4] who's got a huge real estate empire, but is now thinking of running for public office. Seeking something else, some other satisfaction, some other acquisition.

4. This teisho was delivered in 2011 when Donald Trump was considering running for president against Barack Obama.

Another thing about Asura-like people is that they may have great energy, a lot of skills, but they can put them to pain-producing ends. A highly skilled and highly deluded person can do a lot of damage, cause all sorts of havoc. But even if what these Titans do is somewhat beneficial, they may still be completely unsatisfied, because what they achieve is conditioned – it's the same old story – and therefore not reliable or lasting. The Titan relies on a sense of conquest and domination for his thrills. His or her lust is for power. Of course domination is only ever provisional. But even so, the discontent of the Asura can be divine if all that restlessness and energy, and aggression even, can be harnessed in the right way. If we can harness it in the fight against our true enemy, the true cause of all our woes, namely our self-partiality, the ego-mirage. This possibility is recognised in most schemas of the six realms, where the Asura realm is one of the three higher realms, along with the human realm and the deva realm. The other side of it, the more destructive, negative side of the realm is recognised by other schemas which have four lower realms and two upper realms. So there's an equivocal attitude to the Asuras.

We can encounter this in our own practice in that our ego functions of ambition, self-control, directedness and focus can serve us very well in establishing a practice. In Zen one of the things that's highly valued is strong determination; in fact it's seen as an essential ingredient. You need it in order to continue through the many obstacles that are thrown up along the path. Strong determination is a characteristic of the Asuras – the single-minded overcoming of obstacles. But for it to be a positive thing it has to be a single-mindedness in the face of our delusive habits.

On the other hand, we can experience the suffering of the Asuras when we get stuck in the discipline of the practice. Maybe we sit a lot, we arrange our lives in order to be able to practice more, we're very disciplined in the practice itself, and yet we feel there's something blocking us. Discipline is absolutely necessary. Practicing with energy and devotion and active engagement – this is all absolutely necessary. But as long as we have this notion of acquiring something, getting those fruits off that tree, then we will be held back. What's missing here is the element of surrender. The gods are born into the heavenly realm because of their generosity, a giving of themselves, which the Asuras haven't realised yet. They just *want to get that fruit off that tree.* They haven't earned it, in a sense. They haven't yet learnt to surrender. To surrender their ambition. To surrender all their notions about what they are entitled to, what they *should* have, how things *should* be.

The Buddha that appears in this realm holds a flaming sword. Lama Govinda says that this Buddha has a sword because the Asuras can only understand violence. But we can take it positively, too, to say that the warrior spirit is being valued here. And this sword is also symbolic of wisdom, specifically of discriminating awareness.

This discriminating awareness has the power to recognise our delusions. And of course delusions seen are delusions destroyed. This sword has the power to cut through the conceits that hold us back. Manjushri, the Bodhisattva of Wisdom, who's on our altar here, also has a sword. In some renderings this sword, too, is flaming, on fire. But Manjushri's sword, the sword of transcendent wisdom, is known as the sword that cuts in one. Full of energy, full of effectiveness, but not with any kind of outflowing aggression towards the things it cuts. You can think of Manjushri's use of the sword as being more like a dance: a 'working with' as much as a 'working against'.

You can cut away delusions not by actually destroying anything but just with a shift in attention. Every time we dive into the koan, leaving our distracting thoughts alone, we're wielding the sword of Manjushri. Manjushri can dance with everything that comes up in this free, energetic way because he sees the emptiness of all five skandhas, sees his own emptiness, and sees the emptiness of all the dharmas that appear in his mind. He can see the emptiness of purity and defilement as well. He just cuts. Cuts everything back to the bone. The bone of this moment, right here and now.

Day 5

Effort and Surrender (excerpt)

Today we're going to talk a bit more about effort and surrender. This is a question that comes up in practice again and again: Do we make an effort or don't we? There's a story that illustrates this dilemma:

Two disciples of an old rabbi were arguing about the true path to God. One said that the path to God was built on effort and energy. 'You must give yourself totally and fully with all your effort to follow the way of the

Law,' he said. 'To pray, to pay attention, to live rightly.' The second disciple disagreed. 'It is not effort at all,' he said. 'That is only based on ego. It is pure surrender. To follow the way to God, to awaken, is to let go of all things and to live the teaching, "Not my will but thine."' As they could not agree on who was right they went to see the master. He listened as the first disciple praised the path of wholehearted effort and when asked by this disciple, 'Is this the true path?' the master said, 'You're right, You're right.' The second disciple was quite upset and countered eloquently on the path of surrender and letting go. When he had finished he said, 'Is this not the true path?' and the master replied, 'You're right, You're right.' A third student who was sitting there said, 'But master, they can't both be right,' and the master smiled and said, 'You're right, You're right.'[5]

The two disciples were taking positions on opposite sides of what is really a continuum. Disciplined effort and exertion are absolutely necessary, but not sufficient. Eventually self-will has to be relinquished. But we shouldn't think that our effort is just on one side and surrender is on the other and that they're two very different things, because they aren't. It is true to say that often what is required of us at the beginning is the effort. Effort often has to come first. In the Lotus Sutra it says, 'The mind that sets forth and the mind that arrives are not different. But of the two, the former is beset by difficulties.' And we have to work with these difficulties. Struggle with them. Actually the first thing that we need to surrender to is the effort itself. To just make an effort, without any attachment to results. It's really a big step when we realise that it's the quality of our effort that matters, not what we experience in any given round, or in any given sesshin, in terms of its being pleasant or unpleasant, smooth or bumpy.

Here are the instructions that a Chinese Zen master gives on effort:

When you are involved in turmoils and excitements which you have no way of avoiding or eschewing, you should know that this is the very best time to work on Zen. If instead you make an effort to suppress or correct your thoughts, you are getting far away from Zen. The worst thing a student can do is to attempt to correct or suppress his thoughts during inescapable circumstances. Masters in ancient times have said,

No differentiation whatsoever arises.
Only the bright void

5. Christina Feldman and Jack Kornfield, eds., *Stories of the Spirit, Stories of the Heart* (New York: Harper, 1991) p. 307.

Reflects all manifestations within oneself.
Bear this in mind, bear this in mind!

If you use one iota of strength to make the slightest effort to attain enlightenment, you will never get it. If you make such an effort you are trying to grasp space with your hands, which is useless and a waste of time![6]

This Zen master certainly seems to be pouring cold water on all our hopes. Surely we're supposed to do something with our thoughts. Surely we're supposed to make an effort to attain enlightenment. Isn't that what it's all about?

Actually he's giving us very good advice here. First of all he talks about unavoidable disturbances; he calls them turmoils and excitements. He reassures us, 'You should know that this is the very best time to work on Zen.' It's not that we can't arrange the circumstances of our lives the best we can to avoid distraction. Really, sesshin is that. We organise things so that we can quiet the mind and focus it as much as possible. But even with our best efforts, stuff arises. Shit happens. Turmoils and excitements. Difficult states. Anger. Resentment. Jealousy. Old hurts and grudges come up. We chew on them, we turn them over. They can be discouraging. We may think, surely at this point, having done all this work, I should be able to have a quiet mind. Who said? You have the mind you have. And it can be at this point when feeling discouraged, it can be very helpful to remind oneself of what this master is saying: 'You should know that this is the very best time to work on Zen.' When things are at their most chaotic and uncomfortable, that's the best time to work, and often the time when we discover new things and go beyond our normal way of relating to ourselves – when pressed, when up against it, when up against the very things we would very much like to avoid.

The key thing is *how* we work with these things when they come up. Because if we try to suppress our thoughts or straighten them out, correct them, then that's taking us away from Zen. The Master says, The *worst* thing a student do is to attempt to correct or suppress his thoughts. Why is that? Well, you can ask yourself the question, who is it that's suppressing or correcting the thoughts? It's the small mind that wants to do that, the ego-mirage with all its ideas about right and wrong. Shantideva said, 'Self-surrender is the key. If you don't get out of the fire, you're sure to

6. Chang Chen-chi, *The Practice of Zen* (New York: Harper, 1959), p. 66.

be burned.' When we try and suppress or correct our thoughts, we're immediately dividing ourselves in two. There are the thoughts, and then there is the self who is trying to stop the thoughts, or avoid the thoughts. The key in Zen, the essence of Zen, is to become one. That's what this master is talking about when he quotes an even more ancient master. He gives this three-line verse:

> *No differentiation whatsoever arises*
> *Only the bright void*
> *Reflects all manifestations within oneself.*

The bright void that he mentions here is the mirror of our awareness that reflects everything just as it is, without adding anything.

In the second part of this quote, he talks about attaining enlightenment. 'If you use one iota of strength to attain enlightenment you will never get it. If you make such an effort you are trying to grasp space with your hands, which is useless and a waste of time.' Well, we can ask the same question we asked about who is suppressing or correcting thoughts. Who is using her strength to attain enlightenment? We find out when we have a look, Oh, yeah, it's that same small mind again. The mind of gain and loss. The ego-mirage. *Attain* enlightenment. That's really the language of that small self. But that small self is what we need to drop, the acquisitive mind is what must be dropped. What we need instead is the inquisitive mind. Not the mind that seeks to grasp something out there, but the mind that looks within, that *in*vestigates. In Zen we highly value the mind of not-knowing, or as one teacher put it the 'don't-know mind'. This is the mind that investigates Mu, that investigates this moment, however it is, however messy it might be. What is this? Not some future perfect moment, but *this* moment. The mind that looks into sound, whether pleasant or unpleasant, muffled or sharp. Who is hearing? Not grasping at those sounds, but opening to them, letting them in. If there's any kind of grasping, that is inherently unsatisfactory. 'Like trying to grasp space with your hands.' Futile, pointless, because you're trying to grasp what can't be grasped. Practice is letting go.

Sometimes we doubt ourselves, we wonder whether we're capable of doing this work. In that case we can ask ourselves the question, Do we really know that we're *not* capable? Do we know who we are? Sometimes just the conviction, I can't do this, can come up very strongly. It can be very painful. We judge that we don't have what it takes. Of course you

could say that actually we *don't* have what it takes. None of us do. If by
'us' we're talking about our small selves. As long as we're acting out of
self-will, we haven't got a chance. Because it is exactly through relinquish-
ing that identification that the work gets done. Mu realises Mu. We are
breathed by the breath, not the other way around. When we just sit, the
universe is sitting. To apprehend this we have to drop all our manoeuvring, all our plotting, all our attempts at controlling things, all our doing.

Day 6

Emperor Tongguang's Helmet Hood (full teisho)

Today we're going to take up a koan from the *Shoyoroku*, number 97,
Emperor Tongguang's Helmet Hood, and here's the case:

> The Emperor Tongguang said to Master Xinghua, 'I have attained the
> treasure of the central plain; however, no one can set a price on it.'
> Xinghua said, 'Your majesty, please lend it to me so I can have a look.'
> The emperor pulled down the straps of his helmet hood with both hands.
> Xinghua said, 'Who could dare to put a price on the Emperor's treasure?'

First a little bit of background on our two protagonists. Emperor Tongguang, also known as Zhuangzong, came to the throne in 923 after a series
of alliances and and battles to conquer territory, proclaiming himself
emperor of the 'Later Tang Dynasty'. He ruled for just three years before being killed in an army rebellion. The other character here is Master
Xinghua, whose full name is Xinghua Cunjiang. We don't know a great
deal about this master, and the dates I could find for him, 830-888, don't
accord with the dates for the emperor, so perhaps the story is a fiction.
We do know that Xinghua was a Dharma Heir of Master Linji, and in
Zen's Chinese Heritage we get an account of the various milestones in his
training. He trained with Linji first, and after Linji died with a couple
of other masters. I'm not going to go into this account, it's somewhat
convoluted. All you need to know is that it includes a lot of hitting and
shouting, in fine Rinzai tradition.

There is an example of Master Xinghua's teaching, again from *Zen's
Chinese Heritage*, which is actually *about* hitting and shouting. There's
always a danger that a teacher's style, his or her way of expressing the
Dharma, can be imitated by those of inferior understanding and conse-

quently turned into something dead. There's a koan in the *Mumonkan* which looks into this, Gutei Raises a Finger. But here's what Xinghua says to his monks:

> I'm always hearing shouts in the corridor as well as at the back of the hall. I tell you that you musn't blindly shout wild shouts. Even if you shout so loud that it takes my breath away and stops me cold, when my breath comes back, I'll tell you, 'Still not it.' Why? I haven't been passing out precious gems in vermillion wrappings to all of you. What's all the shouting about? [7]

So often we spout what we think is the 'right' answer, blindly, inauthentically. Interesting that he uses the image of the precious gem here, as the Emperor Tongguang does (sometimes 'treasure' in our Case above is translated as 'jewel' or 'gem'). Why does he say he hasn't been passing out precious gems? What if the whole universe is already a precious gem?

There's a little story about the end of Xinghua's life which also features Emperor Tongguang. After trying to present him a purple robe (a symbol of imperial favour), which he refused, the Emperor presented Master Xinghua with a fine horse. While the Master was riding this horse, it startled and reared up, and Xinghua fell off, injuring his foot. The Emperor sent some special medicine to the master to help heal his foot. Xinghua gave instructions to the monastery director to make him a walking stick, and then the master took it and proceeded to hobble around the zendo, and as he did so asked the monks, 'Do you recognize me?' And the monks answered, 'How could we not recognize you?' The Master then said, 'Dharma Master Foot! He can speak, but he can't walk.' He instructed the attendant to ring the bell to assemble all the monks for teisho, and then he addressed them again. 'Do you recognize me?' This time the monks didn't know what to say; they were flummoxed. Then Xinghua threw down the staff and died, sitting in zazen. So he was teaching right until the end.

I wondered on reading this story whether Xinghua had suffered a head injury falling off that horse; perhaps brain swelling or bleeding killed him. Perhaps the Emperor's approval, his favour of the gift, turned out to be fatal. It's dangerous to engage with men of power. Of course we don't know what the interval was between the fall and Xinghua's death. He was

---

7. Andy Ferguson, *Zen's Chinese Heritage* (Boston: Wisdom, 2000), p. 202.

only about 58. But what was his last teaching? What was he exhorting the monks to recognise? It's akin to Bassui's last admonition, 'Look directly!' Can we see clearly what is right in front of us, even as things unravel? Even as our beloved teacher passes away?

So, to our case again.

> The Emperor Tongguang said to Master Xinghua, 'I have attained the treasure of the central plain; however, no one can set a price on it.'
> Xinghua said, 'Your majesty, please lend it to me so I can have a look.'
> The emperor pulled down the straps of his helmet hood with both hands.
> Xinghua said, 'Who could dare to put a price on the Emperor's treasure?'

Now immediately we can notice that there are no blows or shouting here at all, and it's not surprising. Master Xinghua was talking with the Emperor. Most if not all of an Emperor's subjects were not even allowed to look at, let alone lay a finger on him. And also even for those who were in the innermost circle, an exquisite degree of politeness and deference would have been expected. It's probably hard for us to even imagine the kind of power an emperor could wield. Certainly he could command that somebody have their head chopped off in an instant.

The emperor says to Master Xinghua, 'I have attained the treasure of the central plain, however, no one can set a price on it.' So the first point of the koan is to see what the treasure of the central plain is. And there's a footnote that this central plain is a way of talking about all of China, the whole country. Is he talking about having conquered China (literally, the Middle Kingdom)? If it's just worldly treasure he's talking about then we wouldn't really have a koan here, so what could it be, and why is he telling Master Xinghua about it? What's his purpose?

He says no one can set a price on it, on this treasure. What's he wanting from Master Xinghua? Does he want Master Xinghua to put a price on it, to evaluate it in some way?

Xinghua says, 'Your Majesty, please lend it to me so I can have a look.' This is the second point of the koan. What's he asking here in a nutshell? What's he wanting the Emperor to show him?

The Emperor then pulls down on the straps of his helmet hood with both hands. This is the third point one has to look at. What's he doing? What does this mean? It seems rather odd. What's the strap of his hat got to do with the treasure of the central plain?

Xinghua says, 'Who would dare to put a price on the emperor's treasure?' (or jewel in some versions). What's he saying here? Is he approving of this treasure, is he giving an appraisal of it, or not? It is a risky business dealing with men of great power. If Xinghua were to price this treasure too low he could insult the emperor, but if he were to value it too highly, he could fall into flattery. But he manages to navigate between these two. Who could *dare* to put a price...

There's a contemporary commentary on the *Shoyoroku* by Gerry Shishin Wick where Wick tells a children's story which really brings out the fine line that this teacher was having to walk with the Emperor. It's a story about a tiger, a royal tiger who needed to find a new minister of state because he had just eaten the chicken who had previously filled the post.

Three animals applied for the job, a goat, a monkey, and a rabbit. First the tiger faced the goat and exhaled loudly, AHHH. And then he asked, 'Tell me, is my breath foul or sweet?' The goat was gagging and could hardly stand the smell, but he knew that if he told the tiger it was foul, he might eat him, so he said, 'Your breath is very sweet.' The tiger said, 'How can I trust a liar like you to handle my affairs of state?' And he ate the goat. Next it was the monkey's turn. The tiger exhaled, AHHH, and said, 'Tell me, is my breath foul or sweet?' The monkey had learned from the goat, so he said, 'Oh, it's foul indeed!' The tiger said, 'How can I trust so rude a fellow as you to handle my affairs of state?' So the tiger ate him, too. Then it was the rabbit's turn. The tiger asked the same question, but the rabbit didn't answer immediately, he just sat there with his nose twitching. Finally, the tiger said again, 'Tell me, is my breath sweet or foul?' The rabbit just kept twitching his nose. Finally after the tiger had asked a third time the rabbit said, 'Sir, I have this terrible cold and I can't smell a thing.' The tiger said, 'Hah! You're a clever fellow. I think that you will be a fine minister of state.'

In Xinghua's reply, if we look into it, there is at once affirmation, it's encouraging, recognising this treasure that the emperor has put before him, but at the same time there's a gentle corrective in there as well. He says, 'Who could dare put a price on the emperor's treasure?' We can understand that 'dare' there in relation to his being before a man of great power, but there's more to it than that.

Can a price be put on the Emperor's treasure? In telling Xinghua about it, was the Emperor looking for some kind of confirmation of his attainments? Some kind of congratulations from the Master? Master Foyan talks about the sickness of refusing to dismount the donkey — thinking if we have an insight that we are special, that we've got something that other people don't have, something very precious, a treasure. Perhaps since we're dealing with an emperor here we should say he's refusing to dismount his fine horse.

If we raise this treasure up too much, if we put too high a 'price' on it, then people will think that this treasure, this jewel, is something scarce, something very special. On the other hand, put too low a price on it, and people won't appreciate just what a treasure it is. Nansen comments:

It's not expensive or cheap. How can you buy it?

There's a little fragment of a Rumi poem that captures the essence of this beautifully.

A pearl goes up for auction. No one has enough. So the pearl buys itself.

So the pearl buys itself. Only the pearl can buy the pearl. Master Gensha would often talk about one bright pearl. He said:

The entire universe is one bright pearl.

Master Dogen writes:

'One bright pearl' expresses reality without actually naming it — it is the name of the universe. It contains the inexhaustible past, existing throughout time and arriving in the present. At this moment there is a body and mind; they are the one bright pearl. A blade of grass, a tree, the mountains and rivers of this world are not only themselves — they are the bright pearl... We can never escape from the universe, which is nothing but the one bright pearl. Even if it seems to you that you have escaped it for a little while, you are still in time, and all time is covered by the bright pearl... When the right time comes [the essence of the bright pearl can be grasped]; it is suspended in emptiness, hidden in the lining of clothes, found under the chin of dragons, and in the headdresses of kings... How is it possible to doubt that life and death are also the bright pearl? Even if we are perplexed or troubled, it is nothing but the bright pearl. There cannot be any action or thought existing separately from the bright pearl. Consequently, even coming and going in the Black Mountain's Cave of Demons is nothing but the one bright pearl.[8]

8. Kosen Nishiyama and John Stevens, trans., *A Complete English Translation of Dōgen Zenji's Shōbōgenzō*, Vol. I (Tokyo: Daihokkaikaku, 1975), pp. 25–27.

Pain in our knee, niggling worry, birds calling, the creaking of the roof as it cools, all of these are one bright pearl. Rilke in his love poems to God is also always talking about this one bright pearl. In one poem he says:

You are the future,
the red sky of sunrise
over the fields of time.

You are the cock's crow when night is done.
You are the dew and the bells of matins,
maiden, stranger, mother, death.

You create yourself in ever-changing shapes
that rise from the stuff of our days —
unsung, unmourned, undescribed,
like a forest we never knew.

You are the deep innerness of all things,
the last word that can never be spoken.
To each of us you reveal yourself differently:
to the ship as coastline, to the shore as ship.[9]

What the Emperor and Master Gensha and Dogen and Rilke are referring to can't be priced, can't be bought or sold. It can't be taken from us. Nor can we give it to someone else. The poorest most destitute beggar to the richest of the 1% have it. What is this one bright pearl? What is this treasure?

We'll stop here and recite the Four Vows.

Day 7

Lingzhao's Shining Grasses (full teisho)

Today we're going to take up a story called 'Lingzhao's Shining Grasses.' This story appears in *The Hidden Lamp: Stories from Twenty-Five Centuries of Awakened Women* edited by by Zenshin Florence Caplow and Reigetsu Susan Moon, and it involves the Pang family. The Pangs — father, mother, daughter, and son — lived in Tang dynasty (eighth-century) China. The father is known as Layman Pang, or Pangyun in Chinese ('yun' meaning 'lay practitioner'), Hokoji in Japanese. We don't know his wife's name but

9. Anita Barrows and Joanna Macy, trans., *Rilke's Book of Hours, Love Poems to God: Songs of Pilgrimage*, II:22 (New York: Riverhead Books, 2005), p. 177.

she's usually referred to as Laywoman Pang or Mrs Pang. The daughter's name was Lingzhao, which means Spirit Shining, and she's the one who gives her name to today's story, 'Lingzhao's Shining Grasses':

> Layman Pang was sitting in his thatched cottage one day studying the sutras.
>
> 'Difficult! Difficult! Difficult!' he suddenly exclaimed. 'Like trying to store ten bushels of sesame seed in the top of a tree.'
>
> 'Easy! Easy! Easy!' his wife, Laywoman Pang answered. 'It's like touching your feet to the ground when you get out of bed.'
>
> 'Neither difficult nor easy,' said their daughter Lingzhao. 'It's like the teachings of the ancestors shining on the hundred grass tips.' [10]

So before we take a look at this story, a little bit of biographical material on the three Pangs in our story. Layman Pang was born sometime around 740 and died in 808. His biography was written by an official, the Prefect Yu Ti, and it entered into the wider culture in both China and Japan. Zen teachers would quote him, and this has continued right up to today. His most well-known saying is, 'My magical power and spiritual exercise consist in carrying water and gathering firewood.'

There are other laymen who are revered (such as Fu Daishi) but the fact that Layman Pang's wife and daughter were also part of the story and that both were highly regarded for their Zen understanding was pretty unusual at a time when laywomen were not generally able to participate in society and in Zen training in the way that men were. So both Lingzhao and her mother are great exemplars, showing what is possible for women to accomplish.

Most of what we know about Layman Pang comes from the biography by Yu Ti, and it deals mostly with his poetry and his later life, so we really don't know very much about his early life at all, what led him to become interested in Buddhism and to pursue it with all his energy. Nor is there much reference to the era that he lived in, which was a time of great upheaval, with wars, floods, famines, heavy taxes and rapid inflation — circumstances which brought hardship pretty much to everyone. We don't know how these things affected him.

We do know that his father was a Confucian and a minor official in

10. Zenshin Florence Caplow and Reigetsu Susan Moon, eds., *The Hidden Lamp: Stories from Twenty-Five Centuries of Awakened Women* (Boston: Wisdom, 2013), p. 271.

a certain town and then later was transferred to another place where he became the Prefect (a regional administrator). Layman Pang moved to this town with his father and at some point after that he got married and had a son and a daughter, Lingzhao. When Lingzhao was eighteen, there is a story which is related by Ruth Fuller Sasaki as follows:

> When [Layman Pang] was middle-aged, he gave his house away to be used for a temple, and sank his possessions and money in a nearby river in order to be rid of them forever. He apparently regarded the acquisition of wealth as an impediment to the attainment of enlightenment and did not give it away to others for fear it would be a hindrance to them also. It is easy to imagine the surprise and wonder of his neighbours at this drastic renunciation of property. Even today his name is widely known in connection with this incident. Unfortunately we're not told what arrangements he subsequently made for his family, or what his wife thought of this decision.[11]

We might question this action of Pang's. I remember when I first heard this wondering why he didn't give his wealth to the poor. Because surely extreme poverty, indigence, is as much of an obstacle to realisation as wealth. We don't know why he did it, but certainly his dramatic act would have been a teaching for the wealthy people around him who viewed it. And certainly it did seem to set him free.

As Sasaki says, the record does not relate what Mrs Pang or the children thought about this or whether they had a say in it, and in the Confucian culture of the time, it was probably considered completely irrelevant what the wife and children thought. A wife was expected to submit to the rule of her father in her youth, then to her husband and finally in old age to her son. The great Russian novelist Tolstoy did something similar. He was an aristocrat, but at a certain point he decided to give up all his wealth, and he began dressing as a serf. People regard Tolstoy as a kind of saintly character, but left out of this picture are his wife and daughters who were mortified by his decision to live a simple peasant life. His wife had also come from an upper class family, and she and her daughters were not ready to suddenly give away all their possessions, and their jewelry, and their fine clothes, and their comforts, not to mention their status.

---

11. Ruth Fuller Sasaki, Yoshitaka Iriya & Dana R. Fraser, trans., *A Man of Zen: The Recorded Sayings of Layman P'ang* (New York: Weatherhill, 1989), p. 19.

Tolstoy's decision was extremely difficult for them. As for the Pangs, we don't know what their reaction was, but they appear to have just taken it in their stride; at least from what you can infer, the Pang family seems to have been more in sync, and probably they were all ready to take this step together.

Later on Layman Pang wrote this verse:

> *I've a boy who has no bride,*
> *I've a girl who has no groom;*
> *Forming a happy family circle,*
> *We speak about the Birthless.*[12]

Of course, not having any wealth anymore, it would be very hard to find marriage partners for his two children. An imperative of parents in Confucian society was to get their children married off well, and then for those children to produce children to carry on the rites that were so important, rites of worshipping and propitiating the ancestors. But instead of focusing on perpetuating the family line, we see the Pangs focusing on the birthless, the unborn Buddha Mind. Wholeness.

Shortly after disposing of his property Layman Pang went to study with the great Chan master Shitou Xiqian under whom he came to a first awakening. The story appears as follows in *Zen's Chinese Heritage*:

> Pangyun met Zen Master Shitou. He asked him, 'Who is the one who is not a companion to the 10,000 dharmas?'
>
> Shitou quickly covered Pangyun's mouth with his hand. Pangyun suddenly had a realisation.[13]

Later on Layman Pang went on to work with the great Mazu, and he asked exactly the same question: 'Who is the man who doesn't accompany the 10,000 dharmas?' And Mazu replied:

> Wait till you've swallowed in one swig all the water of the West River, then I'll tell you.

And it was at these words the Layman suddenly understood the 'mysterious principle', as the text puts it, and he offered a verse:

> *People of the ten directions are the same one assembly —*
> *Each and every one learns 'wu-wei'.*

12. *Ibid.*, p. 43.
13. Ferguson, *Zen's Chinese Heritage*, p. 94.

This is the very place to select Buddha.
Empty-minded, having passed the exam, I return.[14]

Everyone learns *wu-wei*: This is the effortless doing of non-doing, a term that came from Taoism.

This is the very place to select Buddha – to find Buddha, to be Buddha.

'Empty-minded, having passed the exam, I return'. You could say that passing the exam is seeing clearly into the truth; it's also a reference to the exams that men would have to pass in order to become government officials, as Pangyun's father would have done. But that is an exam where you have to fill your mind with things in order to pass. This one, the Zen exam, is the opposite, to empty out completely and return to our true home that was there all along. Pangyun stayed and practiced under Mazu for two years following this realisation. After that he traveled around China visiting various Zen masters and testing his understanding.

But let's turn now to Mrs Pang, the second protagonist in today's story. It's symptomatic of the patriarchal attitudes of Chinese Buddhism that, although Mrs Pang was clearly an extraordinary woman, we know almost nothing about her, not even her name. But here is one story that we do have. It reveals Mrs Pang as a very down-to-earth and no-nonsense person, and also one who was able to freely and creatively express the Buddhadharma:

> One day Laywoman Pang went to the Deergate Temple and made an offering of food. The temple priest asked her on whose behalf she made the offering so that he could dedicate its merit. She took her comb from the side of her bun and stuck it in the back of her hair. Then she said, 'The transfer of merit is complete,' and she walked out.[15]

Again we see here the unconventional activity of this family. The traditional practice would be to go and make an offering, and then the temple priest would record on a slip of paper your name and what the gift was

14. Ruth Fuller Sasaki, Yoshitaka Iriya, & Dana R. Fraser, trans., *A Man of Zen: The Recorded Sayings of Layman P'ang* (New York: Weatherhill, 1989), p. 26.

15. Florence Caplow and Susan Moon, eds., *The Hidden Lamp* (Boston: Wisdom, 2013), p. 303.

for, and this would be displayed in public so your good deeds would be recognised and the merit would be dedicated to the person on whose behalf the offering was made. But here Mrs Pang just moves her comb from one part of her hair to another and says, 'The transfer of merit is completed.'

This is coming out of her understanding of oneness. Where can the merit be transferred to? It's right here.

The English translation of this story comes, like our main story for today, from *The Hidden Lamp*. This book came out in 2013, and it's a treasure-trove of stories about awakened women in Buddhism over the last 2500 years. I've used many of these stories in teisho in the years since the book appeared, and Mrs Pang, like many of these women, is one of the unsung women that we refer to when we chant our Ancestral Line.[16] It's interesting that in the first 25 years or more of the Rochester Zen Center, when the Ancestral Line was chanted, no reference was made to our female ancestors at all; but then some of the women practicing in Rochester pressed to have something inserted to honour the centuries of awakened women who did not appear in the lineage. So when I trained at Rochester, we would pay homage at the end of the chant to the *'unknown women'* who nourish our practice. Gradually, however, more and more information has come out as female scholars unearth documents, especially Chinese documents, and translate them. So here in Auckland we changed the words from 'unknown women' to 'unsung women' since we do know of many of them now. And now, most recently, we're actually working on a new chant which will include Indian, Chinese, Japanese, and Western female masters by name.[17]

Certainly one of the women who will appear in this new chant is the third and final protagonist in today's story, Lingzhao. As we said, her name means Spirit Shining, and she was born in about 762. As Ruth Fuller Sasaki says, she seems to have had a particularly close and affectionate

16. See Chapter 4, pp. 76–78.

17. This chant (now completed and in use at the Auckland Zen Centre) includes many female masters as well as various male masters to whom we feel a particular connection but who don't happen to be in our specific lineage. Thus it is not technically an ancestral line, but rather we call it a Pool of Radiance after a similar chant that was created by the Swedish Sangha. It recognises and expresses our gratitude for the efforts of the many masters, male and female, who continue to inspire us and teach us even though they are not in our branch of the Zen family tree. At the same time, we also continue to chant our traditional Ancestral Line, since recognising our particular genealogy is important, too.

relationship with her father, and it's also said that she took after her father – she loved books, and she would read with her father and debate with him about the content of the books, and later on when her father went wandering on pilgrimage from temple to temple, she accompanied him. After Layman Pang gave up his wealth, Lingzhao made and sold bamboo baskets as a way to support herself and her father. There's a story in *The Hidden Lamp* that takes place during that time. It's called 'Lingzhao's Helping':

> One day Layman Pang and his daughter Lingzhao were out selling bamboo baskets. Coming down off a bridge, the layman stumbled and fell. When Lingzhao saw this, she ran to her father's side and threw herself to the ground.
> 'What are you doing?' cried the layman.
> 'I saw you fall, so I'm helping,' replied Lingzhao.
> 'Luckily no one was looking,' replied the layman.[18]

So what's going on here? Why does Lingzhao fall down along with her father? And what does he mean when he says it's lucky no one was looking? Was he embarrassed about what Lingzhao was doing?

Actually Lingzhao's giving a beautiful demonstration here of how to help. And the layman's statement, 'Luckily, no one was looking', is integral to what Lingzhao did, to the way in which she was helping. She wasn't standing back and feeling pity for her father who had fallen down. She unselfconsciously got in there, right beside him.

Now we'll turn to our main story, Lingzhao's Shining Grasses:

> Layman Pang was sitting in his thatched cottage one day studying the sutras.
>
> 'Difficult! Difficult! Difficult!' he suddenly exclaimed. 'Like trying to store ten bushels of sesame seed in the top of a tree.'
>
> 'Easy! Easy! Easy!' his wife, Laywoman Pang answered. 'It's like touching your feet to the ground when you get out of bed.'
>
> 'Neither difficult nor easy,' said their daughter Lingzhao. 'It's like the teachings of the ancestors shining on the hundred grass tips.'[19]

18. Susan Moon and Florence Caplow, eds., *The Hidden Lamp* (Boston: Wisdom, 2013), p. 293.

19. *Ibid.*, p. 271.

So we get three presentations here, from husband, wife and daughter. And you might think that these statements contradict each other and that one is right and the others are wrong, but this would be a mistake. Yuanwu when commenting on this exchange says, 'These three Zen teachers each put forth a hand and hold up the bottomless basket.' Bottomless basket is a way of referring to awakened mind. So each of these statements by these three Masters is holding up the bottomless basket.

First we get Layman Pang, who exclaims, 'Difficult! Difficult! Difficult! Like trying to store ten bushels of sesame seed in the top of a tree.'

Who hasn't felt this? Who hasn't exclaimed to themselves at different times, 'Difficult! This is difficult!'

Sesshin is really hard. Life is really hard. It isn't easy being a human, being alive. We suffer. We struggle.

And that's where we start when we come to practice. That's what gets us to practice in the first place, some recognition of our suffering, and some recognition of the part we play in our suffering, that it's not all coming from the outside. But the irony is that the very things that have brought us to the practice are what we have to deal with *when* we practice. We don't somehow check them all at the door when we come into the zendo. We have to face ourselves.

I remember clearly in my first seven-day sesshin, at a certain point just being bowled over by the enormity of the task; seeing clearly the strength and pervasiveness of the ego. It was like a light was shined on it — on how full my mind was of conceits about myself and florid fantasies about what others were thinking of me. One thought would go and then be immediately replaced by another, and the idea of actually reaching a place of stillness seemed impossible. It was like seeing ahead of me the Labours of Hercules, the endless stables that needed to be cleaned out. But there was no turning back, because once you've seen the possibility of awakening, there *is* no going back. You just have to pick up that shovel and start mucking out.

Layman Pang uses the image of trying to store ten bushels of sesame seed in the top of a tree. You can imagine these heavy baskets and trying to climb up to the top of the tree with them, and then somehow trying to balance them up there, and then the baskets falling down and the seeds spilling everywhere. Pretty laborious … and pretty futile. Practice can certainly feel like that.

Difficult!

But this is not the whole story. There's another side. This other side is what Mrs Pang presents when she says, 'Easy! Easy! It's like touching your feet to the ground when you get out of bed.' What could be easier than finding that ground? It can't be missed. It's right there. Laywoman Pang knows this to the core of her being. She sees it. It's not an idea she has, but something she lives out of. She knows that life can be simple. She is herself simple. She knows that we can live a life that is pure, and clear, and peaceful. We don't have to have wild mystical experiences. We really just have to pay attention, and then we can't miss it. Our true nature. We're completely and utterly immersed in it, moment by moment. Why run around seeking it? In our chant 'The Harmony of Relative and Absolute' it says:

If you do not see the way, you do not see it, even as you walk on it.[20]

But even as we walk on it, not seeing it, we're still walking on it. And it's still completely supporting us at each moment.

Easy!

Finally Lingzhao comes in to top the whole thing off. She says, no, not difficult, not easy. The daughter takes the two views of the parents (and remember, difficult and easy are both simply views) and is able to integrate the two. She says:

Neither difficult nor easy. It's like the teachings of the ancestors shining on the hundred grass tips.

Now you can imagine that Lingzhao probably spent quite a bit of time out gathering material for the baskets that she made, so she would often

20. Affirming Faith in Mind (Xin Xin Ming) in *Chants and Recitations* (Rochester Zen Center, 2005); chanted each morning at sesshin.

see the grasses waving in the wind, rising and flattening like wheatfields. It's a beautiful image, and it's a perfect image for the emptiness of form. Yes, there's a form there in the grasses, but it's constantly changing, constantly moving. You can't grasp the shape of that field of grass because it's always in motion, flowing, never still. And it's the tips of the grass that move the most — and yet at the same time there's a stillness too.

These hundred grass tips are all the different forms that our life takes. Now we're at sesshin, sitting another round, now we're at home being a parent or a spouse, now we're at work doing our job, now we're having to deal with the phone company or somebody asking for money at the door. Where are *we*? Where is our self in all of this? Going to dokusan. Dealing with a difficult person at work. The demands of the family. All these changes, all these different roles that we play and tasks that we have to do. Lingzhao says that the Dharma, the teaching of the ancestors, is right there at the tips of those hundred grasses. There's suffering in this world of change, inevitably, but right where that suffering is there's also a way forward. There's something that shines.

Not easy, not difficult.

We get caught up in our ideas of ease and difficulty, but in truth it's neither and it's both.

One master said, 'Difficulty and ease alternate. Therein lies the way.' He didn't say the way lay in difficulty and he didn't say it lay in ease. We have to give up both and join with whatever is arising. We can put our absolute trust in the fact that things will change. None of this is permanent. None of it defines us. And there's light shining right here too.

We'll stop here and recite the four vows.

*   *

*

Hundreds of flowers in spring, the moon in autumn,
a cool breeze in summer and snow in winter.
If your mind is not clouded with unnecessary things,
no season is too much for you.

—Master Mumon's Verse for *Mumonkan,* CASE 19

* * *

CHAPTER 12

Continuous Practice: Daily Life

WHY practice Zen? As we come to our book's final chapter it seems important to revisit this question. Many of us come to Zen practice because our lives feel too harried and full of stress; we hope that the practice of meditation will help us to find some inner calm that will allow us to carry on our lives with greater equanimity and presence of mind, with more kindness and grace, with a deeper feeling of connection to the people and things that surround us. Some of us may even come to the practice with an inkling that our priorities are in need of rearrangement, that our lives are due for some kind of overhaul. All of these are positive, laudable aims which will take us far along the path of Zen. But after many months or years of practice, and very likely after attending a number of sesshins, we may realise that a shift has taken place. We may no longer see Zen practice as an important part of our lives, or as something that can help us in our lives, but rather, we may have come to see our lives as an important part of our Zen practice. This very body that we inhabit, these particular circumstances, the personal past, present and future of this discrete lifetime: all are the coming-into-being of the awakened nature of the universe, an expression of the ancient vows that we have taken we know not when. At this point, life goals in the conventional sense may appear less pressing; what is pressing is to accept whatever circumstances present themselves as an opportunity to drop self-partiality and live out of a much broader and deeper reality.

There are many things about participating in a sesshin that may bring about such a shift. One is the experience of spending a week with so many of our choices taken away from us. Just as sesshin is not arranged in the way we would choose for our optimal comfort, so life is not always the way we want it to be! This is of course the first and essential element of our lives that the Buddha identified: *dukkha*. And the next essential element of the Buddha's teaching is that, instead of immediately moving to try to fix our unsatisfactory circumstances, we might look to our mind and our own reactions instead. In sesshin, since we are mostly powerless over our circumstances, we have no other choice than to follow this advice – and this turns out to be wonderful training for when we leave sesshin. We have seen that this dropping of preferences can actually work!

Similarly, the experience of working with makyo[1] in sesshin can be great training for our post-sesshin lives. In daily life most of us are not likely to experience the grosser forms of makyo – visual or auditory hallucinations – but we will certainly continue to experience sudden surges of emotion, as well as all manner of urges, compulsions and perplexing circumstances. If we have been able to take on board Roshi Kjolhede's advice that it is beside the point whether such experiences are to be called real or illusory, then we can begin to work with whatever may arise as passing phenomena to which there is no need to over-react. Co-author Kathryn reports an experience she had a few days after her fourth or fifth sesshin:

> I was driving in the car, on my way to an appointment, and I had not left myself enough time. Of course there was some kind of road work that made the traffic much worse than usual, and I found myself getting more and more anxious and upset until I was actually in tears, cursing myself for my bad

1. See pp. 219–223.

habit of not allowing enough time to get where I needed to go. Suddenly in the midst of my spiraling emotions, the thought broke in – 'I'm having a makyo!' Immediately the situation appeared as no more than it was, and I was able to calm down easily.

There are other ways, too, in which sesshin can bring about big shifts in our lives. In sesshin we have the chance to explore the mind at a new depth. This, along with the 'speeded-up karma'[2] that we may experience in sesshin, can result in a radically altered view of our lives and our selves. In particular, the sudden insights or breakthroughs that may come to us in sesshin may leave us feeling changed, renewed, even 'washed clean'. As we leave sesshin the world may sparkle with an aliveness we have never known before, as if scales have fallen from our eyes, and we may feel full of new understanding and confidence.

While the inspiration that we draw from such experiences is invaluable, at the same time we need to be aware that anything we experience in, or indeed after, sesshin is still just an experience. Our mindstate is not a stable thing, and old habits, views and reactions die hard. Buddhist writer Jack Kornfield has published a book with the wonderfully suggestive title, *After the Ecstasy, the Laundry*. The experience of sesshin can be revelatory on many levels, but how do we integrate such experiences into the fabric of our everyday life? Unless we have some really useful, practical tools for doing so, we may soon find ourselves discouraged and overwhelmed by the realities of our day-to-day existence and the resurgence of our old habits and thought patterns.

If we look once again at the Noble Eightfold Path taught by the Buddha, we could say that the eighth aspect of the path, Samadhi or Concentration, is the pre-eminent concern for sesshin and, more generally, for our formal, on-the-mat practice. But in daily life it is the seventh limb, Mindfulness (*smṛti* in Sanskrit or *sati* in Pali), which must come to the fore. Mindfulness is a vast topic, but we can pull together some of what this term covers by pointing out that the root of the Sanskrit and Pali words *smṛti/sati* (as well as of the words used to translate these into other Asian languages) all have the basic meaning of 'remembering'. What is it that we are to be remembering as we move through our daily lives?

We often get the impression, particularly if we are working on a koan, that continuous practice means that we should try to keep the koan in

2. See Chapter 10, p. 224.

mind at all times. Though this may be a statement of an ideal, and though this may be possible occasionally, for instance when we are in sesshin, we need to make our peace with the fact that practice outside of sesshin and outside of formal rounds is not the same as inside. This doesn't mean we don't make an effort to return to our practice whenever we can. There are many times, such as sitting on a bus, waiting in a doctor's office, or even at a red light, when we can happily take advantage of the opportunity to dive into our practice. A conscious decision made in advance to use such times for taking up the practice rather than for reading magazines, listening to music or snapping on the car radio, is an important first step towards making our practice more continuous.

But there remain many other times in our daily lives when we need to concentrate fully on an activity that requires discursive thinking, or on a conversation with family or colleagues, and in these situations the koan or other formal practice must drop away – and may not be remembered again any time soon. We do need to make our peace with this fact, and also to realise that at these times the koan or other practice is not 'gone'; it is more like an underground stream which has temporarily disappeared from view but which will re-emerge at the appropriate time. We need to have confidence that, if we are sincerely committed to our practice, then it continues to work on us even when we are not consciously aware of bearing it in mind. No matter how often or for how long we lose track of the practice, this attitude of confidence will serve us better than an attitude of frustration, shame, or anxiety about the situation, all of which reinforce our sense of self.

Besides using the moments of waiting that crop up during our day as times to revive our practice, there are various other mindfulness exercises that we can introduce into our routine which can help us bring the concentrated presence of formal meditation into situations of daily life. Such practices are commonly taken up by participants in Term Intensives at the Auckland Zen Centre (see Chapter 7, p. 144). Mindful eating is an example: When we eat can we *just eat* – really being aware of the smell, taste, texture of our food and our reactions to these? Or we may choose to bow before we start eating, bringing to mind our gratitude and sense of oneness with all beings. Other examples include taking a breath before answering the telephone, or taking a moment of mindfulness before starting the car or when passing through a doorway. These can be helpful practices in encouraging us to return to a place of balance and awareness, if even for just a moment, many times throughout the day. But, just as with koan work, such practices can also give rise to anxiety, frustration, or obsessive-compulsive behaviour. To some extent we can see such things as a sort of shadow side of Zen — and some people may be more prone to such traps than others. But, either way, finding a way to work skillfully with our own minds is precisely the point.

In addition to working with discrete mindfulness practices, some of us may be in a position to make more global shifts to our home life or daily schedule. We can look to traditional monastic or full-time Zen training programmes for hints in making such changes. In such programmes we find three key aspects: first, silence as default mode, that is, speaking only as necessary and eliminating the distraction of electronic devices; second, leaving no traces, in other words maintaining an orderly, clean and spare (visually undistracting) environment; and finally, a set schedule that allows plenty of time for sitting, as well as set times for chanting, meals and work.

The truth is that most of us would not be able to function well in our day-to-day roles if we were to fully adopt such a regimen. We do need to use our computers and phones, to chat with people, to feel comfortable in all sorts of environments, and to respond flexibly to the needs of others and to changes in our schedules. At the same time, however, it may be very helpful to examine our lives from time to time and to consider how we might introduce changes that will move us in the direction of more quiet, order, and discipline. It is simply a fact that our physical circumstances and our daily routines have a profound effect on our minds. How much news do we truly need to consume each day to remain informed? Might it be possible to clean the dishes after each meal instead of letting them pile up in the sink? Can we, as a baseline, make a commitment to a daily sitting routine and to regular attendance at formal sittings? But while changes to our routine can be immensely helpful supports to our inner work, even more important is our willingness, even as we become more deeply engaged in the formal aspects of Zen practice, to cultivate a mind that does not value the formal practice over the other parts of our lives. When we step up from the meditation mat, rather than heaving a sigh that we must now leave our practice behind, it can be helpful to tell ourselves, 'Now is the chance to *really* practice.' The formal practice can be seen as effective to the extent that it lessens our sense of alienation from our own circumstances and our sense of separateness from others. As we move through our lives, more important than, for example, remembering to take a breath each time the phone rings is to remember the fundamental teachings of non-separation and non-harming.

Thus, as lay practitioners, it is vital that we not view our families and our jobs as distractions from our practice rather than as its centre. We should avoid falling into the error of believing that it is only monastics or those in full-time training programmes who are doing the 'real' practice. On the contrary, living with family can be a full and fully real way to practice. In a teisho from 2004, Sensei Wrightson quoted an article by Kyogen Carlson, a Zen teacher in Oregon, USA. He started off as a monastic and then fell in love with a fellow monastic, so disrobed and got married. In the article he wrote:

> Over the years we have found that marriage can be a wonderful expression of Sangha.

This very simple statement really caught Amala-sensei's attention as being something very obvious but also something that one doesn't hear much about in Zen. She said:

> Certainly for me, for the first four years of our practice, after attending a workshop in Sweden and then going home to New Zealand, Richard and I were Sangha to each other. We did sit intermittently with another group, but mostly we supported each other. It's so much easier when you are practicing with even one other person. You might not be feeling like sitting but the other person does, so you end up sitting, and of course you're glad afterwards that you did. If you hadn't had that one other person you might not have; and then you are the same for that person when they're not feeling like sitting, so right there you receive and give support.
>
> In Christianity marriage is a sacrament. It's addressed as a central ritual of that religion. In Buddhism we might imagine that marriage is devalued. It certainly looks that way. When you look at our foundational myth, right there near the beginning, what does the Buddha do? He leaves his wife and baby. Doesn't look good for marriage. But we shouldn't misunderstand this. One way of seeing it is that at that point in his life the Buddha's need to connect with all beings meant that he couldn't be confined within the nuclear family, or within his father's kingdom. These were too narrow a field for his endeavour to come to awakening. But part of the story that isn't told as often is that not only his wife but his son and his step-mother

eventually joined the Sangha. So there was a parting but then a return where the family was included in this bigger context.

It's important for us to remember this second part of the story. But this doesn't mean that our goal is to get all of our family members practicing, too. We need to have a more sophisticated understanding of Sangha in the broadest sense, seeing the ways in which our family members play a role in our spiritual life. Marriage can be a matrix for enlightenment, for *dana*, for going beyond the small self.

Likewise it is important to see caring for children — as well as caring for elderly parents — as an expression of *dana*, as an expression of Sangha, and as a matrix of enlightenment. The love and care that we feel for our children has been taken as archetypal in Buddhism and in Zen. The Metta Sutta (see inset overleaf) refers to the love that a mother feels for her only child as a model for how we should relate to all of our fellow beings. And in one of his best-known works, the *Tenzo Kyokun* or *Instructions to the Cook*, Master Dogen tells us:

> *Rōshin* is the mind or attitude of a parent. In the same way that a parent cares for an only child, keep the Three Treasures in your mind. A parent, irrespective of poverty or difficult circumstances, loves and raises a child with care. How deep is love like this? Only a parent can understand it. A parent protects the children from the cold and shades them from the hot sun with no concern for his or her own personal welfare. Only a person in whom this mind has arisen can understand it, and only one in whom this attitude has become second nature can fully realize it. This is the ultimate in being a parent. In this same manner, when you handle water, rice, or anything else, you must have the affectionate and caring concern of a parent raising a child.[3]

In his commentary on Dogen's text (published under the title *How to Cook Your Life*), Zen teacher Kosho Uchiyama tells us:

> ... the *Tenzo Kyōkun* teaches us that the Self inclusive of the whole world is nothing other than the very things, people, or situations that we presently encounter and know, and helps us to discover our lives through these things, and, in turn, pour all our life ardor back into them.[4]

3. Zen Master Dōgen and Kōshō Uchiyama Rōshi, *How To Cook Your Life: From the Zen Kitchen to Enlightenment*, trans. by Thomas Wright (Boulder, Colo.: Shambhala, 2005), pp. 17–18.

4. *Ibid.*, p. 52.

The Buddha's Words on Loving-Kindness
translated from the Pali by
The Amaravati Sangha

This is what should be done
   By one who is skilled in goodness,
And who knows the path of peace:
   Let them be able and upright,
Straightforward and gentle in speech,
   Humble and not conceited,
Contented and easily satisfied,
   Unburdened with duties and frugal in their ways.
Peaceful and calm and wise and skillful,
   Not proud or demanding in nature.
Let them not do the slightest thing
   That the wise would later reprove.
Wishing: In gladness and in safety,
   May all beings be at ease.
Whatever living beings there may be;
   Whether they are weak or strong, omitting none,
The great or the mighty, medium, short or small,
   The seen and the unseen,
Those living near and far away,
   Those born and to-be-born —
May all beings be at ease!

Let none deceive another,
  Or despise any being in any state.
Let none through anger or ill-will
  Wish harm upon another.
Even as a mother protects with her life
  Her child, her only child,
So with a boundless heart
  Should one cherish all living beings;
Radiating kindness over the entire world:
  Spreading upwards to the skies,
And downwards to the depths;
  Outwards and unbounded,
Freed from hatred and ill-will.
  Whether standing or walking, seated or lying down
Free from drowsiness,
  One should sustain this recollection.
This is said to be the sublime abiding.
  By not holding to fixed views,
The pure-hearted one, having clarity of vision,
  Being freed from all sense desires,
Is not born again into this world.

In seeking to develop and 'remember' this parental mind in all of our daily activities, we need to find the most effective balance of formal and non-formal practice, without undervaluing either. In the Introduction to *How to Cook Your Life*, translator Thomas Wright points out two traps into which practitioners can easily fall: first 'in taking literally the idea of zazen being the most important activity in our life as opposed to all our other activities and trying to do as much zazen as possible to the neglect of everything else', or conversely 'of deluding themselves into believing that since all their activities are zazen there is no need to sit and face the wall and do zazen'.[5]

Thus our goal is not to tot up the largest possible number of hours of sitting, but rather to bring the spirit and mind of zazen into all of our activities – while, at the same time, practical experience teaches us that we have very little chance of doing so without a steady dose of daily sitting practice. Sitting gives us a space in which we are able to notice the mind without immediately moving into reactivity: if something itches, we notice rather than scratching, if we are bored, we notice rather than getting up, if we are in pain, we notice rather than changing position, if we are prey to afflictive emotions, we notice rather than complaining, throwing things, or telling someone off. If we can bring this habit of noticing the mind – of 'remembering' the mind – into our daily life and our interactions, then we can create for ourselves just that little moment of time that may be needed for us to identify our own situation, feelings, and reactions without *identifying with* them, and without automatically jumping into blaming or hurting others. This doesn't mean that we don't communicate with others. But if we can be clear about when we are upset and when we are calm, and if we can learn to to wait for the calm times to do our communicating, then we may be less likely to speak and act in ways which we later may regret.

The Buddha taught about four *Brahmaviharas* or Divine Abodes, four qualities that, when cultivated, can create a heaven-on-earth within and around us: these qualities are loving-kindness, compassion, joy at the happiness of others, and equanimity. The last of these, equanimity (literally 'even-mindedness' or 'equal-mindedness'), is interesting; though we may be tempted to think of it as a state of calm detachment, it is actually taught

5. *Ibid.*, p. xiii.

as the culmination of the other three qualities, referring most fundamentally to the ability to view all other beings equally, and to cherish each one as we cherish ourselves or our own families and friends. This is a radical state of non-differentiation and of the dropping of preferences, of likes and dislikes. And yet it is not an arid state of indifference or of distancing oneself from the joys and sorrows of this world. Rather, it is in cultivating compassion, loving-kindness, and sympathetic joy in our lives every day that we may begin to experience a taste of this equal-mindedness.

At the same time, it is not just in our interactions with others that we can cultivate these qualities. We can learn to ground our formal practice in them as well, approaching our own minds with gentleness and love, and our meditative work with joy and a willingness to surrender to whatever arises. In doing so we find our practice coming to life in a new way, along with an increased capacity to manifest more love, compassion and joy in the world. As we recognise these Divine Abodes as our true home and make them our dwelling place, the boundary between our formal practice and our practice in daily life begins to dissolve, and we can begin to experience the seamless wholeness of things as they really are.

Since ancient times, Zen masters have presented the path of Zen by means of Ten Oxherding Pictures. In this sequence of ten sketches, a man is seen searching for an ox, finding its tracks, catching the beast, taming it, and riding it home.[6] Of course the pictures present a metaphor for our Zen practice, and for our relationship to our practice and to our True Nature. At a certain point in the series, the ox — and then even the man — disappear: no more separation from the practice; no more sense of a separate self. The ninth picture is entitled 'Returning to the Source'. In this sketch no ox or man appears, and the accompanying text begins with the words, 'From the very beginning there has not been so much as a speck of dust.' This is a state of deep enlightenment. Significantly, however, to dwell in such a state is not the endpoint of Zen practice. In the tenth picture, there is the man again, laughing as he 'enters the marketplace with helping hands'.

6. See, for example, Roshi Philip Kapleau, *The Three Pillars of Zen* (New York: Anchor, 2000), pp. 332–345.

TEISHO

* * *

No Season is Too Much
(2013–07–16)

Today I'd like to take up a verse from the *Mumonkan* as the starting point
for this teisho. Each of the 48 koans in the *Mumonkan* is accompanied
by a commentary and a verse written by Master Mumon, who assembled
the collection. The verse we'll look at today accompanies Case 19 and
it goes as follows:

> *Hundreds of flowers in spring, the moon in autumn,*
> *A cool breeze in summer and snow in winter.*
> *If your mind is not clouded by unnecessary things,*
> *No season is too much for you.*

This verse seemed like a good one for us in the depths of winter. Today
is a beautiful day, but we've had some pretty cold, wet weather lately. Can
we appreciate that cold weather? Can we appreciate it without grumbling
audibly or to ourselves? Historically in Japanese culture there's a strong
aesthetic tradition of appreciating the seasons. Perhaps nowadays this is
blunted somewhat by urban living, but traditionally it has been expressed
in poetry, especially in haiku, or by having a flower arrangement or scroll
in the alcove of the house that is in tune with the season, wearing clothing
with designs that harmonise with the seasons. To be able to appreciate all
the little changes that occur and the things that are especially meaningful
in each season – as it says in this verse, the flowers in spring, the moon
in autumn, a cool breeze in summer, snow in winter. Of course here in
Auckland we don't get snow – except once last year for about five minutes – but to be able to appreciate what we do receive! Sun in winter is
particularly beautiful, to be able to sit with the sun on one's back on a
cold day. Dogs and cats know this very well.

Of course, this verse has more to it than just the literal meaning. When
Mumon talks here about seasons, he's talking about all the different kinds
of changes that we go through: birth, growth, aging, dying, as well as
struggles of all kinds. And we could also include here any of the mental

weather systems that come our way: anger, boredom, dullness, confusion, anxiety, discouragement, excitement, elation, enthusiasm.

If your mind is not clouded by unnecessary things,
No season is too much for you.

Often we don't even allow ourselves to experience what's going on because we jump so quickly to our opinions about what's happening, to our thoughts, or to trying to fix things. In one of his books Jon Kabat-Zinn suggests a little exercise, which is just to say to ourselves, to remind ourselves from time to time, 'This is it.' This is it. Whatever we are experiencing, this is it. Kabat-Zinn reminds us that acceptance of the present moment has nothing to with resignation. 'It simply means a clear acknowledgement that *what is happening is happening.*'[7] We can't act wisely without this basic awareness, and it is where the primary koans 'Mu' and 'What is this?' are anchored. Right now, if this is it, *what* is it? What is mu right here and now? We ask these questions of whatever we are experiencing in this moment.

Kabat-Zinn describes a *New Yorker* cartoon which I also remember seeing and smiling about, and which was on the bulletin board at the Rochester Zen Center for a while. It shows two Zen monks sitting next to each other; one's young and fresh-faced and the other is really old and wrinkly like a prune, and the young one is looking bleakly at the old one who's saying, 'Nothing happens next. This is it.' Kabat-Zinn writes:

> Ordinarily, when we undertake something, it is only natural to expect a desirable outcome for our efforts. We want to see results, even if it is only a pleasant feeling. The sole exception I can think of is meditation. Meditation is the only intentional, systematic human activity which at bottom is about not trying to improve yourself or get anywhere else, but simply to realize where you already are. Perhaps its value lies precisely in this.[8]

It doesn't matter what practice we're doing, whether it's breath, or koan, or shikantaza, it's necessary to do it just for its own sake, to be fully engaged with this present breath, not thinking about how some other breath is going to be, or some other moment.

7. Jon Kabat-Zinn, *Wherever You Go There You Are* (New York: Hyperion, 1994), p. 16.
8. *Ibid.,* p. 14.

But hearing this, you might very well be asking yourself, well what is the point? Surely I *do* come along wanting to get something out of this practice. It might be to relax, or to experience deeper states, to become a better person — or just last Saturday at the workshop we heard many people talk about wanting to work with very painful things in their lives, to work with suffering, to find some freedom from old habits and compulsions. And actually all of these are valid reasons for taking up a meditation practice, but they can become problematic if we expect that everything's going to change just because we're meditating now. Actually sometimes when you start to do a meditation practice, it feels like your mind is worse than before. And this comes about because you're now beginning to pay attention to your mind and are seeing its defilements more clearly. Often things do have to get worse before they can get better.

But if we can't let go of our thoughts about what we want to get out of the practice, then it's as if we are always taking the lid off of the pot, checking to see how it's going, and a watched pot never boils. It's very easy to get discouraged when we're always looking for signs of progress. It's counterproductive. Who is it that wants progress? I've mentioned before some very good advice that Vajrayana teacher Alan Wallace was given by his teacher, when he was puzzling about this. He went to his teacher saying, Surely I'm striving for awakening, surely that's a necessary thing. And his teacher told him, Let that aspiration get you onto the mat to do the practice, but once you're on the mat and doing the practice, then forget about that and just do the practice. Very good advice. In other words we don't want to turn our aspiration, which is really a dynamic, changing thing, into a fixed idea. Jon Kabat-Zinn says that in meditation practice, the best way to get somewhere is to let go of trying to get anywhere at all.

We work by indirection in our practice, not by confronting our thoughts and feelings head-on, not by doing battle with them, but rather by recognising thoughts as thoughts and feelings as feelings and returning positively to our practice focus. For most people the focus is the breath, this process which happens so beautifully without our conscious involvement. In fact the breath is a kind of a bridge between our conscious mind and our unconscious mind, as well as uniting our so-called inside and outside. We can bring our awareness to the breath; we can even control it if we wish, though that is not our approach in Zen practice. But even when we don't bring our awareness to it, our breathing goes on. It happens when we're doing some complicated activity, it happens when we're talking, it happens when we're asleep. Functioning perfectly! Very often we can get fixated on what is wrong, but the breath can be a reminder, every time we come back to it, of the perfection, of the *thusness* of this moment. This is it! Actually we don't have anything else but this to work with.

Ajahn Brahm, a western-born Thai Forest Tradition monk tells a really good story about this tendency to pick out from any experience what is wrong. When his community first started building their monastery in Perth, in Western Australia, they were very short of money. They couldn't afford to hire labourers, and so had to learn how to build everything themselves. One of the things he learned was how to lay bricks, and he said it was much harder than it looks. You'd put the mortar on and try to get the brick into place, but it would invariably go up on one side and down on the other and you'd have to nudge it back into position. He said that being a monk he had a lot of time on his hands, and so he took his time with this and tried to get every single brick level. Eventually, going along like this, he finished this wall, but when he finally stood back to admire it, he noticed that there were two bricks in the middle of the wall that were really bad. They were on an angle and spoiled the whole wall. But it was too late, the cement had already hardened and the only way he would have been able to fix this wall would have been by knocking part of it down and building it again. And he actually wanted to do that, but he was told no, there were many other things they had to do and he needed to just leave it. So he left it, but he says that when he'd take visitors around the monastery, whenever he would go past that wall, he would cringe. He hated it, because he would see those two crooked bricks.

Then he tells how at a certain point some months after he had finished making the wall, he was showing a visitor around, and the visitor said, 'That's a nice wall.' And then Ajahn Brahm said, 'No, what are you talking about? Can't you see those two bad bricks that spoil the whole wall?' and the visitor said, 'Yes, I can see those two bad bricks, but I can also see the 998 good bricks as well.'

And Ajahn Brahm relates, 'I was stunned. For the first time in over three months I could see other bricks in that wall besides the two mistakes. Above, below, to the left and to the right of the bad bricks, good bricks, perfect bricks. Moreover the perfect bricks were many, many more than the two bad bricks. Before, my eyes would focus exclusively on my two mistakes. I was blind to everything else. That was why I couldn't bear looking at that wall or having others see it. That was why I wanted to destroy it. But now that I could see the good bricks, the wall didn't look so bad after all. It was, as the visitor had said, a nice brick wall. It's still there now twenty years later, but I have forgotten where those bad bricks are. I literally cannot see those mistakes any more.'[9]

There are so many situations in which we only see what is wrong. When we fixate on other people's imperfections it can affect our relationships with them, and it can affect our relationship to our work and our relationship to ourselves. We often do this with our practice, too. And there are many reasons for this common habit, but perhaps one is that we live in a culture of dissatisfaction. In our consumer society we're constantly being enticed to seek out what's new or improved, or 20% more for the same price. We are deeply conditioned to see growth and expansion as essential, so we are always wanting improvement, when in the natural order of things growth is not a constant but part of a cycle that includes decay and death. The human race is in denial about this. When Mumon talks about our mind not being clouded by unnecessary things, we are reminded to let go of our thoughts about progress, about attainment, about 20% more. Instead of getting caught up in those concepts, can we just become so involved in *this* that our ideas about the process and about ourselves dissolve?

The Taoist sage, Zhuangzi says:

In the age when life on earth was full, no one paid any special attention to worthy men, nor did they single out the man of ability. Rulers were simply the highest branches on the tree, and the people were like deer in the woods. They were honest and righteous without realizing that they were 'doing their duty'. They loved each other and did not know that this was 'love of neighbor'. They deceived no one yet they did not know that they were 'men to be trusted'. They were reliable and did not know that this was 'good faith'. They lived freely together giving and taking, and did not know that they were generous. For this reason their deeds have not been narrated. They made no history.[10]

Of course there was probably never actually a time when this was the

9. Ajahn Branhn, *Opening the Door of Your Heart* (Melbourne: Lothian Books, 2004), p. 7.
10. Thomas Merton, *The Way of Chuang Tzu* (New York: New Directions, 1969), p. 76.

case, but Zhuangzi is using this idea of a Golden Age as a rhetorical device in order to point out what true ordinariness is like. To be ordinary, to have a mind unclouded by unnecessary things, is to live in a way that is completely unaffected, where we're just being honest, not thinking, 'I'm an honest person,' where we're just being generous, not thinking, 'I'm a generous person.' When we're sitting we're just sitting.

There's a Zen story in which a master has a government official as a student, and at a certain point this official is appointed to a new position, and the teacher asks him, Well, how are you going to rule? And the official says, 'I will rule with wisdom and compassion.' And then the teacher says, 'Oh, I pity your poor subjects if that's the case!'

Our verse for today was written to go along with *Mumonkan* Case 19 which is called 'Ordinary Mind is the Way'. And the case goes like this:

> Joshu asked Nansen, 'What is the Way?' Nansen answered, 'Ordinary mind is the Way.' Joshu asked, 'Shall I try to seek after it?' 'If you try to seek after it, you go away from it,' answered Nansen.
> Joshu: 'If I do not try for it, how can I know the Way?'
> Nansen: 'The Way is not a matter of knowing or not knowing. Knowing is illusion; not knowing is blankness. If you attain to this Way of no-doubt, it is as boundless as vast space, so how can there be right or wrong in the Way?'
> At these words Joshu was suddenly enlightened.

This is one of the dilemmas that comes up in practice time and again. If we're not to seek after the Way, if it really is just what's right here in front of us, then what are we supposed to be doing? How do we seek the Way without seeking? Nansen says, 'The Way is not a matter of knowing or not knowing. Knowing is illusion; not knowing is blankness.'

The problem with knowing, what makes it illusory, is that it's dualistic; there are a knower and a known in knowing. The world is split in two, and along with self and other all the other dualities that we get hooked on also arise; have/have not, success/failure and all the rest. But then to just reject knowing is also a mistake, because that's just ignorance, blankness. The secret really is to join with the practice, to become the breath, to become the koan, to just be so completely absorbed in this moment that the self is forgotten.

'If you attain this way of no doubt it is as boundless as vast space.' In the commentary, Mumon says, 'Questioned by Joshu, Nansen like melting ice and disintegrating tile dissolved, and could not offer a plausible explanation.' This may sound like a criticism, but in fact it is Mumon's frequent ploy of giving praise through what sounds like slander. You find this style of humour all through the *Mumonkan* and it is an expression of Mumon's intimacy with the masters whose stories he tells. But then Mumon says something that's not teasing at all, but is very to the point. He says, 'Even though Joshu has come to a realisation, he must delve into it for another thirty years before he can understand it fully.'

This ordinary mind, *this* – this right here [taps lectern] – is unfathomable. We might get a glimpse of the nature of this ordinary mind, and yet we'll need to delve into it for another thirty years, to truly live out of that simplicity, to live out of that immediacy.

The great Chinese lay practitioner Layman Pang (740–808, see above pp. 246 ff.) wrote the following verse, the last two lines of which are particularly well-known:

> *In my daily life, there are no other chores than*
> *Those that happen to fall into my hands.*
> *Nothing I choose, nothing reject.*
> *Nowhere is there ado, nowhere a slip.*
> *I have no other emblems of my glory*
> *Than the mountains and hills without a spot of dust.*
> *My magical power and spiritual exercise consist in*
> *Carrying water and gathering firewood.*[11]

'I have no other emblems of my glory than the mountains and hills without a spot of dust.' No need for titles. No need for recognition. But what extraordinary adornments, the mountains and hills. The fields and the forests. The sky and the clouds.

'My magical power and spiritual exercise consist in carrying water and gathering firewood.' Carrying water. Gathering firewood. Paying the bills. Washing the dishes. Playing with our grandchildren. Writing a letter. Making a phone call.

To really be able to just do what's in front of us, to do what needs to be

11. Quoted in John C. H. Wu, *The Golden Age of Zen* (New York: Doubleday, 1996), p. 71.

done, while at the same time being aware of the boundlessness and spaciousness within each moment.

> *Hundreds of flowers in spring, the moon in autumn,*
> *A cool breeze in summer and snow in winter.*
> *If your mind is not clouded by unnecessary things,*
> *No season is too much for you.*

We'll stop here and recite the Four Vows.

* *

*

GLOSSARY

ANATTĀ: *see under* THREE DHARMA SEALS

ANICCĀ: *see under* THREE DHARMA SEALS

ANUTTARĀ-SAMYAK-SAMBODHI: The Complete Perfect Enlightenment of the Buddha.

BHIKKHU, BHIKKHUNĪ: A traditionally ordained celibate male (bhikkhu) or female (bhikkhunī) monastic, pledged to following the approximately 227 bhikkhu or 311 bhikkhunī precepts (numbers vary in different traditions), which are found in the sacred texts known as the *Vinaya*.

BODHICITTA: The aspiration to awaken for the sake of helping sentient beings; this impulse is central to the teachings of the Mahāyāna. Bodhicitta is further divided into 'relative bodhicitta', the cultivation of loving-kindness and compassion for others, and 'ultimate bodhicitta', the cultivation of non-dual wisdom or seeing into the Emptiness (*q.v.*) of all phenomena, that is, that nothing exists apart from anything else. These two, compassion and wisdom, are seen as equally necessary elements of awakening.

BODHIDHARMA (483–540): The founder of the Zen (Chan) School. Known as the twenty-eighth Indian ancestor (see Chapter 4, p. 76), Bodhidharma is said to have brought the practice and teaching of Zen from India to China (see further under Chan below). He is famous for his fierce and uncompromising approach to practice and teaching, typified in reports of his initial encounter with the Chinese Emperor Wu (quoted below), of his sitting and facing a wall in a cave at Shaolin without speaking for nine years, and in the legend of his cutting off his eyelids to prevent himself from falling asleep while meditating. (As the eyelids hit the ground, the first tea plants sprang up.) The first koan in the *Hekiganroku* (*q.v.*) begins as follows:

> Emperor Wu of Liang asked the Great Master Bodhidharma, 'What is the first principle of the holy teachings?' Bodhidharma said, 'Emptiness without holiness.' The Emperor said, 'Who is standing before me?' Bodhidharma replied, 'I don't know.' The Emperor did not understand.

Bodhidharma's reply of 'I don't know' has been called the most famous response in Zen; Zen practice continually throws each of us back on our own not-knowing.

NOTE: For reference, all words in the Glossary are listed with full diacritics (accent marks). Diacritics are not used in the main text, except in the case of Māori words. Note that the pronunciation of Sanskrit ś is like English 'sh'. In the main text this sound is spelled out as 'sh'; for example, Śila is spelled Shila in the main text.

BODHISATTVA: A bodhisattva is anyone in whom the spirit of bodhicitta (*q.v.*) has arisen, and who has therefore taken a vow to achieve enlightenment for the sake of all beings. In the Theravāda tradition in particular, 'the Bodhisatta' refers to the Buddha during the years (and lifetimes) before he had attained his Complete Perfect Enlightenment. In the Mahāyāna tradition, many great archetypal bodhisattvas are venerated, such as Kannon (Avalokiteśvara), the Bodhisattva of Compassion; Mañjuśrī, the Bodhisattva of Wisdom; and Samantabhadra, the Bodhisattva of Skilful Means or Enlightened Action. Additionally, however, the Zen teaching is that each of us who sincerely makes the effort to walk in the path of the Buddha is also a bodhisattva.

BRAHMAVIHĀRĀ: 'Divine Abode'. One of the four qualities that the Buddha taught which, when cultivated, can create a heaven-on-earth within and around us, namely: loving-kindness, compassion, joy at the happiness of others, and equanimity. See Chapter 12, pp. 266–267.

BUDDHA: Literally, 'the one who is awake', Buddha is the word used by Shakyamuni when he was asked to explain who he was. In the Mahāyāna view, Shakyamuni, the Buddha of our own age, is only one of countless billions of awakened Buddhas who populate the universe offering support to sentient beings. The word can also be used to refer to the awakened nature of the universe which is inherently present within each one of us. See also under Three Jewels.

CHAN: The word 'Zen' is the Japanese form of the Chinese word 'Chan,' which is, in turn, the Chinese form of the Sanskrit (Indian) word 'Dhyāna' meaning 'meditation' or 'concentration'. In the Buddha's teaching, Dhyāna is one of the eight essential aspects of the path to liberation (see under Eightfold Path), and the Chinese Chan school of Buddhism is the one that put special emphasis on this aspect of the practice. The evolution of the word Dhyāna to Chan and then to Zen follows the historical path of the teachings as they moved from India to China and Korea and then to Japan. Bodhidharma brought this school of Buddhism to China in the fifth century, and it reached Japan in the twelfth century.

DAISAN: Private interview offered by a senior student rather than a teacher (cf. Dokusan). See Chapter 4, p. 76.

DĀNA: 'Giving,' the first of the Paramitas (*q.v.*). Colloquially, 'dāna' is often used to refer to donations to a Dharma Centre or to a teacher, priest or monastic, and in particular to the food offerings of the laity upon which monastics depend for their sustenance, as they do not handle money.

DEPENDENT CO-ARISING, or DEPENDENT ORIGINATION, *see under* PRATĪTYASAMUTPĀDA.

DHAMMAPADA: One of the most beloved of the Pali Sūttas (*q.v.*), the *Dhammapada* consists of a series of *gāthās*, or verses, which pithily express the core teachings of the Buddha.

DHARMA: The teachings of the Buddha, the Law of the universe, or simply 'the way things are' (which is what the teachings of the Buddha reveal); dharma (with a small 'd') is most often used in the plural (dharmas) to mean 'things, phenomena, the stuff of our physical and non-physical world'. See also under Three Jewels.

DHARMA HEIR: One designated by their teacher in a public ceremony as having embodied the transmitted teaching and as having the aptitude, spiritual maturity and upright character required to teach others effectively.

DŌGEN ZENJI (Zen Master Dōgen) (1200–1253): The founder of the Japanese Sōtō Zen School (see under Sōtō and Rinzai). As a young man, Dōgen trained under Rinzai Masters Eisai and Myōzen, then travelled to China where he studied Chan with Master Rujing. After returning to Japan he established the Sōtō school at Eihei-ji temple. He was a prolific writer, and his written works are still studied intensively, both by Zen practitioners and by religious historians, as masterpieces of Zen expression.

DOKUSAN: The Japanese word *dokusan* means literally to 'go alone', and in Zen training it refers to a one-to-one meeting between a teacher and student. See Chapter 4, pp. 75–76.

DUKKHA: Suffering, unsatisfactoriness. A possibly false but oft-quoted etymology makes the word 'dukkha' refer to an axle-hole that is not properly fitted to its axle. In other words, dukkha encompasses not just the more obvious types of pain and loss, but also the way that our lives and circumstances so often feel off-kilter or in need of fixing. The Buddha delineated three types of suffering, related to the Three Dharma Seals (*q.v.*): the suffering of suffering (painful physical and emotional experiences), the suffering of change (impermanence), and the existential suffering of being. The last stems from our sense of separation or alienation – our belief in our own independent existence.

EIGHTFOLD PATH: The Way to liberation as taught by the Buddha. For a list and explanation of its eight aspects see inset p. 121.

EMPTINESS (Śūnyatā): The teaching that all things are empty of a separate self or of an absolute, independent, or eternal existence. From the positive perspective this is the doctrine of Pratītyasamutpāda (*q.v.*) or Interbeing. Insight into Emptiness is a goal both of practice and of Madhyamaka philosophy (*q.v.*) and the Prajñāpāramitā Sūtras. The great Indian teacher Nāgārjuna (*q.v.*) was instrumental in the development of these last two (see Chapter 5, p. 100, and inset pp. 162–163). See also under Bodhicitta.

FOUR NOBLE TRUTHS: The Four Noble Truths are: the truth of suffering, the truth of the causes of suffering, the truth of the cessation of suffering, and the truth of the way out of suffering. (See Chapter 2, pp. 40–42.) Though these truths have long been referred to in English as the Noble Truths, an equally valid or perhaps preferable translation would be Ennobling Truths. This captures the way in which these truths may act upon us when we start to live by them. (See further the Wikipedia article on the Four Noble Truths under 'Truths for the noble ones'.)

FOUR SIGHTS: An old person, a sick person, a corpse, and a monk in meditation: these are the sights Prince Siddhartha (the future Buddha) saw on his first journeys outside of the palace grounds where he had been raised. His encounter with the truth and universality of suffering led to his renunciation of his life of luxury and his quest for enlightenment. See further at Chapter 10, p. 197.

FOUR VOWS (or Four Bodhisattvic Vows): These four vows of the bodhisattva (*q.v.*) are recited at the end of each formal sitting:

> *All beings without number I vow to liberate,*
> *Endless blind passions I vow to uproot,*
> *Dharma gates beyond measure I vow to penetrate,*
> *The Great Way of Buddha I vow to attain.*

HARADA, DAIUN SOGAKU (1871–1961): *see under* SŌTŌ AND RINZAI.

HEART SŪTRA: Probably the most frequently recited sūtra of Mahāyāna Buddhism, this brief text (see Chapter 8, pp. 162–163) expresses the essence of the Prajñāpāramitā (Perfection of Wisdom) teachings on Emptiness (*q.v.*).

HEKIGANROKU: The *Blue Cliff Record* is a koan collection compiled by Xuedou Chongxian (980–1052; Setchō in Japanese). It was later commented upon by Yuanwu Keqin (1063–1135; Engo in Japanese). Though chronologically an earlier collection than the *Mumonkan* (*q.v.*), it is generally the second book of koans taken up by students in dokusan.

INTERBEING, *see under* PRATĪTYASAMUTPĀDA.

JUKAI: The ceremony in which one formally enters on the Buddhist Path. The heart of the ceremony is the taking of the sixteen Precepts (*q.v.*). Practitioners participate in this ceremony not just once, but on a regular basis, as a way of renewing their vows and affirming an ongoing commitment to ethical conduct. For a more detailed discussion, see Chapter 5.

KANNON: The Bodhisattva of Compassion. See Chapter 8 teisho and under Bodhisattva.

KAPLEAU, RŌSHI PHILIP (1912–2004): Founder of the Rochester Zen Center and author of the Zen classic *The Three Pillars of Zen* as well as many other books.

KARMA: In English the word 'karma' is generally used as a shorthand for 'karma-vipāka' or action-result. Buddhism teaches that all things exist dependent on causes and conditions, and, moreover that our own actions are causes of future conditions. See further at Chapter 6, pp. 123–125.

KINHIN: Walking meditation. See Chapter 3, pp. 56–57.

KJOLHEDE, RŌSHI BODHIN (1948–): Current Abbot of the Rochester Zen Center. Dharma Heir of Rōshi Kapleau and teacher of Amala-sensei.

KOAN: A koan is a Zen teaching story. The word 'koan' is the Japanese form of the Chinese word 'gongan', a term that comes from Chinese law, where it means a 'public case' or precedent. Koans most often take the form of a pithy story recounting an incident or verbal exchange between a master and student, or between two masters. These anecdotes were gathered into teaching collections in medieval China; standard collections worked on by Zen students today include the *Mumonkan* (*q.v.*), the *Hekiganroku* (*q.v.*) and the *Shōyōroku*. Students who have been assigned a koan in dokusan have the task of demonstrating to the teacher their grasp of the essential meaning of the incident or exchange. See further at Introduction, p. 8, and at Chapter 1, Note 6 (p. 27). For more on the process of working on a koan, see Chapter 10, p. 199; Chapter 11, Day 3; and Chapter 12, pp. 259–260.

KYŌSAKU: The stick, or encouragement stick. The use of the stick during formal rounds of meditation is said to date to ancient China where it was introduced as a way to rouse sitters who had nodded off while sitting. Today it is used more generally to rouse energy and determination, and to cut off the wanderings or daydreams of the mind. Sitters are struck twice on each shoulder on the trapezius muscle, the spot known in Chinese medicine as the 'triple warmer' acupuncture meridian. Receiving the stick is always optional; it is never used as a form of punishment.

LINJI: Linji Yixuan (d. 866), or Rinzai Gigen in Japanese, was one of the most renowned Chinese Zen masters of the Tang Dynasty period (often known as 'the Golden Age of Zen') and the founder of the Linji teaching lineage, which became the Rinzai school in Japan (see under 'Sōtō and Rinzai'). Linji was known for his fierce style of teaching which included many shouts and blows. His sayings and teachings are recorded in the *Linji-lu* or *Record of Linji*.

MADHYAMAKA: The 'Middle Way' philosophy of the Mahāyāna (*q.v.*) branch of Buddhism has its origins in the work of Nāgārjuna (*q.v.*). Madhyamaka teaches that no single philosophical position can be constructed and defended as ultimate by logical means; rather arguments pro and con may always be marshalled. In particular neither a nihilistic nor an absolutist view of reality can be ultimately defended. (See further at Chapter 8, pp. 161–165.)

MAHĀYĀNA: *see under* THERAVĀDA, MAHAYĀNĀ, VAJRAYĀNA.

MAÑJUŚRĪ: The Bodhisattva (*q.v.*) of Wisdom.

MARA: The Buddhist tempter; a personification of evil and death. Mara appeared to the Buddha, as he does to us, as the inner voice questioning our own worthiness or ability to persevere on the spiritual journey. See Chapter 9, p. 184, and Chapter 11, p. 231.

MU (Chinese 'Wu'): Literally 'no' or 'not', 'Mu' is the famous reply of Zen Master Jōshū (Zhaozhou) in the first case of the *Mumonkan* (*q.v.*):

A monk asked Joshu, 'Has the dog Buddha nature or not?'
Joshu said, 'Mu.'

Through the centuries this koan has gained fame as the one most commonly assigned as a first koan to Zen students taking up koan work. Students are advised not to contemplate the exchange as a whole, but rather, as Master Mumon instructs in his commentary to the case, to 'cut off the mind road' and 'make your whole body a mass of doubt, and with your three hundred and sixty bones and joints and your eighty-four thousand hair follicles concentrate on this one word, Mu. Day and night, keep digging into it.'

MUMONKAN, MUMON: The *Mumonkan,* called in English the *The Gateless Barrier* or *The Gateless Gate* is one of the collections of koans that are part of the Zen koan curriculum, and in the *Mumonkan* each koan is accompanied by a commentary and a verse written by Master Mumon (1183–1260, Wumen in Chinese), who assembled the collection.

NĀGĀRJUNA (*c.* 150 – *c.* 250 C.E.): Foundational philosopher of the Mahāyāna. He was instrumental in the development of Madhyamaka (Middle Way) philosophy (*q.v.*) and the Prajñāpāramitā (Perfection of Wisdom) sūtras. See also under Emptiness.

NIRVĀṆA (Nibbana in Pali): Literally 'extinction' or 'snuffing out' as of a candle, nirvāṇa is the extinction of a sense of separate self and the complete liberation from Saṃsāra (*q.v.*) or the Wheel of Birth and Death. This may be viewed as a state of non-returning to a human or other form, or (in the Mahāyāna teachings) as a state of liberation within the world of Saṃsāra, where all dualistic notions (pain and pleasure, gain and loss) have been transcended. See also Three Dharma Seals.

PALI AND SANSKRIT: The classical languages of the Buddhist scriptures. The words of the Buddha were transmitted orally for approximately the first five hundred years after his Parinirvāṇa, but were eventually recorded in the Pali language in the first century c.e. These texts of the 'Pali canon' form the basis of Theravāda (q.v.) teaching and are accepted by Mahāyāna practitioners as well. At close to the same time that the Pali canon was coming into being, other writings also appeared which reflected the teachings of the then-developing Mahāyāna school. These writings were mostly in Sanskrit, the most ancient classical language of India. Pali is closely related to Sanskrit, but is somewhat more simplified and modernised. See also Sūtta, Sūtra.

PĀRAMITĀ : The *pāramitās*, most commonly listed as six in number, are the 'perfections', or qualities to be perfected by a bodhisattva (q.v.) on the path to realisation. They are sometimes called the bodhisattva trainings. For a list of the pāramitās see p. 147, and see further discussion at Chapter 7, p. 146, p. 149 and *passim*.

PARINIRVĀṆA : The nirvāṇa that occurs upon the death of someone who has achieved liberation.

PRAJÑĀ : *see under* THE THREEFOLD TRAINING.

PRATĪTYASAMUTPĀDA : Dependent Co-arising or Interbeing, (See Chapter 9, pp. 178–179). The Links of Dependent Co-arising is a subtle and complex teaching exploring the origins of our world, our lives and our consciousness, and the ways in which they actually co-arise. Depending which Sūtta is studied, there may be a different number of links given, but the most popular presentation is of Twelve Links as follows: ignorance, karmic formations, consciousness, name-and-form, sixfold sense bases, contact, feeling, craving, attachment, becoming, birth, suffering. The links are very often depicted, each with a traditional illustration, in the form of a wheel (the Wheel of Life). The circular presentation helps to emphasise that the links do not (or do not solely) appear in temporal fashion, one after the other, but that they co-arise. At the centre of the wheel are three animals representing the Three Poisons (q.v.) which drive the whole system; the Three Poisons are encircled by the Six Realms of Unenlightened Existence (q.v.), and these are encircled in turn by the Twelve Links. The whole wheel is held in the clutches of Yamarāja, the Lord of Death. One particularly helpful explication of the Twelve Links is offered by Lama Govinda in *The Foundations of Tibetan Mysticism*, p. 245. He emphasises that the links may be best understood by working backward step by step from our current state of suffering:

> The Buddha spoke only of a *conditioned* or *dependent* origination, not however a law of causality, in which the single phases of development follow each other in ever the same way with mechanical necessity. He started with the simple question: 'What is it that makes old-age and death possible?' And the answer was: 'On account of being born we suffer old age and death!' Similarly, birth

is dependent on the process of becoming, and this process would not have been set in motion if there had not been a will to live and a clinging to the corresponding forms of life. This clinging is due to craving, due to an unquenchable 'thirst' after the objects of sense-enjoyment, and this again is conditioned by feeling (by discerning agreeable and disagreeable sensations). Feeling on the other hand, is only possible by contact of the senses with their corresponding objects. The senses are based on a psycho-physical organism and the latter can only arise if there is consciousness! Consciousness however, in the individually limited form of ours, is conditioned by individual, egocentric activity (during countless forms of existence), and such activity is only possible as long as we are caught in the illusion of our separate egohood.

PRECEPTS: May refer to the Ten Cardinal Precepts, or more broadly to the Ten Cardinal Precepts plus the Three Refuges and the Three General Resolutions (listed at Chapter 5, p. 103). These precepts are descriptions of the ethical behaviour that is the foundation of Buddhist practice. For a detailed examination, see Chapter 5, pp. 104 ff. and Chapter 6.

RAKUSU: A traditional Japanese garment that represents the Buddha's robe in abbreviated form. The sewing and wearing of a rakusu represents a commitment to the Buddhist Path and to a particular teaching lineage, and there are different styles and colours of rakusu for lay practitioners, for priests, and for teachers. See Chapter 5, pp. 106–107, for more detail.

RINZAI: For the Rinzai school, see 'Sōtō and Rinzai'. For Zen Master Rinzai, see under Linji.

RŌSHI: 'Rōshi' is an honorific term translating roughly as 'old teacher'. In English, the term is often placed before the person's name (Rōshi Kapleau, Rōshi Kjolhede), but the traditional Japanese format is to attach the term to the end of the name (Yasutani-rōshi, Harada-rōshi). For more on the terms Sensei and Rōshi, see Chapter 4, pp. 78–79.

SAMĀDHI: *see under* THE THREEFOLD TRAINING.

SAṂSĀRA: The world of unenlightened existence, of cause and effect and karma. This is the world depicted by the Wheel of Life (see under Pratītyasamutpāda) and marked by suffering, impermanence and instability. See also under Nirvāṇa.

SAMU: Work practice; see Chapter 7, pp. 144–146.

SANGHA: The community of Buddhist practitioners. At various times and places 'Sangha' has had somewhat varying connotations. Historically in the Theravāda it has often been used to refer to the ordained monastic Sangha only, with lay people seen as supporters of the Sangha. However there are also early references to the Arya Sangha, meaning just those practitioners (whether ordained or lay) who have attained enlightenment, as well as to the Fourfold Sangha of male monastics, female monastics, laymen and laywomen. In the Mahāyāna, and particularly in the West, the term is most frequently used for any Buddhist community that practices together as well as for the community of all Buddhist practitioners worldwide. Even more expansively, all those who are working to uncover truth and to live in accordance with ethical principles may be seen as Sangha, whether or not they subscribe to specifically Buddhist teachings. See also under Three Jewels.

ŚĀNTIDEVA (Shantideva): Great eighth-century Indian teacher and author of *The Way of the Bodhisattva*, a work which continues to inspire practitioners with its call to compassion and bodhicitta (*q.v.*). Among many famous verses from this work is one which is said to be a favourite prayer of the Dalai Lama:

> *For as long as space remains,*
> *For as long as sentient beings remain,*
> *Until then may I too remain*
> *To dispel the miseries of the world.*

SENSEI: The title 'Sensei' simply means 'teacher', or 'one who walks ahead' in Japanese. In Zen it is used by those authorised to teach as a Dharma Heir (*q.v.*) in a particular lineage. As with the title 'Rōshi' it can be placed before the teacher's name in English (Sensei Wrightson), but the traditional Japanese format is to attach the term to the end of the given name (Amala-sensei). See Chapter 4, pp. 78–79.

ŚĪLA: *see under* THE THREEFOLD TRAINING.

SIX REALMS OF UNENLIGHTENED EXISTENCE: There are traditionally six realms into which those still bound to the Wheel of Birth and Death may be born: the Hell Realms, the Hungry Ghost Realm, the Animal Realm, the realm of the Asuras or jealous gods, the Human Realm and the realm of the Devas or happy gods. Birth in the human realm is considered precious because it can provide optimal circumstances for attaining enlightenment: sufficient suffering or dissatisfaction to spur us to practice, combined, ideally, with sufficient leisure and opportunity to pursue it. While birth in the blissful Deva realms may seem preferable, the Devas remain attached to their pleasures and comforts which will, however, eventually fade, even if only after many eons. Today the Six Realms are often interpreted from a psychological perspective as representing different mind states to which we are all subject, or as states which human beings are capable of creating for themselves here on earth through violence, addictions and so forth. See also under Pratītyasamutpāda, and further at Chapter 11, Day 2 teisho pp. 229–230.

SŌTŌ AND RINZAI: The two major schools of Zen in Japan. The Sōtō school is descended from the Chinese Caodong school founded by Dongshan Liangjie in the ninth century. Master Dōgen (*q.v.*) travelled to China in the thirteenth century and brought the teachings of this school back to Japan. Today the sect is associated especially with the practice of *shikantaza* or 'just sitting', a practice taught in China as 'silent illumination' by the twelfth-century master Hongzhi as well as by Dōgen's own teacher, Master Rujing.

The Rinzai school is descended from the Chinese Linji school, founded by ninth-century master Linji Yixuan (*q.v.*). Historically associated with a fierce and dynamic teaching style, the school today emphasises the investigation of koans. Several other Chinese schools of Chan either died out or did not take root in Japan. In twentieth-century Japan, Daiun Sogaku Harada, a priest of the Sōtō school, came to feel that the Sōtō sect placed an insufficient emphasis on the possibility of awakening to our True Nature, and to this effect he pursued koan work with a Rinzai teacher. Harada-rōshi's Dharma Heir (*q.v.*) Hakuun Yasutani, was likewise ordained originally as a Sōtō priest, but, after working with Harada-rōshi, founded a new lineage, the Sambō Kyodan, or Three Treasures Order. This teaching lineage seeks to hand on the best of both the Sōtō and Rinzai traditions in an amalgam sometimes known as 'Integral Zen'. The Harada-Yasutani lineage has been powerfully influential in Western Zen. (For a complete list of Dharma heirs in this lineage see http://www.ciolek.com/WWWVLPages/ZenPages/HaradaYasutani.html). Rōshi Kapleau (*q.v.*) studied in Japan with both Harada-rōshi and Yasutani-rōshi (his main teacher).

Śūnyatā (Shunyata): *see under* Emptiness.

Sūtra, Sūtta: 'Sūtra' is the Sanskrit form and 'sūtta' the Pali form of the word that refers to texts containing the words of the Buddha.

Teisho: A Dharma talk delivered by a Zen teacher during a formal block of sitting. See Introduction, pp. 6–8.

Theravāda, Mahāyāna, Vajrayāna: Buddhism as practiced today in different parts of the world can be divided into three main branches: Theravāda ('the way of the elders'), Mahāyāna ('the great vehicle') and Vajrayāna ('the diamond/thunderbolt vehicle'). The first is most commonly practiced in Southeast Asia, the second in East Asia, and the third in Tibet and adjacent regions. As its name implies, Theravādan Buddhism is the most historically conservative. Its teaching and practices hew closely to the Pali canon (*q.v.*). The traditions of the Mahāyāna developed in ancient India alongside those of the Theravāda, but emphasised a perhaps more popular stream of teachings, focused on the veneration of great Bodhisattvas (*q.v.*), the liberation of all beings and the conviction that all are inherently Buddhas. Vajrayāna is the youngest tradition of the three. Its teachings were brought from India at a time when Tantric or esoteric practices were dominant there, and these form the hallmark of the Vajrayāna. Some scholars classify the Vajrayāna as a branch of Mahāyāna Buddhism, while others see it as a separate branch altogether. All Buddhist practitioners accept as valid the teachings of the Pali canon; practitioners of the Mahāyāna and Vajrayāna adhere as well to the teachings of the Mahāyāna Sūtras, while Vajrayāna practitioners add in also their own later texts and traditions. See also under Pali and Sanskrit, and further at Chapter 5, pp. 98–99.

THREE DHARMA SEALS: Impermanence (*aniccā*), No-self (*anattā*), and Suffering (*dukkha*). Any system of teaching or instruction which does not acknowledge these three characteristics of existence is said to be a non-Buddhist teaching. However, teachers of the Mahāyāna sometimes replace *dukkha*, suffering, with *nirvāṇa* or the end of suffering. See also under *dukkha* and *nirvāṇa*.

THREE JEWELS (also Three Treasures, or Triple-gem): The Three Treasures of Buddha, Dharma and Sangha (*q.v.*) may be expounded on various levels from the more literal to the more abstract or cosmic. For the literal level, see Introduction, p. 3; for an exploration of some of the deeper connotations, see Chapter 5, pp. 101–104. To take refuge in the Three Treasures is the means of formally setting out on the Buddhist path (see under Jukai above), and many Buddhists recite the Three Refuges on a daily basis. The order of teachers, priests, and lay people established at the Rochester Zen Center by Rōshi Kjolhede is known as the Three Jewels Order; Amala-sensei and those ordained by her are members of this order.

THREE POISONS: Greed, hatred and delusion are known as the Three Poisons. Just as the precepts are descriptive of enlightened action, so the Three Poisons are descriptive of the unenlightened mind. We believe that we are separate from 'things out there' (our basic delusion), and so we react to things either by liking or disliking, by grasping or pushing away, by saying 'I want this' (greed) or 'I don't want that' (hatred or aversion). But as we learn to recognise these poisons in our own minds, we need to see also how they lie at the base of our social ills: wars, exploitation, and environmental degradation; and we need to acknowledge not only the inner work but the outer work that still remains to be done.

THE THREEFOLD TRAINING: Śīla (pronounced 'Sheela', ethical behaviour), Samādhi (development of meditative concentration) and Prajñā (wisdom). Progress along the Buddhist path is taught as equally dependent on each of these three elements. The last, Wisdom, can refer both to the study of Buddhist scripture and teachings as well as to the transcendental wisdom of enlightenment. See further at Chapter 6, pp. 119–122.

TWO TRUTHS: Buddhist teaching speaks of 'relative truth' and 'absolute truth'. Relative truth is concerned with the world of karma, of cause and effect, of scientific truth. Absolute truth sees into the ultimate emptiness of the relative world and reveals a perspective of oneness. Awakening reveals that these two aspects of reality are in fact inseparable.

VAJRAYĀNA: *see under* THERAVĀDA, MAHĀYĀNA, VAJRAYĀNA.

VIPASSANĀ: Insight or seeing things as they are. 'Vipassana' is also the name of a widespread school of modern (mostly Western) Theravāda Buddhism which teaches Insight Meditation.

YASUTANI, HAKUUN RYŌKŌ (1885–1973): *see under* SŌTŌ AND RINZAI.

CHINESE AND JAPANESE NAMES

Most Zen koans or teaching stories come to us from ancient China, and their protagonists are most often Chinese students and masters. When the Japanese re-told these stories, the Chinese characters (*kanji*) were pronounced using the sounds from the Japanese syllabary. For us as English speakers, the Japanese forms of the name are often more familiar and easier to remember. In the lineage of the Auckland Zen Centre, koans from the collections known as the *Mumonkan* (*The Gateless Barrier*) and the *Hekiganroku* (*The Blue Cliff Record*) are studied using the Japanese names, while those from the *Shoyoroku* (*The Book of Equanimity*) are studied using the Chinese names. Thus, depending on the particular koan, the teishos in this book may refer to the protagonists either in Japanese or in Chinese. You may consult this appendix to find the alternate name.

CHINESE	JAPANESE
Baizhang Huaihai	Hyakujō Ekai
Danyuan Yingzhen	Tangen Ōshin
Daowu Yuanzhi	Dōgo Enchi
Dasui Fazhen	Daizui Hōshin
Dongshan Liangjie	Tōzan Ryōkai
Foyan Qingyuan	Butsugen Seion
Guishan Da'an	Isan Daian
Guishan Lingyou	Isan Reiyū
Guiyang school	Igyō school
Huizhong, *see* Nanyang	
Linji Yixuan	Rinzai Gigen
Mazu Daoyi	Baso Dōitsu
Nanquan Puyuan	Nansen Fugan
Nanyang Huizhong	Nan'yō Echū
Pangyun	Hōun
Ruiyan Shiyan	Zuigan Shigen
Shitou Xiqian	Sekitō Kisen

Tiantong Rujing	Tendō Nyojō
Wumen Huikai	Mumon Ekai
Xinghua Cunjiang	Koke Sonshō
Xuansha Shibei	Gensha Shibi
Xuedou Chongxian	Setchō Jūken
Xuedou Zhijian	Setchō Chikan
Yangshan Huiji	Kyōzan Ejaku
Yantou Quanho	Gantō Zenkatsu
Yaoshan Weiyan	Yakusan Igen
Yuanwu Kequin	Engo Kokugon
Yunyan Tansheng	Ungan Donjō
Zhaozhou Congshen	Jōshū Jūshin

JAPANESE	CHINESE
Baso Dōitsu	Mazu Daoyi
Butsugen Seion	Foyan Qingyuan
Daizui Hōshin	Dasui Fazhen
Dōgo Enchi	Daowu Yuanzhi
Engo Kokugon	Yuanwu Kequin
Gantō Zenkatsu	Yantou Quanho
Gensha Shibi	Xuansha Shibei
Hōun	Pangyun
Hyakujō Ekai	Baizhang Huaihai
Igyō school	Guiyang school
Isan Daian	Guishan Da'an
Isan Reiyū	Guishan Lingyou
Jōshū Jūshin	Zhaozhou Congshen
Koke Sonshō	Xinghua Cunjiang
Kyōzan Ejaku	Yangshan Huiji
Mumon Ekai	Wumen Huikai
Nansen Fugan	Nanquan Puyuan
Nan'yō Echū	Nanyang Huizhong

Rinzai Gigen	Linji Yixuan
Sekitō Kisen	Shitou Xiqian
Setchō Chikan	Xuedou Zhijian
Setchō Jūken	Xuedou Chongxian
Tangen Ōshin	Danyuan Yingzhen
Tendō Nyojō	Tiantong Rujing
Tōzan Ryōkai	Dongshan Liangjie
Ungan Donjō	Yunyan Tansheng
Yakusan Igen	Yaoshan Weiyan
Zuigan Shigen	Ruiyan Shiyan

ACKNOWLEDGEMENTS

FROM KATHRYN ARGETSINGER: First and foremost my thanks go to my husband Mark, who has supported me, both financially and emotionally, through nearly two decades of Zen training, including frequent and lengthy journeys to the other side of the world, innumerable absences to attend sesshin, and months of solo retreat here at home. His support has continued through the past two years of my work on this book, and in addition he has selflessly taken on responsibility for its design and production, attending to every detail of the book's final form with great sensitivity and professionalism.

Deep bows also to my two dear Ann(e)s, Ann Duncan in Auckland and Anne McKinnon in Massachusetts, who, besides the gift of their friendship, have offered their brilliant and orderly minds to read the book in manuscript and to provide feedback, suggestions and copy-editing. It was Ann in Auckland who originally had the idea of compiling a volume of Amala-sensei's teishos. Hanya Gallagher, then manager at the Auckland Zen Centre, made the project a reality by assigning it to me as my 'work' during my final year of training there, and by making time in the Centre's schedule for Amala-sensei to work on the project as well. Both Hanya and staff member Robin Gardner-Gee gave extra effort to the many tasks required to keep the Zen Centre ticking over while one or both of us were involved in the writing process.

Thanks to Richard von Sturmer for poring through years' worth of his wonderful photographs to find just the right images to support and reflect the themes of each of the book's chapters, as well as for the Dharma Talk included as part of Chapter 4. It serves as only one example of the many delightful and creative talks Richard has delivered at the Centre through the years.

Finally I must try and fail to find adequate words to express my gratitude to my teacher, Amala-sensei. In the fifth decade of my life, without any sense that I was searching for anything in particular, I unexpectedly found my teacher. Something that had been hidden was suddenly revealed and I knew I must dedicate my life to its unfolding. It has been an unimagined privilege to attempt to convey, through the medium of this book,

Sensei's particular presentation of the Dharma, her insights, her faith, and her encouragement to each of us to practice and to uncover that which is beyond any words and letters offered here.

FROM AMALA WRIGHTSON: Many bows from me too to all those people Kathryn mentions above, but with added thanks to Richard von Sturmer, for his having introduced me to Zen in the first place (little did he know at the time what a momentous effect that introduction would have upon our lives), and for his love, inspiration and support in so many ways over the past 42 years. It seems fitting that some of his words and images are included in this book, along with Mark's elegant design.

Many bows also to Kathryn for all her work in assembling and organising the materials for this book, including our countless hours of discussion over the internet, carving out time for the project from two very full lives. Without Kathryn's care, energy and persistence the book would not have happened. I came across this statement by Roshi Pat Enkyo O'Hara recently which applies to our long and close collaboration. 'If you study with a teacher for a long time, with both of you earnestly serving the Dharma, wonderful things can happen. Positions can change, and suddenly one day the teacher is the student and the student is the teacher.' This has happened not just once but many times over the years. Nevertheless I take full responsibility for any errors or omissions to be found in these pages.

Thanks also to the Auckland Zen Centre members who took part in the photo session which generated the posture images in Chapter One, and to all the Zen students whose struggles, concerns and questions, along with my own, inform the teaching presented here.

This book ends where it began, with much gratitude for Roshi Bodhin Kjolhede, Abbot of our mother temple, the Rochester Zen Center. We can never requite our deep debt of gratitude to him, to Roshi Philip Kapleau, to our Dharma ancestors, or to the Rochester Sangha, present and past, for creating and sustaining such a wonderful practice community. We can only carry on the endless work of waking up to *this*.

ABOUT THE AUTHORS

Sensei Amala Wrightson is the resident teacher and Spiritual Director of the Auckland Zen Centre. She began practicing Zen in 1982 after she and her husband, Richard von Sturmer, attended a workshop with Philip Kapleau, author of *The Three Pillars of Zen*. In the late 80s she and Richard left New Zealand and their work in experimental theatre to pursue residential Zen training at the Rochester (NY) Zen Center (the centre founded by Kapleau), as no similar training was then available in New Zealand. Working in Rochester with Kapleau's successor, Roshi Bodhin Kjolhede, Wrightson was ordained as a Zen priest in 1999 and authorised to teach Zen in 2004. She then returned to Auckland intending to make available in New Zealand the training she had received, and was sanctioned as a full Dharma Heir of Roshi Kjolhede in 2012. Sensei Wrightson has offered meditation instruction, talks on Zen, and opportunities for practice and retreat both at the Centre and at other locations around Auckland for the past fifteen years. She was a founding member of the New Zealand Buddhist Council as well as its chairperson for a decade, and she is a member of the American Zen Teachers' Association.

Kathryn Argetsinger began studying Zen under Sensei Wrightson in 2001 and has been her student since that time, completing several years of residential Zen training and assisting in Auckland with the administration of the Centre as well as with meditation workshops and retreats. She is a lay member of the Three Jewels Order and currently leads sitting groups in Western Massachusetts (USA). Prior to taking up full-time training, Kathryn taught Classics for many years at the University of Rochester (NY), and first met Sensei Wrightson at the Rochester Zen Center.

Richard von Sturmer is a New Zealand writer and longtime Zen practitioner. Together with Sensei Amala Wrightson he founded the Auckland Zen Centre.

www.ingramcontent.com/pod-product-compliance
Lightning Source LLC
Chambersburg PA
CBHW021236060726
47590CB00005B/1781